Progress Without Poverty

PROGRESS WITHOUT POVERTY

SOCIALLY RESPONSIBLE ECONOMIC GROWTH

By

PETER S. ALBIN

Basic Books, Inc., Publishers   *New York*

The author gratefully acknowledges the publisher's permission to reprint selections from *The Political Economy of Public Service Employment*, edited by Harold L. Sheppard, Bennett Harrison, and William J. Spring (Lexington, Mass.: Lexington Books, D. C. Heath and Company, Copyright 1972, D. C. Heath and Company).

Library of Congress Cataloging in Publication Data

Albin, Peter S
  Progress without poverty.

  Includes bibliographical references and index.
    1. United States—Economic conditions—1971–
  2. United States—Social conditions—1960–
  3. United States—Economic policy—1971–
  4. United States—Social policy. 5. Economic
  development—Social aspects. I. Title.
  HC106.7.A36   330.9′73′0926   77–20425
  ISBN: 0–465–06407–8

TO MY PARENTS

CONTENTS

PART FOUR
THE ORPHANS OF GROWTH

PART FIVE
POLICIES FOR PROGRESS

PREFACE

This book developed over a number of years and reflects many influences, criticisms, and kindnesses. Institutional support was received from New York University through its Arts and Sciences Research Fund, Schools of Business Research Fund, and Institute of Labor Relations; and in the last stage, there has been a healthy spillover of ideas from work on formal characteristics of technology carried out under a grant to me from the National Science Foundation. A grant from Resources for the Future, Inc., assisted at an early stage of the research. John Jay College of the City University of New York provided support in the final stages of the work, and the University of California at Berkeley in intermediate stages. I owe a special debt to the University of Cambridge for the many courtesies extended to me over a sabbatical year and several summers in residence. Individual acknowledgments are an incomplete index of the intellectual support and renewed education that I received there. Perhaps I am a slow learner or perhaps it was the strength of my original neoclassical education, but it took some years for me to realize the power of the tradition and style of work which derive from and extend Keynes's original insights into the driving forces of capitalism. I have tried to write about how the system works and might be controlled rather than about how a system would have to work were the ideological claims made on its behalf to be realized.

Many individuals have left a mark on this book. I would like particularly to thank Tony Atkinson, Will Baumol, Alex Belinfante, Christopher Bliss, John Eatwell, Robin Marris, James Meade, Hy Minsky, Geoff Heale, David Newbury, and Joan Robinson for thoughts and criticism on the theoretical analysis along with Pat Albin, Roger Alcaly, Bennett Harrison, Carol Jusenius, Bob Mier, John Mason, and Thomas Vietorisz for guidance on matters of political economy.

The sections on poverty and public assistance reflect a long and productive collaboration with Bruno Stein, and the sections on educational policy borrow from joint work with Shirley Johnson. Finally, much material on macroeconomic policy was developed in the course of my affiliation with the Unicorn Group, through continuing debates with Walter Peters and my association with Hy Minsky.

The book as a whole has received careful attention from Martin Kessler of Basic Books; his comments and criticisms, although not always welcome, were invariably correct. The book presents a new perspective on the structure of the economy, and I was surprised to find that most of the qualitatively important parts could be presented without recourse to jargon, specialists' terminology, or thinly disguised paraphrases of journalese and mathematics. Actually "shocked" comes closer to describing my feelings. It did not occur to me as a veteran producer of arcana that a serious original statement in economics could be made in the common tongue without compromise of precision and content. Martin guided me to this realization ("guided" is a mild word), and I was pleased to find that once the decision was made to write in English, it became possible, as well, to deal naturally, directly, and nonsuperficially (I hope) with critical issues of power, politics, and political economy.

A generation of students has left a mark on this work, but I would like to give special thanks to Yung Lee and Mary Joe McCullough for special contributions. In addition, I would like to acknowledge the secretarial assistance of Karen Austen, Mike Cooper, Elizabeth Griffith, Linda Hurst, and Helen Ray; each somehow managed to find words among my scribblings and each had much to do with the completion of this work. Finally, I would like to thank Harvard University for permission to reprint materials that appeared in different form in the *Quarterly Journal of Economics*, and the editors of *Urban Studies* for permission to reprint sections of an earlier article in that journal.

1

Introduction: The Social
Dimensions of Growth

THIS book confronts a number of the most persistent problems in American society: a hard core of poverty and welfare dependency, urban crisis, the growth of the technically oriented corporation, environmental cliffhanging, and chaos at all levels of education. It is the thesis of this book that these problems are closely intertwined—that in fact they are unforeseen and misunderstood consequences of a characteristic pattern intrinsic to the dynamics of modern industrial society. This pattern is not simply an expositional contrivance that allows the author to fit a full array of current and relevant topics between the covers of a single book. Rather, the pattern is fundamental, and its implications force a rethinking of the process of economic growth and the rationale of economic policy.

The misunderstandings extend further. The past decade has been a time of economic stagnation, serious threat of depression, and unprecedented inflation. These are shown to be the outcome of policy failures directly attributable to misunderstanding of the growth process and mismanagement of the forces that contribute to growth. The allegation of mismanagement is broad; it covers the grotesqueries of the Nixon-Ford administrators, Burns, Simon, Greenspan, et al., and extends to include an opposition which failed to present to the public an intelligent comprehensive counterview. The nominal change in administrations hardly alters the situation. The legacy of cultivated public ignorance remains; the benchmarks of what constitutes satisfactory economic performance are obscured if not forgotten; and there is no evidence that policy is being constructed on a coherent general view of the development of the economy and society.

Of course policy makers still retain their basic kit of tools, and it is quite possible that a limping approximation of the postwar pattern of growth could be achieved despite energy constraints and the obstacles presented by the international economy. But this prospect does not arouse enthusiasm, for there is every reason to believe that even under a benign administration the dynamics of the system will again be misunderstood, and destructive and perverse forces will again be fostered.

These are sweeping statements. They constitute a claim that the policy makers, social critics, and academics have been wrong in their perceptions and theories of the process of economic growth. The claim goes further. As a result of these errors, the prescriptions of the economic policy establishment distorted outcomes and led to the destabilization of the larger system. The term destabilization is used both in its narrow technical sense and for its broader political connotations which embrace the potentialities of coup (as directly threatened by the Nixon forces [1] *) and the exacerbation of divisions over aid to the cities, racial questions, and the position of the unemployed poor.

"Wrong" is, of course, a fighting word. It is also a dangerous word to use in the social sciences, where standards for judging what is correct are subjective and mutable. Errors of judgment or omission and mistaken points of view, rather than errors of fact and technical analysis, are involved; and this is a difficult sort of mistake to pin down. For example, it appears that the ways in which most economists view income distribution make it extremely difficult for them to pinpoint the causes of contemporary poverty or, more generally, to associate social change with economic causal agents. In similar fashion, the standard explanations of business behavior basically focus on issues of pricing in the short run and actually impede analysis of the role of technical change within growth. As a result, policies and programs have been misdirected. Procedures

* Footnotes designated by stars and daggers provide side comments and brief explanations where appropriate. Numbered endnotes are assembled chapter by chapter beginning on page 221. These give citations, bibliographic comments, or technical explanations. The latter fill out points of economic analysis that are too cumbersome or too mathematical to fit a book that has been designed to be read rather than studied. The non-economist should ignore these elaborations, but many economists will want to see how critical points can be worked through with some rigor and precision. I have tried to spot such notes at points where I as a specialist reader might feel uneasy if there were no evidence that the author was aware of how analysis that is standard in the discipline could be applied.

appropriate to the stabilization of a 1950s type economy have foundered on the poverty problems of the 1960s and 1970s and even appear to have led to deterioration in the intrinsic productivity of the system.

Errors in management and guidance can be far-reaching. For example, the country at present seems to be in the process of "de-educating" its work force, and there is even a semblance of rationality to the process. The prospective student sees that education has lost its magic payoff in income, status, and security; while to those who pay the bills, educational institutions appear as inefficient and costly drains on private and public budgets. The error here is one of omission. At least three basic perceptions have been lost: first, the perception of how knowledge, education, and skills contribute to growth and technical progress; second, how, during times of temporary stagnation, the economy sends false signals on the relative advantages of education; and third, how the apparent cost of education will be influenced by broader productivity trends. In short, the standard analysis does not provide a framework that properly integrates the educational and technical-change factors within economic growth. And even though de-education threatens to undercut the basis for economic progress and to cede technological and knowledge leadership to Japan and West Germany, these factors are not appreciated or given their full weight either in national policy formulations or in debates over district school bonds.

This is not an isolated phenomenon. The misdirection of conventional analysis and policy reflects in part the misdirected humane impulse of a concerned public. The ecological, energy, resource, and food crises have engendered public skepticism, if not antagonism, toward the whole growth objective. Yet *giving up now* on growth means dooming our posterity to excruciating poverty and sacrificing significant possibilities of social advancement in the present.[2]

In reaction to such prospects, this book firmly endorses the basic growth objective; but the endorsement carries a caveat. Economic growth is needed to provide the material basis for ameliorative social change, but growth of the sort we have had in the past has been strikingly ineffective in meeting distributional objectives and has actually intensified social pathologies. It should be possible to restore growth—the failures of past administrations notwithstanding—yet it would be inexcusable to just feed the fires and let the system take off on its own to duplicate the errors of the past. Management and guidance are essential, and we must contemplate types of planning and control that are without significant precedent in this country. An even stronger statement is necessary. The planning and the theory that underlies it must fully comprehend and incorporate the social dimensions involved in economic change.

THE SOCIAL CONSEQUENCES OF GROWTH

Certain "social consequences" of economic growth are self-evident. If growth means industrialization, it is also likely to mean a society structured to promote the smooth working of the industrial system in its most critical aspects. Urbanization, factory and office organization, intricate transportation and communication networks, and the integration and rationalization of markets are part and parcel of this type of growth. Such growth-accommodating or growth-propelled changes have been chronicled, deplored, or applauded in an immense literature of economic history and social commentary. Similarly, since economic growth essentially means increasing material well-being, it must also connote changing styles of life and social attitudes. It is immaterial whether such changes are thought of as side consequences of economic expansion or constitute the rationale for such expansion. They are intrinsic to growth and require no special elucidation.

What does require elucidation, however, is the nature of processes that can translate "urbanization" into either a Zurich or a Bedford Stuyvesant; "factory organization" into a workers' cooperative or a Lordstown; "changing styles of life" into anomie or integrated participation. Our concern then will be with perverse patterns and syndromes in the growth process that can swamp the primary positive effects of industrialization and expanding output.

Consider the case of poverty in the United States. Although the data are subject to varying interpretations, it is clear that growth in overall income since the Korean War has bypassed a large population who were then in deep poverty, who remained in poverty through the growth years of the 1960s, and who remain in poverty today. This seems to run counter to what one would expect in an advanced economy which as a whole has had a history of expansion. Why has poverty persisted and, on some interpretations, become more intractable? Discrimination and inadequate social services are surely important factors that explain a significant part of the poverty syndrome. But it is the claim of this book that hard-core continuing poverty is a built-in consequence of the way in which the economy is organized around growth—that the growth process is selective as to whom it benefits and that, by and large, it is biased against those who start off poor. Growth involves the creation and rapid diffusion of technical change and, in general, the poor are excluded from the worker groups who participate in such change and share in its returns. They start off "left behind by technology" and fall further and further to the rear. Ultimately, as in the recent past, they become categorized as a drag on the economic engine, the cause of stagnation, the source of deteriorating productivity, and are exposed to unreasoning vindictiveness.

Examine the economy of cities. Here again the situation contradicts our preconceptions of what should happen in periods of growth. For reasons we shall explore in some depth in later chapters, rapid growth in the economy as a whole creates excruciating pressures on the finances of the typical American city. Far from being helped by growth, cities (particularly the older Eastern cities) tend to decay rapidly during periods of strong national expansion. The costs of necessary services escalate while the ability to meet these costs steadily deteriorates. In the process, social discord reaches crisis levels. Cities such as Newark are in the final stages of this process, but many, if not most, American cities are threatened by this syndrome, which is indeed intrinsic to our present system. The *fiscal* crisis which can occur during a period of stagnation is the final stage in a process initiated by forces released by growth. In this setting, the standard policy remedies turn out to be patchwork expedients; effective policy initiatives do exist, but they require serious revisions in one's conception of the ways in which growth forces work.

As the book develops we shall encounter many other critical effects of the pattern of growth on the social fabric. The interactions of education, income distribution, and growth require particular elucidation, as do the relationships between the investment behavior of major corporations, their use of educated work forces, and the resultant patterns of technical change and industrial development. As far as the policy maker's standard perception of the economy is concerned, these effects come out, at best, as afterthoughts or side events. As a result, social policy appears as an *ad hoc* corrective without organic links to what is labeled "economic policy."

In contrast, the operating premise of this book is that where critical social trends and changing patterns of life and welfare are directly associated with economic dynamics, the analysis must incorporate explicit and direct consideration of the behavior in question.

To take just one example, consider the critical policy area of "manpower planning," an applied discipline which involves the translation of targets for future production into preparations to train and recruit the personnel needed to accomplish the targets. On the surface there is nothing wrong with the approach. As practiced in this country it exemplifies rationality with its calculated anticipation of future requirements. The defects, however, lie deep. The manpower approach is essentially passive with regard to technology. It implicitly accepts an output or broad growth projection and accommodates the work force to the dictates of technique. In effect, the manpower projection translates technical production recipes into a projection of social structure and income distribution; for that is the meaning of its delineation and description of the future work force. Of course there can be situations in which the growth projection and its associated manpower plan can represent an idyllic future. But this need not be so—the futures currently being laid out for many in the present generation are anything but pleasant.

Is there another way? Clearly, there is no circumventing the realities of modern technology: once a machine is installed the number and variety of work positions attached to that machine are fixed within narrow limits. What is usually missed in the standard style of manpower planning is the possibility of altering production techniques at the design stage so that the structure of work opportunities implied by the machine more closely fits a desired societal pattern. This is by no means a preposterous suggestion. Designs have nearly always been adjusted to the detailed specifications of the customer and they are now routinely adjusted to externally imposed restrictions on energy use and environmental impact. Yet, surprisingly, although manpower requirements are a subject for planning, the most important determinants of the structure of employment opportunities and job characteristics are excluded from the process.*

The issue here might seem simple; yet the analysis and its interpretations are intrinsically complex: To understand a specific applied problem such as the manpower issue, we must establish a framework that links social effects with growth policy. But to understand the limits of growth policy we must perforce track the system as it is: that is, as it has malfunctioned under conventional guidance. Dilemmas will accumulate: descriptive and historical analyses expose standard growth and passive planning as processes with profoundly disturbing social consequences; yet the underlying conditions are such that the resources to overcome the social

---

* Or perhaps the omission is not so surprising. Also at issue here are social conditions within the workplace. The manner in which a production technique is designed constitutes a political statement in the battle for authority on the factory floor; and one typical statement is an assertion of hierarchy. The ostensible neutrality of the standard manpower approach is itself a comment on where power lies in industrial relations.

problems of poverty and inadequate public services can only be obtained through growth. To be sure, we will identify socially constructive lines of some promise, including a solution to the manpower problem just posed; but a solution would have no value if it did not take into account the warnings of a recent history in which growth has been an instrument with dangerous bias.

In fact, as we focus on policy in the broadest sense, we will recognize other reasons to be pessimistic or ambivalent about growth. First of all, there is the difficulty of finding intelligent management for growth policies (even of the standard type) and of obtaining general political support for growth objectives. At an even more fundamental level, we must ask if environmental and ecological concerns preemptively invalidate growth as a social remedy. These issues must be considered at the outset; for if managed growth is institutionally infeasible, or if growth of any sort is ultimately destructive of biological life, the matter is closed.

CAVEATS TO THE GROWTH OBJECTIVE

The Practicality of Managed Growth

We must first recognize that growth has ambiguous standing as a societal goal. In fact, in little over a decade the opinions of policy makers and the concerned informed public have swung from ignorance of controlled growth, to growth enthusiasm, to deep pessimism on growth prospects. The growth view in this country developed out of the Keynesian revolution and the practical successes of Keynesian policy in seemingly eliminating the violent swings of the business cycle. With the stabilization problem apparently solved, a longer view was taken on policy. The view manifested itself in a number of ways, from simple-minded extrapolation of past successes in the financial press to sophisticated growth theory in the economic journals. But in all cases, a projection of continuously expanding output, economic activity, and employment was taken seriously as the proper way to view the future. In the early to middle sixties, the most sanguine saw no horizon; but even the growth pessimists saw no objection to the process continuing over decades, and projections to 1975, 1984, 1990 and 2001 were seriously advanced. On the basis of such projections, batteries of experts inferred the relative future power of nations— with current growth rates, in effect, establishing the morning line in a Gross National Product (GNP) race among the United States, U.S.S.R., Japan, and Western Europe.

On a more humane note, the projections served as the basis for a program of social remedies. In the standard view, poverty and deficient social services in the United States could be obliterated by assigning only a small portion of the increasing outputs and energies to neglected areas and people. One evoked the image of a pie that grew each year: everyone could have a larger slice, so conflicts over scarce morsels would be diminished. The "haves" would have more and would hardly resist social changes and reallocations that would improve the positions of the "have-nots." One could even extend the image of a slice for social advancement to the world at large; and many projections saw advanced country growth as the vehicle to free resources for the underdeveloped nations. The image of growth remained unflawed as successes came to the growth men of postrecovery Western Europe and Japan and to the managers of the socialist countries in the Soviet bloc. Growth optimism reached its height in the middle and late sixties following the successes of the Kennedy and Johnson administrations in maintaining continuous economic gains quarter after quarter, year after year, long past the point where conventional business-cycle reasoning predicted the inevitable downturn. Business forecasting became the art of predicting changes in the economy's growth rate; that the growth rate itself would be positive and substantial was never doubted.

However, a chill was felt in the late sixties, and in the early seventies growth optimists were drenched in a cold shower bath. The steady expansion of personal incomes ceased, anticipations were frustrated, and economic policy appeared ineffective and misdirected.

We will consider causes for the policy failure in some detail in a later chapter. The list of contributing factors is long and includes such elements as the preemption of critical resources by the war in Indochina; an unresilient international monetary system; agonies over the inflation-unemployment trade-offs; signs of weakness in corporate financial structures; resource and energy shortages; and, finally, ignorant mismanagement of the policy tools, along with ideological self-indulgence in an environment of outright corruption.

My own feeling is that the failure to sustain growth was not inevitable and that sensible and intelligent management could have overcome the basic structural problems. Nevertheless, the fact of failure must be given prominence. Growth processes rely on a conviction that growth, once started, will continue in a relatively orderly fashion. Firms invest on a working expectation that future profits will validate their commitments. Individuals commit themselves to education and professional or vocational development on a conviction that places will be found for them. Similarly, purchases are made on projections of income increases that, in turn, imply projections of technical advance. This closes the circle, since the projected technical advance is itself an outcome of investment and educational decisions which contribute to the economy's productivity. In other words, growth begets growth. Ideally, the policy actions taken by government will be supportive and integrative: first, to maintain aggregate demand so that the performance of the economy validates earlier anticipations; second, to promote critical technological developments so that there is a technical basis for expansion; and, finally, to help coordinate expectations of the various participants in the system.

The parts all fit together, but what happens if government fails in its supportive role and people experience frustration of their growth expectations? The markets of the 1970s lack the buoyancy that was predicted for them in the 1960s. The job opportunities for the 1978 graduate are not those that were envisioned in the student's college-preparatory years. The effects of such failed expectations can be profound and, regardless of their cause, may result in a drastically changed economic environment. If sustained growth is not viewed as a practical certainty, firms and individuals will tend to hedge their commitments and trust; planning periods will be shortened and greater attention given to contingency options and liquidity. All of these conservative reactions, which can be summarized as a "crisis of confidence," have as their inevitable consequence a reduction in the ability of the economy to generate and sustain growth.

Consider some of the dimensions of the policy failure we have experienced. In 1974, per capita real GNP dropped 5 to 6 percent. This loss of product must be weighed against an increase of 5 or 6 percent which would have been realized had the growth-rate extrapolations of the 1960s been sustained. The one-year shortfall amounted to upwards of $100 billion, the rough equivalent of some five million jobs plus a substantial increase in living standards. Moreover, we must reckon that the shortfall below anticipations for the entire period of the Nixon-Ford administration is many times this amount. If the economy had sustained growth of only 3 percent in real per capita income over the 1968–1976 period of virtual stagnation, the average living standard would have increased by nearly 25 percent by the end of the period, while the accumulated gain would have amounted to nearly 90 percent of a full year's GNP.

There are other disruptions to consider. Record inflation and the disarray of the international goods and financial markets add to the perceived pressures and risks. Let us suppose for the moment that many, if not most, major firms can freely choose between a strategy of long-term expansion or a strategy of short-term market exploitation and profit seeking—there should be very little doubt as to which option will be taken when there is uncertainty as to future growth. The same reasoning applies in the human domain. What is the sense in taking a chance on an extended education if there is no firm promise of employment at the end of the process and money is short now?

Growth, then, requires coherence in expectations and confidence that basic projections will be achieved—in fact, a distinct consciousness oriented to economic advance. On this reasoning, the policy failures of the past few years carry a cost beyond the product that "might-have-been" had the economy been geared up to potential capacity. We must also reckon on losses extending over years if it turns out to be difficult to reestablish such growth consciousness.

This book will argue for a return to a growth economy (noting, though, that the growth processes envisaged here demand a different conceptual setting from that conventionally held). A reformulation of social objectives and policy directions is also necessary; yet there is no escaping the fact that it will take some time for confidence in any sort of growth policy to reestablish itself, and we may have to suffer through some difficult years before we can be satisfied that the system can be propelled and controlled along a sensible and effective path.

This unhappy thought will recur throughout the policy sections of the book. The policy designs that are presented here may seem relatively insensitive to the mismanagement risk, but there is no such thing as total immunity. Quality of leadership and administration can no longer be treated as a given, and this represents a fundamental wrench to the standard perception. Economists in their communications with one another had gotten into the habit of assuming benign and intelligent governance by authorities that are committed to making efficient, informed, politically responsive choices.* It is hardly news that skeptics have criticized the naiveté of this stance; but disillusionment with the potential for policy has grown to the point that it must now be considered as an important institutional element.[3] Geoffrey Barraclough, a distinguished historian, enunciated skeptical views that are voiced with

---

* In this view the details of policy are simply matters of technique whilst tradeoffs between competing goals are matters to be solved by pluralistic interest-group politics within the zone of consensus. The assumption of dispassionate, responsive, rational governance has been somewhat strained by disclosures from the *Pentagon papers* through Watergate and beyond.

increasing frequency—that economists, politicians and planners are bound to do more harm than good and that there are no explanations of major economic events and trends other than in the magical forces of the cycle.[4] If views of this sort gain general credit, the acceptability and likely implementation of constructive, informed policy is itself diminished. James Tobin, a leading American growth economist and then a strong critic of the Nixon-Ford program (or nonprogram), was singled out for criticism by Barraclough as an exemplar of the failed technocrat qua "new economist." But Tobin's position was simply that of advocating a rational response to a world in crisis—that the real requirements of earth's billions necessitate an expansion of sustenance, that redistribution and restraint can help but not suffice. It is particularly ironic that the failures of an administration which had been antagonistic to the principle of intervention were used as evidence in the case against management, guidance and planning. However, this kind of skepticism is in the air and represents still one more obstacle to the possibility of informed guidance. We may differ with Tobin and other growth economists on the particulars of how growth should be managed and on social strategies, but not on the necessity of intervention and on the essential solvability of the *technical* problems of management. In short, we are forced to assume intelligent leadership since the game must be played out; but the presumption is more of a hope than a practical certainty.

The Growth Objective and the Risk of Ecological Disaster

Another source of growth pessimism is the popular belief that destruction of the environment is an inevitable consequence of economic growth. Appalling cases of destruction include the creation of wastelands by strip mining or river blockage, intensive use of nondegradable substances, myopic irrigation or fertilization practices, overcropping and overgrazing, urban sprawl, profligate automobilization, and overloading a vast area of ocean, land, and atmosphere with pollutant wastes.

Surely one must block off a path that leads over a precipice. Yet, in the face of intimations of disaster, we must consider the case for growth. The humane potential of economic growth is in the improvement of personal welfare, and there is a vast population which is right now living under desperate conditions. To forego the possibility of growth is to condemn this population to an inhuman state. (The greatest luxury and self-indulgence is to say, "I have made it, and growth can stop.") The number of poor is large: a population of 30,000,000 within the United

States and billions elsewhere in the world. The social product is not yet so large that we can contemplate a stop to expansion and rely on redistribution of the existing product. As we will see, there are many areas in which maldistribution is the issue but it must be recognized that not even the present total product of the advanced nations would suffice to solve the world poverty and development problem. The have-nots would end up with a few additional crumbs of crust, but there are not enough slices of pie, even poisoned pie, for everyone.

Thus, the growth objective cannot be dismissed out of hand. Considerable management and planning skills will be required to negotiate the environmental risks and it is madness to faithfully expect the spontaneous emergence of radical, new, clean, and cleansing technologies to rescue the earth. Instead, we will have to rely on population controls, hard environmental standards, and both direct and indicative planning for new technological development.* Again we are forced to place considerable reliance on intelligent management of the instruments of control and on an underlying article of faith that significant clean growth is possible. It is not necessary for there to be conflict between growth and commitments to preserve the environment: *If ecological concern is powerful enough to stop growth, the same humane interest should be capable of directing the system toward clean growth and patterns of development that will, in fact, provide powerful material and social benefits.* In fact, growth is necessary to effect the necessary alterations of technology. Vigilance, novel techniques, and an unusual degree of control will be required; and within this book, at least, we must proceed on the presumption that these conditions can be met. For without growth, the injustice of poverty remains; while without clean growth, the planet itself may die.

Adverse Social Consequences of Growth

We now come to a final caveat that takes us, in turn, to the core of this book. Let us assume for the sake of the argument that the prerequisites of effective politics, intelligent management, population and ecological control, and technological guidance can be met. There is still the question of social impacts to consider. We must face up to the possibility that policies of growth (managed according to the conventional

---

* There might have been a time when population growth seemed to encourage significant economic expansion, but there is now a large enough catalogue of economic stimulants so that this particular incentive can be disregarded. Population control is not the subject matter of this book. It is treated, instead, as the prerequisite for humane policy.

protocols) are likely to exacerbate social trends which, in their way, are as dangerous as the ecological consequences now commanding attention. These social consequences (which are most glaring in the United States economy) include the following:

(1)   Tendencies rooted in the basic structure of U.S. growth that intensify hard-core poverty and freeze the income distribution;

(2)   Tendencies that discourage a wide variety of occupations, including skilled crafts, public service, education, and many performing arts;

(3)   Tendencies toward particular forms of social organization, none of which are wanted for their own sake. Urban sprawl and ghettoization are glaring examples. More subtle cases include: alterations in family and household structure, attitudes toward authority, man–machine–production relationships, and even sexual practices.

It is the task of this book to describe the relationship among important social tendencies, growth processes, and policies to promote growth. We will see that many policy actions framed on the conventional understanding of the processes are likely to lead to profound (and adverse) social consequences; but we will also see that it is possible to tailor one's thinking and trim policies to obtain a sensible and humane outcome. This is an extremely delicate area: the argument is that the potential of ecological disaster must be faced, given the profound human needs for improved economic welfare. If, however, we cannot make economic growth meet these human needs, then there is a strong case for arguing that the risk of fostering growth should not be taken.

THE NATURE OF GROWTH: "DUALISTIC IMBALANCE"

We now move from assertions and abstract strategies toward specifics. This book attempts a major reconstruction, and it is necessary to rethink the linkages between theoretical constructs, the policies for which they provide the rationale, and the social dimension.

We begin with the assertion that economic growth (as yet undefined) rarely occurs in a uniform fashion; certain sectors and activities appear as driving forces in the economy while others lag. This unevenness can be stereotyped as a simple division of activities into those that are technologically progressive and those in which there is little technological change. In the former, technological change is continuous and effective; in the latter, older techniques survive, and there is little physical evidence of productivity increase. In other words, the incidence of activities with relatively high or relatively low growth potential is not random with respect to industries, geographic areas, socioeconomic divisions, and occupational groupings. In fact, there are many significant associations to consider. In particular, one sees links between technically progressive production activities, their location within major industrial firms, and their association with a skilled and educated work force and with high-level scientific, administrative and technical personnel. On the other side of the coin, one sees links between stagnant industrial activities, small "competitive" firms, and an uneducated labor force at or near the poverty level. According to this picture, "general economic growth" is a misleading concept. Increases in the national product seem to emanate from the technical choices and investment activities of a "progressive sector," while the benefits of growth are not generally distributed but tend to flow to progressive-sector participants. Increased national product cannot simply be viewed as the uniform growth of a pie stuffed with benefits for all; certain people's slices grow with surprising vigor and the shape of the pie can become monstrously distorted as expansion continues.

We will encounter variations on this basic pattern throughout the book: critical activities lead and twist the expansion process, employment is determined by the nature of technical advances within the progressive sector, while income distribution is the resolution of forces that hold the sectors, activities, and labor forces apart. This is the "dualism" side of the picture, a blend of mechanisms that tends to divide productive activities and the general population into two major sectors and associated social divisions. The "imbalance" side concerns trends in costs, prices, and wages that derive from this production pattern. We will see that these trends tend to favor the progressive activities, and for a number of institutional reasons they also tend to worsen the position of services provided by the public sector relative to goods provided by the mainstream private economy. In this situation the hard-core poor, if they are employed at all, are linked to the stagnant activities. Programs which might benefit them and expedite social and economic mobility are penalized by the cost trends and thereby inhibited. Thus, what is perceived to be general economic growth is, in fact, growth that is restricted to the progressive sector. Spillovers of this growth to the stagnant sector are insignificant and, on the imbalance argument, result in damaging cost pressure on education and other activities which might help to effect social transformation.

POLICY AND PLANNING

The nature of the argument becomes clearer if we examine it in another context, that of planning and policy design. Suppose that an administration decided to try to build confidence that growth could be restored and that there was good reason to expect steady increases in real per capita GNP. How could such a prospect be realized? At the moment we would expect that plans for this hypothetical future would be designed around the conventional policy instruments: financial incentives, tax incentives, management of aggregate demand, productivity guidelines, and the like. In fact, such plans have been under official consideration for some time. Yet the realization of such plans would, most likely, resurrect forces which have been quiescent during the long period of stagnation. The conventional policy instruments are designed to propel what we have labeled the progressive sector. If they are used, it is a virtual certainty that the economy will continue on the path of dualistic imbalance and that social problems will only worsen. That is: the gap between the hard-core poor and the rest of the economy will remain open, the urban problem will be intensified, while the social services and the quality of life will further deteriorate.

Of course, some ameliorative policy steps are possible. Certain tax structures and cost- or revenue-sharing systems are less likely to amplify the imbalance factor. The welfare system can be better adapted to the needs of the poor, and subsidies and special programs can remedy certain perceived deficiencies in the social services. However, these expedients can only ease the pressures; they will not redirect the system or work cooperatively with the basic forces. For this to occur a different active policy stance is required.

However, our dualistic-imbalance structural description points to a few critical variables that can be acted on to effect significant social changes without disrupting the basic growth impulse. The key issues are control over the character of technical change and continued support to education as a vehicle of social transformation. Necessarily, a critical reorientation in the way one looks at policy is required. Growth does not have to mean an extrapolation of the present social structure or an accommodation of human conditions to a predetermined progression of techniques. It is possible to break out of this trap and establish programs that will incorporate social transformation as an explicit goal. This will require highly selective programs and also a new quality of planning. The most important "practical" contribution of this book is its specification of blueprints for this effort. The individual programs that make up the scheme will not be of any radically new type. Even the program for control over the manpower dimensions of technology uses familiar guidance techniques. What is unusual is the way in which all programs are integrated into a comprehensive system that ties together economic and social processes and provides guidelines to focus programs on critical sectors of the industrial economy and critical labor-force and social groupings.

Explicit planning is needed since the ordinary guidelines for market processes—economic signals in the form of prices, cost projections, and interest factors—are set to the standards of the existing system and favor the established patterns of imbalance. Later chapters will go into details of this syndrome; for the moment we will take a broader, historical perspective, concluding this chapter with a general view of the process of industrialization. We must ask why the system, when left on its own or when guided by the conventional rules of conduct, can be successful from the standpoint of perceived efficiency, yet can be so damaging in terms of social and human outcomes.

GROWTH INDUSTRIALIZATION AND HISTORICAL CAUSATION

Michael Harrington has called the last one hundred years "The Accidental Century." The "accident" (or rather, series of compounded accidents) is the transformation of social structures by decisions made on technical or economic grounds.[5] Each decision might have appeared "correct," "rational" or "optimal" at the time that it was made; nevertheless, each decision had unforeseen effects on institutions and the physical and social environment. It was in the nature of the accident that these effects compounded themselves into powerful trends that predetermined the scope and range of outcomes of subsequent decisions.

We are all aware of a few such patterns. Take the case of the automobile. Initial decisions resulted in the development of an infrastructure of roads, service stations, and other investments. The existence of such facilities made subsequent expansions of the automobile mode profitable to firms and desirable to individual citizens. Vested interests created by previous growth influenced the path of development further. The end results—or perhaps we haven't reached the end of the path yet—are a physical environment completely transformed by the automobile (the Los Angeles landscape) and the total transformation of our social institutions.

The point is not that all of these effects are bad in some way or that their net social impact is negative. Rather, Harrington's chilling argument is that the basic shape of our automotive society was arrived at through a chain of accidents, without conscious planning or any contemplation of feasible alternatives. The case of the car is, of course, only a starting point. The real power of his essay is in the far broader proposition that the industrial system itself is the result of a compounded sequence of "accidents."

This accidental revolution is the sweeping and unprecedented technological transformation of the Western environment which has been, and is being, carried out in a casual way. In it, technology is essentially under private control and used for private purposes; this situation is justified in the name of a conservative ideology; and the by-product is a historical change which would have staggered the imagination of any nineteenth century visionary. In following their individual aims, industrialists blundered into a social revolution. There is indeed an invisible hand in all of this. Only it is shaping an unstable new world rather than Adam Smith's middle-class harmony.[6]

The dominant force in Harrington's system is the modern industrial economy, feeding on technological change to produce further technological change. Each step of development is justified by individual decisions taken on economic criteria internal to the system; but because of the "accidental" bias that inevitably favors extensions of the existing economic order, each step further enhances the power and range of the system. That is, the efficiency of the industrial order rests on the evolved structure of business relationships, the development of markets, transportation modes, and communication media, along with the parallel growth of educational and research facilities. The characteristics of these facilitating institutions are such that further extensions of markets, modes, and media are naturally seen as profitable and enhancing productivity, while activities which do not adapt to production within the industrial order are evaluated as having limited potential productivity and profit.

The continuously increasing productivity of the industrial order means that workers and managers who are part of this order have a lifetime prospect of growing material welfare, and this suffices to bid them away from alternatives outside of the order, which by definition are incapable of such improvement. In short, once society elects industrial organization, it perforce accepts a regime of self-impelled technological progress, and efficiency is defined within this regime.[7] Efficiency judgments may turn out to mean that certain individuals are shunted out of the mainstream of the economy and relegated to inferior status on what to them (or others) appears to be harsh and capricious grounds. Harrington, in his earlier book, *The Other America*, coined the description of the poor as those "left behind by technology," the victims of accidental choices made at past crossroads in the path of technological development.[8] Similar accidental judgements may bias or control the form of outputs of the economy; as in the automobile example, society ends up with unwanted clutter and cloverleafs because it seemingly cannot afford to do without them.[9]

However, alertness to the destructive potential of growth-propelled change must be coupled with an awareness that a growth process, once understood, can be influenced, controlled, or even counteracted. Ideally, it should be possible to retain many of the strong forces of the industrial system and yet redirect them so that there will be a broader distribution of social gains and a break in the syndromes of poverty, urban blight, and starved social services. In short, this book will attempt to show that a growth approach to social change is worthy of resuscitation. Two lines of analysis are necessary to establish this position: first, we must examine the ways in which social damage results from unrestricted growth; and second, we must see whether, and how, a redirection of the growth impulse is possible. The first part of the book is devoted primarily to description of the conventional patterns: we will see that the strongest trends are typically "unforeseen" by the actors who initiate them; though they are generated by a single, coherent, and relatively uncomplicated growth process. The picture of this process given here incorporates the cogent social categories, takes full account of the role of the large firm, and represents the institutions that create technical progress and guide the dynamics of the system. From the middle section of the book onward, the process is examined for keys to constructive policy, and the final chapters are devoted to a program for controlled and managed growth that can operate within the framework of objectives and hopes which began this chapter.

In other words, this book provides a common logical scheme and theoretical picture that underlies both a critique of the system as it stands and a program for its reconstruction. This scheme is the essence of the book and its most important doctrinal contribution. For some time there has been a division between economists who work in the social problem areas and those who work on the "large questions" concerning fundamental production processes, broad growth, and system characteristics. The division is of consequence and is not just a manifestation of a "breakdown of communication," an "ideological division," or the "distinction between the theoretical and the applied." The division has meant that most of the work on social problems cannot be directly expressed in terms that relate to the fundamental processes of the economy: capital accumulation, productivity generation, adaptation to prices. It has also meant that, with very few exceptions (primarily in Marxist literatures), work on the large questions has taken place in a social vacuum. The policy suggestions that emerge derive from study of hypothetical economies different from the one that actually exists in the social domain; so it is not surprising that the impacts of such policy are what they are.

I believe that the system described here provides a conceptual bridge between the social dimensions and fundamental economic and production processes as most in the discipline understand them. The text presents this system discursively and intuitively, concentrating on the social questions and related policies and explaining them in language that will, I hope, be clear to most readers who are concerned with the issues themselves. The formal scheme itself is presented in complete and comprehensive form within the appendix. Most of its important properties are described there in a way that will permit direct comparisons with the styles of analysis in common use and expedite employment of the system as an instrument for planning and for the design of actual policies.

PART ONE

THE GROWTH ENGINE
MISFIRES

2

The Misperceived Economy

In this chapter we will reflect upon the sources of growth and upon a peculiar condition wherein these and other basic facts of economic structure have been ignored and misinterpreted in the development of what passes for economic policy. The focus for our discussion is the dualism condition, a fundamental split in the economy which amounts to its disjunction into two nearly distinct subeconomies. According to a view which we will examine in considerable detail in subsequent chapters, the operating core of the system is an active, "progressive" sector characterized by large firms, technological change, skilled educated work forces, and an atmosphere of growth. This is juxtaposed against a stagnant sector of unsophisticated technology, underdeveloped human resources, declining employment, marginal career opportunities, and hard-core poverty. The dynamics and forces for change in the society as a whole emanate from business decisions taken within the progressive sector. Yet these forces have not been effectively directed at reducing the drag of the stagnant component, improving the material well-being of those tens of millions left behind within it, or otherwise assimilating them by expanding the industrial core. The outcome is dramatic inequality and desperate poverty within the world's largest economy, and within a society that takes pride in its myths of equality, equity, and opportunities for social mobility.

The prospect of the permanent encapsulation of an impoverished, underdeveloped society within the body of the economy is disquieting at the very least. For those condemned to an unrelieved perspective of poverty the sentence represents the abrogation of an implied social contract which promised equitable participation in the functioning of the society. But set against the destruction of the myth of equality and mobility is the paradoxical malfunctioning of the mainstream economy itself. The progressive sector although maintaining its qualitatively distinct form has sputtered and failed to keep up to the standards of its own best historical performance or the standards established by comparison with industrial Europe and Japan.

It is hard to understand why the situation has been allowed to persist. If the core of the economy were functioning smoothly, one might be tempted to describe the dualistic structure as a manifestation of purposeful action, a program of immiseration or intended neglect carried out by a ruling elite or other dominating force or class. However, this and other similar strawman reductions which treat the state in its policy role as a simple instrument of a dominant economic interest are unconvincing since the deterioration of the economic core affects the putative oligarchs themselves. In short, we must examine the possibility that some of the most prominent features on the socioeconomic map are there in spite of rather than because of economic interest and political power.

COARSE-TUNING THE ECONOMY

Why has state policy failed to produce a climate of business advance, effective social correctives, or even effective exploitation? A possible answer is that the technical operations of the economy are misunderstood and misperceived in fundamental ways by all major participants in the system: seekers of power, wielders of power, apologists, academics who attempt to rationalize the actions of power, and critics. As a result, economic controls have been ineffective, making political power itself transient— lost as each regime fails to master the economy. Were the operational functioning of the system better understood, the state itself could become a far more effective apparatus for the exercise of power and thus a basis for its continuity (whether for an oligarchy, a leader of a moderate coalition, a charismatic populist, or a putative despot). The ineffectiveness of economic controls and the resultant elusiveness of stabilization targets as attempted by a succession of regimes has had the outcome of destroying political power itself. Obviously there is a great deal more behind the falls of Johnson, Nixon, and Ford (and the scattering of Carter's promise and promises in compromise and accommodation) than has been suggested here; but in each case their powers might well have been retained had their administrations exhibited some semblance of economic mastery. The failure to develop a direct affirmative policy has led to the image of an autonomous state with unrealized power of its own, but operating within a constraining field generated by the several major political and economic interests.[1] No one of these interests has shown itself capable of sustaining its hold on state power by activating its potentialities. Yet despite the fouling of the reins of executive power, several interests do hold negative or constraining power over tentative initiatives of the ostensible regime. The nature of negative power is such that all or most of the leading interests may perceive themselves and may be perceived to have significant influence. It bears noting that such influence in no way equates with model pluralistic governance. The veto power of individual groups has not been translated into participation within coherent coalitions capable of sustaining affirmative programs.

This focus on confusion, misunderstanding, and misperception does take us outside the dimensions within which current topics of economic policy are conventionally analyzed. However, it should be recognized that attributions of error are familiar enough in *historical* analyses of like phenomena. For example, it is commonplace now to remember the inconsistencies of early New Deal policies or to treat the Jackson-Biddle conflict over the Bank of the United States as a complex misunderstanding in which the lines of advocacy which were drawn on perceived interests would have been rejected by their respective sponsors had there been understanding of the actual monetary mechanisms and their implications.

The possibility of basic error or disoriented perception does not seem to come to mind so easily in analyses of contemporary phenomena. In fact, I am suggesting that the critical focus is misplaced in such current controversies as those between Keynesians and monetarists of varying degrees on methods of stabilization, and those between radicals and moderates of varying degrees on the question of the locus of political control. The divisions on these issues correspond to meaningful political and economic divisions, but the positions taken do not lead toward the realization of ostensible objectives and interests. There is no denying the loose association within conventional Democratic politics of a labor interest with a modified Keynesian view toward employment stimulation through fiscal policy, nor the loose association within Republican politics of a business and commercial interest with anti-inflationary bias and certain monetary predilections and formulae (nor the ramifying and overlapping of individuals' positions on subsidiary issues). Yet policy formulated on either main position will fail in the specific context of the dualistic structure of production and growth. Both varieties of policy lack the leverage to reorient the economy so that the simpler mechanisms of stabilization can work. Thus, the broader criticisms turn out in large measure to be aimed at a system which is malfunctioning on its own terms. What we have been observing in recent years is not capitalism as capitalists might want it to be nor a mixed pluralistic economy that is constructively responsive to constituent power; rather, the system has been coarse-tuned into ineffectiveness.

According to this description, the state possesses the means to be effective in the conventional policy instruments, whether the state is activated by conventional politics or by the deeper political direction of major economic interests. But because of misperception of the operating forces and misunderstanding of the actual effects of policy, governance itself has been unconstructive. If this view is correct, even in part, the manifest decay of governance is a matter of inappropriate instrumental policies and techniques rather than the inevitable consequence of a confrontation with intrinsically unsolvable problems or ultimate contradictions in the system. However, this emphasis on surface phenomena as opposed to deeper structures should not be taken as a dismissal of the major issues in political economy. Of course, power structures are such that the dominating interests can take maximum advantage from events —even adverse ones—though they lack a clear enough view to shape events constructively.*

These views dictate a peculiar logic: first that we consider policy as it might be formulated under the mythical systems of politics, governance, and social objectives were the workings and key behaviors of the basic economy properly comprehended and perceived. It also focuses analysis on a specific set of system phenomena which form the constraining framework for current policy but which have evolved through several generations of systematically misapplied interventions. These critical phenomena include industrial dualism, dichotomous social structures, and the dismantling of the growth engines of the economy.

Social dichotomy and industrial "dualism" are hardly novel concepts: they appear frequently in descriptions of the economy and critical studies.

---

* The causal agents and agencies are obscure. In the case of the urban crisis—as well as in the more general economic failure—specific interests and powers appear to take profit or relative advantage from disasters. For example, banks and certain identifiable landlords may emerge unscathed while a victory over municipal workers in a retrenchment battle will signal potential gains in a general employer campaign to reassert discipline over the work force. Although there is a temptation to see causation where benefits are realized, it may be a mistake to attribute the death to the actions of the vultures who are seen at the final feast.

However, the concepts have not been incorporated in the types of analysis that provide guidelines for general policy; nor are they ordinarily taken into consideration by policy makers themselves. The neglect is significant here. The glaring policy debacles of the recent past, including declining real incomes, stagflation, lost technical leadership, deteriorating growth forces, and defeat in the war on poverty, can be attributed in large part to a failure to comprehend the compartmentalized structure of the economic system and the implications of dualism. Policy has been developed on a presumption that the economy is homogeneous enough in its structure so that the favorable effects of policy would ultimately be transmitted to all groups and elements of the society. Divisions are implicitly treated as transient phenomena or aberrant market imperfections that will be overcome with time. However, these are dangerous presumptions; only a portion of the economy is driven by the standard controls while the split is not a momentary aberration that can be corrected by ordinary market forces, by a trickle of benefits, or by waiting out the cycle. To the contrary, we will see that the trends generated during the moments of growth when the system is apparently working most efficiently are those that intensify the divisions: solidifying the advantages in production of the progressive sector and, paradoxically, worsening the relative opportunities for advancement of depressed groups.

In effect, we are enmeshed in a syndrome in which misdirected policy has played a significant part. It is possible to sketch abstract designs for constellations of policies that would break the syndrome, but this brings us back again to the issues of misperception and confusion. The facts of economic structure have been covered up to such a degree (while the stereotyped lines for public policy debate are so displaced from reality) that there is hardly a basis for informed discussion.

LOSING SIGHT OF HISTORY: EDUCATION AND PRODUCTIVITY INCREASE

Perhaps the most significant specific example of the misperception phenomenon is the growing confusion regarding interactions between education and growth. Recall that during the growth era of the 1960s, post-secondary education, whether general or technical, was championed both as an instrument of individual advancement and, in its composite "human-capital" manifestation, as a means for national development. Yet in the

1970s era of economic stagnation, perspectives on education had altered dramatically. From the standpoint of the individual student, the prospective gains from continued education appeared to have been reduced considerably except in a few isolated areas such as medical training. At the national level, support for educational finances on the part of the public, public officials, and government generally became noticeably unenthusiastic, if not grudging. In about the period of time it takes a student to complete a college-preparatory program, human capital appeared to have lost its productivity; educational development, its rationale; and the educational system, its constituency.

There is no paradox here, nor had there been a fundamental alteration in the nature of production during the interim period. Sustained growth in an advanced industrial society is the outcome of a complex process that combines technical and entrepreneurial innovation, rapid assimilation of new techniques, effective management, and (usually) large-scale capital investment. Active research and development and an adaptable work force are a foundation for the process and a promoting element. To the extent that compensation flows to critical agents it would not be surprising to find that a substantial proportion of the gains from rapid growth flows directly and indirectly to the growth-active sectors—in terms of personnel, this means to the management and support staff of the progressive sector, the technically sophisticated and educated work forces. In this way productivity gains and growth become registered in the data as returns to education. However, although the educational component is a necessary element in advanced industrial development, it is not of itself a sufficient driving force to maintain development and growth. Depressed investment expectations, insufficient stimulation of aggregate demand, or constraints on critical sectors can inhibit or destroy the dynamics of the system. Naturally with growth inhibited, the flow of gains to the growth-active sectors is slowed; and perforce, those returns to education associated with the growth process are much reduced.

We also have here a first hint of the dualism syndrome as well. Education at intermediate levels, on-the-job training, and skill development during the periods of peak labor demand are primary vehicles for initiating entry of the lowest social strata into mainstream economic activities. The linked upthrust of social strata and creation of job opportunities had been natural primary characteristics of past growth and development, and to a considerable extent returns to education had been an index of opportunities for social advance. The recent breakdown of growth has had a multiple-levered adverse effect for this population. Not only was there slack in the pull of expanding industry but the characteristics of production have been altering so as to simultaneously reduce the number of minimum-skill entry-level jobs and increase the educational and skill levels within the remaining central activities. The combined effect is again one in which the ostensible returns to education fall dramatically and inducements to upgrade the skill, training, and knowledge foundations of the lowest population strata disappear entirely. The situation becomes desperate for them; the system apparently closes down the channels which offered promises of opportunity and participation to previous generations. They are further isolated with the distraction of attention from their situation to the problems of the mainstream sectors.

There is a great deal more to the story than is conveyed by this capsule account, but it indicates the first-order-of-magnitude effects in the growth-distribution-education nexus, and also the source of confusion in its analysis. The apparent payoff to education will be relatively high during periods of high employment and sustained growth, reflecting the active participation of educated personnel in critical phases of the process. The significance of this element diminishes if growth flags (as it did after 1969), and returns to education as measured in terms of wage, salary, and income differentials fall—even to the extent that educated personnel are in apparent oversupply.

This is the point at which the most significant misperception has occurred: the error is that of overlooking interactive causality, and the danger is that of accepting the "market" signals of apparent oversupply and the associated budgetary pressure as a basis for action. The actions indicated by market signals are just those that will diminish the nation's development potential once (and if) a growth policy is reestablished. The reduced emphasis on education and research of recent years is compatible with the requirements of a low-growth economy and consistent with lowered overall expectations; but the long-term effect of undercutting the development of the human resource is a Procrustian solution, one that brings material potentialities in line with humdrum expectations and literally forces the social outcome.

The argument turned around, however, becomes the basis for constructive planning; it suggests that at a high rate of national growth there would be much higher demand for educated personnel both in industry and in support activities. In other words, if the economy had sustained the growth of the 1960s, the 1970s glut of Ph.D.'s, M.A.'s and B.A.'s would most likely have been absorbed in jobs that corresponded reasonably closely to the expectations of students at the time of matriculation.

This is not to say that there are no limits to educational expansion nor that an oversupply of educated personnel could not occur under conditions of reasonable growth. Rather, the point is that education is interactive with growth and that the personnel status of the society must be assessed in conjunction with macroeconomic performance. Apparent oversupply of educated personnel, low rates of productivity associated with education, and diminished inducements to break the poverty syndrome are linked phenomena that may well be manifestations of a rate of aggregate growth that is inappropriately low given the potentialities of the system.

In this context, it is helpful to think of public reactions to the general and specific "oversupply" phenomena as analogous to the pre-Keynesian misdirection of policy in the depression phase of a business cycle. The symptoms of depression are ostensible oversupplies of both capital and labor; but reacting to the symptoms (e.g., by allowing wages and prices to fall) constitutes a "therapy" of bleeding the patient. Budgetary austerity in reaction to hard times can further undercut aggregate demand and worsen the situation. In the context of growth, reacting to diminishing realized growth with "budgetary economies" leads to the discouragement of public expenditures on education, technical development, and research. This, in turn, leads to undermining the foundations of potential growth—another instance of a self-fulfilling prophecy.

The accumulation of errors on this issue typify a class of misperceptions surrounding growth which derive implicitly from failure to focus on the sources of increased productivity for the society at large. The error of omission here is not itself surprising, since for a great many years steadily increasing productivity could, for all intents and purposes, be taken for granted as an intrinsic characteristic of the U.S. economy. Whatever the underlying causes of the mythic bias towards progress— capitalist dynamics, the presumption of social mobility, technical virtuosity, favorable resource endowments, or broad accessible markets—the economy seemed to emerge from all but the very worst cyclic episodes somewhat stronger than when it entered the phase. However, spontaneous generation of productivity increase can no longer be presumed, nor can we expect its conscious cultivation to be trivially accomplished as a by-product of fair approximation to short-term macroeconomic stabilization.

In fact, we will see that the productivity factor itself must now become a subject for explicit, as opposed to rhetorical, management; and the basic mechanisms underlying productivity increase must be comprehended as first principles.

A LOST OPTION—MANAGEMENT OF
GROWTH AND PRODUCTIVITY

Understanding of the process begins with reflections as to the effective meaning of "productivity." The term is defined as the ratio of an economic output to an input—usually the labor input. Productivity is also intimately associated with growth. Where economic growth is understood to mean an improvement in general material status, e.g., more product per person derived from the operations of the domestic economy, it follows that growth in this sense must involve productivity increase. In the popular understanding, a substantial component of productivity increase is a consequence of better machines, more machines, better communication, better organization, technical advance, operation at high capacity levels, and a superior work force. In this instance the popular understanding is largely correct, as is also the intuitive understanding that the participation of an educated and skilled work force in conjunction with active research and innovative management is necessary in order to exploit the potentialities for gain. These are home truths—how could productivity increase develop otherwise?

We will examine significant details of mechanisms that generate productivity in a number of later sections; let it just be noted for the moment that despite the intuitive character of the linkages between productivity increase and the education, research, and development elements, the general perception of their importance does not extend to recognition of the need for their conscious management. But this is hardly surprising since the umbrella of misconception also covers the domain of simple aggregate demand management and stabilization policy. Chapter Eleven will examine problems of perception and consciousness in this particular context. For now our concern is with an apparent failure to make the transition from a situation in which spontaneous development was the rule to an economic environment in which conscious management is a necessity.

The basic story line is written in the historical data of national economic growth. Table I gives comparative growth rates in per capita, GNP per worker over the periods 1870 to 1950, 1960 to 1965, and 1965 through 1971. The 1870–1950 U.S. experience provides an exemplar of growth that was sustained over many cycles but was in essence unplanned.

TABLE 1

Comparative Rate of Growth in GNP per Civilian Person Employed,
Percentage per Year, Selected Periods, 1870-1971

Country	1870-1950	1950-1965	1965-1971	Output per Man Hour—Rates of Change 1970-1975
United States	2.4	2.5	1.3	2.1
France	1.7	4.6	4.9	6.6
West Germany	1.6	4.8	4.3	5.3
Belgium	1.6	3.0	3.7	6.7
Netherlands	1.1	3.7	4.7	8.5
Italy	1.5	5.5	5.7	5.1
United Kingdom	1.6	2.2	2.5	3.6
Unweighted average for the 6 Western European countries	*1.5*	*4.0*	*4.3*	—
USSR (Russia)	1.7[a]	4.2	4.3	—
Japan	1.4[a]	6.8	9.6	14.2

SOURCE: Michael Boretsky, *U.S. Technology: Trends and Policy Issues* (Washington, D.C.: U.S. Department of Commerce, October 1973); fourth column figures from Seymour Melman, "Decision Making and Productivity as Economic Variables: The Present Depression as a Failure of Productivity," *Economic Issues* 10 (June 1976).

[a]Growth in per capita GNP.

We have here the record of the U.S. economic achievement: eighty years of growth averaging nearly 2.5 percent per annum, a rate significantly above those in other industrial nations, and accomplished in the face of dramatic natural population increase, extraordinary immigration, and significant reductions in working hours. In the process one can clearly identify as critical economic factors the continuing upgrading of the labor force, technical advance, innovation, modern organization, and capital improvement. Or as Dennison puts it in his classic empirical study:

It is clear that economic growth, occurring within the general institutional setting of a democratic, largely free enterprise society, has stemmed and will stem mainly from an increased labor force, more education, more capital and the advance of knowledge, with economies of scale exercising an important, but essentially passive, reinforcing influence.[2]

In the American experience the drive toward industrial development was by-and-large uncoordinated and occurred outside of conscious direction, with the active forces rooted in the organizational objectives of capitalist enterprise. The educational development of the society was equally unplanned but, as has often been noted, consistently supported both tacitly and philanthropically by industry and institutionalized in myths of advancement and social mobility—myths which came true often enough in their time despite the violent swings of the industrial economy itself.

However, the moment for haphazard and spontaneous development seems to have passed and the extrapolation of past productivity trends is now very much in doubt. The spontaneous forces are losing potency and the myths must be viewed with a skepticism which is prompted by a closer look at the data. As Table I shows, U.S. growth from 1950 to 1971 and from then to the present time was far from uniform. The country was able to maintain its historic growth rate for the 1950 to 1965 period but growth rates elsewhere jumped dramatically. More recently, 1965 to 1971, the U.S. rate dropped while rate acceleration continued abroad. In the years since 1971 the gap in favor of the rest of the world remains; although most absolute growth rates have dropped slightly, in response both to stagnation of U.S. demand and the dislocations of the energy crisis.

There are probably as many legitimate answers to the question of what happened to abort U.S. growth as there are economists with theses to advance and ideologists with systems to advocate, but certain factors emerge as significant. By 1950 most of the industrial nations were well through the bitter and austere stages of their postwar recoveries and were activating explicit long-term growth plans aimed specifically at productivity growth, work force development, and technological advance.

One might say that growth in the U.S. was supported by a degree of demand management: unambitious, but sufficient perhaps to more-or-less offset the emerging tendency to channel resources towards the unproductive military uses of the intensifying cold war.[3] Demand management had become an established policy principle abroad however, and for many nations, economic management went beyond simple Keynesian public finance to include explicit programs for technological development, infrastructural support, educational planning, technical organization, coordination and encouragement of capital accumulation. Presumably because some of these policies worked, significant sustained growth was achieved. For a brief period in the early mid-6os, the U.S. appeared to be entering a parallel path of development, but the moment was essentially lost with the intensification of the Viet Nam war. No profound revitalization of policy has appeared since. The outcome is seen in the final column of the table, and the figures have not appreciably improved in the years since then.

Although I am suggesting that the stagnation of the post Viet Nam era is largely due to lack of attention to the basic productivity factors,

I am not about to argue that conscious plans to improve productivity are automatically fulfilled as an appropriate reward to virtue; the Socialist and Tory parties in England both botched their attempts at productivity management and there is more to this exception than proof of a rule.* Political and class strains along with intrinsic resource limitations can bind any economic mechanism. Even so, such restrictions would not seem to apply to the U.S. case and there are still good reasons to view the U.S. economy as one which is capable of sustaining growth were the perceptual gaps to be closed. The long-term growth record is a significant fact, at the very least, shaping a basically optimistic pattern of anticipations; so a return to growth might easily be expedited once policy is adjusted. Such would appear to have been the lesson of the high growth years of the 1960s in which the achieved growth and productivity rates were well above the historical average and approximated rates abroad. In addition, although U.S. technical leadership is reported to have diminished in many areas, it is still true that in a number of emerging fields such as integrated-circuit technology, U.S. industry and applied science retains the ability to dominate and pioneer technical advance. Finally, one has the growth potential implicit in the skill and educational level of the present work force, the strength of the education system, and the sheer scale and complexity of the capital stock and infrastructure. These elements are quiescent, if not deteriorating, at the moment; but, as we shall see, they stand as a potential base for renewed increases of productivity and technical advance.

In short, the U.S. economy resembles a modern growth economy but one that has declined substantially in productivity and realized growth. The proximate causes for stagnation are neglect of demand management in favor of stop-go stabilization policy along with neglect of growth enhancing structural policies in favor of military and other unproductive programs. These errors of omission themselves appear to date from the 1950s, when the rest of the world seemed to have completed its shift from fortuitious to planned growth. The avoidance of the planned route and misperceptions of the growth process itself can be attributed in part to U.S. ideological conservatism; but the institutional and political economic setting is such that correct perceptions are obscured at best. The range of policy errors encompasses most of the active elements in the economy, but one generalization seems to hold: that a calculus based on individual

---

* Or so it would appear, but the accounts on the Concorde project are not yet complete, and there is still the chance that the North Sea oil and gas finds will pay for all.

and corporate decision making hopelessly fails to capture the essential ingredients needed to foster a socially acceptable pattern and rate of growth. Again the mishandling of educational policy is a central illustrative case.

To a significant extent, education has been thought of as an individual act, and a private and individualistic calculus is commonly employed in an analysis of educational development. Yet, the economic impact of the educational level itself is a social or public concern and requires analysis and calculation at this level.

During the earlier growth years there was no significant conflict between the private calculus and the public calculus; but the situation changed during the postwar years. Tuition cost trends, largely attributable to the growth process itself, imposed apparent burdens in the private calculus; but the offsetting gains at the public level were ignored for institutional reasons. The gains derive from the direct association of educational levels with general productivity and result from both the improved productivity of the individual worker and the ability to operate more progressive techniques on a broader scale. Neither effect is recognized and the role of education is ignored where productivity increase and technical progress are presumed to be gifts of the gods, the natural rewards of enterprise activity.

Paradoxically, European nations with elitist educational traditions are engaged in systematic expansion and broadening of their educational systems for tangible productivity gain; while in the United States, with a tradition favoring open educational opportunity, the process of educational broadening has been checked even though the process had been a determinant of past progress. Thus, what was both a significant source of productivity gain and a major instrument of social mobility has been disabled.

This brings us, at last, to the source of the dualism phenomena within the present U.S. system. The advanced industrial activities seem at times to be at the verge of developing momentum; but the metaphor is the rolling stone gathering no moss, not the snowball growing to an avalanche. At an earlier stage of our development, economic growth could be characterized as "adhesive" in the snowball metaphor: in the sense that, as the leading productive sectors expanded employment and career opportunities, the population stuck to the growth snowball and was transformed through assimilation into the advancing industries. At the present time, ostensible economic expansion can occur within a few activities, but the pattern tends to be "nonadhesive": exclusionary toward the remainder of society. Compartmentalization of industrial activities and the hardening of economic strata tend to be the rules; as indicated by the fact that the most recent periods of expansion have not had pronounced or lasting impact in ameliorating the condition of the poor.

The nonadhesiveness of enterprise directed, progressive-sector growth poses a significant policy dilemma. With no consistent macroeconomic stimulation, the economy lapses into stagnation, as witness specifically the eight years of the Nixon-Ford administration and, more generally, the comparative stagnation of the full postwar period. With stimulation of the growth-active sectors, the economy shows itself capable of sustained but compartmentalized growth, as during much of the Kennedy-Johnson administration. There have been some policy attempts to break down the division as suggested by the emphasis on human resources in the language and spirit of the Great Society programs; but, as we shall see, it is not at all certain that a policy directed primarily toward transforming the characteristics of a social group can be successful unless it also encompasses planning direction over the conduits of production and technical development. It is a truism that the structure of technical development determines the number of open paths to opportunity in the society. Our examination of the technical characteristics of the industrial system will suggest socially constructive control potentialities; but the examination will also show that in its current mode of operation, direction, and control the industrial system with its underlying reliance on individualist and enterprise mechanisms for generation of productivity tends to reinforce the hardening of socioeconomic divisions.

SOURCES OF PRODUCTIVITY GAIN

What then constitutes a correct perception of the growth process? The first principle to stress is that the education-skill-manpower factor plays an absolutely critical role. Let us again think back to fundamentals. Productivity increase as we have been using the term, connotes an increase in output per worker within an activity or enterprise. Whether the enterprise is a small firm or a vast bureaucratic complex it is, at the core, no more than an assemblage of workers and machines. Present productivity and prospects for productivity improvement will be determined by the numbers and types of workers employed and how they do their jobs with the numbers and types of machines they confront on the factory floor. In turn, productivity gains can only be generated through a few simple mechanisms involving improvements in the designs of machines and tools used by workers, more intense concentration of machinery and tools per worker, the "learning-by-doing" experience factor,[4] improving worker skills and abilities, and increasing efficiency through superior organization, administration, or communication.

Much understanding can be gained from reflecting on handy and familiar cases. In my favorite example, automobile performance data provide an intuitive index and image of economywide productivity change. Records have been kept for lap speeds at Indianapolis, Monte Carlo, and other major tracks with long racing histories. Accept for the moment that the steady increase in speeds—amounting to 2.5 percent per annum on some layouts—is in some way a proxy measure for "productivity increase" (leaving the concept of "productivity" itself unexplained and undefined). What sort of intuitive understanding of the sources of performance improvement can one gain from this homely example? First of all there is the matter of *design*. The cars have been altered continuously and radically to reach the present mid-engine "winged" configuration of the pure racing vehicle. But the design does not drive or maintain itself, and attached to any lap record is a history of experimenting, and of *learning* how to drive and modify the key design (and learning which designs to reject). The new designs develop in part from suggestions emanating from the works, pit crew and driving teams. These, naturally, were aimed at improving the performance of the car, but creations developed on other motivations (for example, plastics from a home-furnishing industry) are incorporated into the new vehicle as well. The staff has to be alert, skilled, and technically adept to integrate these various potentialities.

The major effects are highly interactive: for example, the productivity gains from a remarkable new technological advance could be frustrated if the economy were unable to finance the installation of new machines incorporating the advance; or if its work force were unable to adapt to the change; or, of course, if considerations of preserving monopoly or job rights caused its suppression.* Occasionally, one constraint may be dominating—in certain underdeveloped economies, capital shortage may be the primary restriction on growth of any sort—but interaction is more generally the rule in advanced industrial systems. The greatest insight into this in-

* This discussion ignores the effects of the state of the markets for final goods on the search for productivity opportunities. Ebullient prospects and a flood of new product types might expedite the renovation of the stock of machines, but it might also deflect attention from the production process and retard learning.

teractive structure is gained through focus on the technological-advance factor and its relationship to the education and skill levels of critical elements of the active work force. The lesson is that the education factor, in the broad sense of the term, plays a determining role in each of the major mechanisms.

Consider the foundation event, the Industrial Revolution in England. The Industrial Revolution was founded on technical advance in a pattern of new design and active learning-by-doing through the succession of innovations in textile machines, ceramic methods, and stationary steam engines. For example, Landes has pointed out that capital accumulation at the time of the textile revolution was not remarkably high; thus technical advance was the key.[5] The "revolution" was a revolution because of the enormous productivity increases resulting from each successive design and the rapid adaptability of work processes and modes of industrial organization to the new techniques. Of course, the act of installing a new machine was by definition an act of "investment." However, it would be incorrect to view the financier's search for investment opportunities as more than an accommodating passive element in the process.[6] In fact, investment motivated primarily by the search for simple financial gain was directed more towards peripheral activities or to the implantation of less-advanced technology abroad.

The focus, then, is on the enterprise in the most dramatic areas of innovation. First of all there was a predominant "leading-edge" phenomena. Learning and design innovation were most effective in those cases where they built on what were already the most-advanced designs. There is nothing startling in this general observation; there are, after all, very few ways in which one can improve upon a technology based on hand tools, and experience with hand tools is imperfect preparation for making the jump to a considerably more advanced technology that does offer design-learning prospects. The point is that productivity improvement is likely to be greatest where worker productivity is already high and where the activity operates with a definite commercial advantage.

The technical leading edge tended to sharpen with time since the holders of the most-advanced industrial designs also held commanding commercial positions from which they could support and encourage further productivity change.[7] In the English phase of the Industrial Revolution and in the later German phase, the process of innovation and learning tended to be self-reinforcing in this way and concentrated in locations where industrialization along with commercialization were already most advanced.[8] Historically, the design-learning mechanism was, and perhaps still is, such as to amplify and magnify the advantage of a leading technology.[9] *

There are a number of ways in which we can conceptualize the association between technique and work force. In the abstract, we can think of capital equipment as produced in two formats: one suitable for unskilled workers, the other for highly skilled and/or responsible workers (a hand shovel *vs* a power shovel). The possibilities for design improvements are exhausted in the former case but are wide open in the latter. The skilled worker will therefore be intrinsically linked to technical advance. In another model of the mechanism the view is that considerable sophistication is needed to properly evaluate and adopt new advances and techniques of operation and control. Even when new techniques emanate from sources outside of the enterprise or are to be used by unskilled basic labor, an "educated staff" must be on hand to implement them and to adapt routines to them. On this view the skill factor, at least within a critical core of the enterprise, is a precondition for technical advance. On reflection one sees that this mechanism characterizes the modern leading-edge technologies.

These patterns characterize past leading-edge phenomena as well. Landes, summarizing a widely held view, associates English dominance in the early years of the Industrial Revolution with the existence of a trained and active work force of technicians and mechanics who produced the new designs, adapted to them quickly, and expedited their diffusion.[10] Technical dominance passed to Germany as a result of a historical shift towards industrial activities based on chemical and metallurgical processes and, with it, shifts from an empirical to a scientific knowledge base with a different style of work force development. The small workshop-laboratories of the Midlands with an educational base of *ad hoc* apprenticeship-training relationships and private technical schools operated at a severe disadvantage in relation to the German large-scale industrial laboratories and their base in university education and technology institutions with objectives coordinated to those in the major industries. On this historical view the education-skill characteristics of the work force determined the qualitative aspects of growth—in particular an ephemeral attribute which has been labeled technical leadership. Of course, capital accumulation is

* To this we should add that when innovation becomes a value in its own right that is supported by the implicit values of industrial society; it is *institutionalized* and the distinction between the exogenous and endogenous sources becomes blurred. Harrington's construction goes far in this direction.

still an important instrument of growth, but in the absence of technical leadership, capital accumulation becomes a passive carrier of growth styles which are initiated by the leadership industries of other nations.[11] Thus an English style of industrial development was imported into the continent during the middle years of the Industrial Revolution and a German style subsequently dominated until the emergence of the American style and its international (multinational) outgrowths.

Style is something less than a rigorous term but it carries a number of implications: a particular way of solving a technical problem, a particular level of capital intensity, an implied organizational structure, a presumed skill level for the workers who will operate the technique, a particular coordinated catalog of techniques. The ultimate transplantation of technological style is the modern "turn-key" installation, a complete plant and production system shipped to an industrial site anywhere in the world and there unpacked, assembled, and placed in operation. But the operation must reflect the style of the institutions and relations of production of the leadership industry and nation. If style can be impressed on transplanted technology it must denote the organization and structure of industrial activities within the leadership economy itself.

Examining the production style and work force relationships of the U.S. system in this regard, we find the culmination of the trend toward the mobilization of the technical work force is the amalgamation of the immense modern firm with the *technostructure* factor, Galbraith's term for organized technical, managerial, and planning skills.[12] If Galbraith's views are correct as to the course taken in management and control during and after World War II, technical change is not only primarily determined by the knowledge factor but is also subject to far greater direct and conscious control than ever existed in the rough and tumble technological competition of the English midlands or the cultivation of scientific expertise that characterized the old-line of German heavy industry. The key to the new situation is the planning role of the technostructure, particularly where such planning can be made effective by means of control over the markets for final product.[13] The rate and style of technical advance had formerly been a matter of historical accident (in Harrington's sense). In the technostructure model, the modern firm has substantial control over the rate of technical advance, the manpower and employment implications of such advance, and the product and industry areas to emphasize.*

---

* For the moment, we are ignoring the important question of the role of small enterprises in generating significant technical improvements. The matter will be considered in later chapters.

The modern enterprise at the core of the economy is characterized by its committment to technical progress and utilization of an educated, technically proficient work force when and if the economic environment provides opportunities for growth. Ostensibly, these factors would seem to be positive for general growth, but such need not be the case. An argument that we will examine in the chapters that follow suggests that the planning of individual firms and constellations of firms is directed towards revenue growth but is largely biased against increases in the scale of work force: The enterprise will foster productivity increases, but these will not significantly increase employment within the firm and may generate cost and price relationships that can extinguish activities outside of the firm. In effect, each firm pursues a similar style of planning; the constellation of like-styled firms forms a more or less homogeneous subeconomy; the subeconomy expands its product but not necessarily its scale of employment. This subeconomy is ostensibly a growth economy; in fact, it is *the* growth economy within the United States. It carries an educated sophisticated labor force that is capable of generating technical advance and productivity increase when appropriately stimulated; the problem is that it *need* not grow in breadth and extension in reaction to such stimuli; and when it is seemingly most productive on its own, it is most destructive of outside activity. Thus dualism is a symptom of the nonabsorptive growth of the enterprise.

This then is another major neglected element in the social problem involved with growth. The enterprises are the propagators of growth, but in their choices of production techniques (which constitute implicit plans for labor intensity and utilization), they may effectively check absorption of the educated work force while propagating cost pressures on other productive activities and education itself, the ultimate source of the productivity gains. These critical mechanisms derive from our simple intuitive picture of the education-productivity nexus and the placement of the modern industrial firm at the planning focus.* The structure of misperceptions centers on the neglect of this or like schemes. Needless to say, the conventional views on policy ignore the possibility of placing technostructure guidance of technical progress under social control. The appropriate instrumental scheme is again intuitively based. The educational level of the population is a determinant of the scale of the technostruc-

---

* The representation of education as a factor that facilitates technical change implies that a description of the economy requires at least two distinct production specifications: one for progressive technology, one for stagnant activities. This approach is subversive to the conventional neoclassical view (see the Appendix p. 185) but, as argued here, seems significantly more in touch with the facts of production.

ture-eligible work force. By implication, control over the educational level becomes a way to influence the technically progressive sector and thus, indirectly, the overall rate of productivity change. But this, of course, is only part of the story. The existence of a skilled work force is a pre-requisite for critical forms of technical change; and expansion of the skilled work force would appear to be a prerequisite for expansion of the relative size of the progressive sector within the economy. Ultimately, however, these potentialities are realizable only with appropriate steering of the investment choices and strategic plans by the enterprises involved. Accordingly we must ask how firms can set the pace and style of technical progress, how firm activities can influence the degree of dualism within the system as a whole, and how policy intervention might reverse tendencies leading toward rigid compartmentalization.

In short, we have proceeded from a plausible and unexceptionable description of production processes and productivity factors to an implied line of policy that is actually quite unusual when suggested in the context of a developed industrial economy.

3

The Style of Growth in Modern

Industrial Capitalism

THE lesson of the preceding chapter is that growth and sustained productivity increase are to a very large extent the outcomes of processes involving technical advances as innovated, implemented, and adapted by a sophisticated and highly educated work force. In the United States, the organization of this work force tends to be under what has been labeled "technostructure" planning control. This style of organization is associated particularly with firms that possess dominating market power. Such organization can be creative; it can also mobilize resources effectively and adapt to new developments with remarkable effectiveness; but one should not presume that this creativity, efficiency and effectiveness will be focused on social reconstruction. On the contrary, their style of technical development can be such that growth will tend to be encapsulated within dominant firms and exclude the rest of the society.

These associations are intrinsic to the industrial process and would seem to apply in most, if not all, advanced systems whether capitalist or socialist. In the United States the class of technically progressive enterprises overlaps the class of large firms with dominant market positions: i.e., the *Fortune*-listed firms, the major firms in oligopolistic industries, the major technology developers. Of course the overlap is not perfect; there are declining and stagnant larger firms, and a significant number of the brightest and newest technologies emanate from vigorously competitive, vest pocket enterprises on their way up. But it is the general pattern that significantly determines the pace of technical developments, the bias toward labor saving, and the distribution of gains from productivity increase.

DOMINANT FIRMS AND TECHNICAL PROGRESS

In terms of the creative process, market power is not needed for invention or technical advance. However, the path of corporate development has been such that the attributes which characterize enterprises with market dominance are just those which foster *adaptation* to technical advance. The association is complex as we shall see in later chapters. At the moment, we simply note that at a minimum there are tensions within the firm between those behaviors that encourage technical advance, productivity, and growth, and those profit-seeking behaviors that seek to gain maximum advantage from today's market. Even so, technical development may ensue, almost despite the inclinations of the enterprise. The American steel industry, for instance, has long been convincingly criticized for its resistance to new technical developments that might upset the stability of a cozy shared monopoly.[1] Yet when the basic oxygen process was literally forced upon the industry by the threat of foreign competition entering the Midwest steel markets, the American firms were found capable of making the adaptation and gaining the productivity advantages—albeit belatedly. Relative to Japanese and European competitors, they remain high in cost and stolidly oriented towards protection. But compared to their own earlier operations, they have managed to record substantial and continuing productivity increases. The new production techniques were theirs to use or reject simply by right of being in the commanding market position.

Propagation of Technical Advances

Accepting the fact that technically progressive enterprises also tend to be firms with dominant positions in their markets, how do productivity advances within this class of firms propagate themselves across and through the larger system?

In effect, they do so through weight of influence. Now, "weight of influence" is something more than relative size and conventional market power. The 500 largest firms produce more than half of the manufacturing and mining output, and many among them stand as dominant firms in highly concentrated industrial markets; but their economic influence extends beyond their potential ability to extract the dues of monopoly within static markets. The remaining output of the economy is to a very large extent shaped by the major firms acting as buyers, sellers, creators of technology, creators of job opportunities, and major elements in the labor market. Although these aspects are separately distinguishable, they should nevertheless be thought of as manifestations within a more general system of influence. Of course, as national sellers of finished consumer items a number of major firms directly influence what goes on the final shelf or rack at the retail level.[2] Perhaps the direct effect of brand name associations may be sufficient to turn a significant component of the retail and consumer service industries into little more than conduits for the major producers (informal dealerships in effect); however, the dynamic and historical influences that flow from an initial dominant seller's position are potentially of greater importance.

The direction taken in product research and innovation is one such source of dynamic influence. Consider a rather simple example, a decision that favors the development of one artificial fiber over another. The effects of such a decision within a dominant firm can significantly and rapidly shift the levels of activity among cleaning establishments, hand laundries, machine home laundries, or laundromats. In the case of synthetic fibers, the actual choices appear to have created a bias in favor of machine laundry systems, the production of which is another progressive sector activity. We need not engage issues of whether or not the choices conformed to consumer preferences, whether they improved consumer well-being, or reflected styles and fashion; the point is that decisions taken within the progressive sector are more likely than not to have levered secondary effects throughout the economy.

However, our concern is with how the productivity cost relationships of progressive sector firms are transmitted to other activities in the economy. For example, consider what happens when a national progressive sector firm creates a substitute for potato chips. The ersatz chip is made with a new technology that offers potential production efficiencies stemming from the use of bulk-handled inputs and a packaged output that offers a favorable weight-to-volume ratio and good handling characteristics.* Inevitably, further productivity advantages will develop for the new product

* This means that potato paste is processed like toothpaste and that plastic chips pack neatly.

so that its future cost relative to the standard chip must be favorable. Whether or not the prospect of favorable cost advantages can overcome a taste disadvantage is almost unimportant; makers of the old chip must take these cost prospects into account. They can compete directly by producing their own variant of the new product, or move into an advertising and marketing war, or stay with the old chip and a lower share of the market.

The last, however, is a potentially dangerous option. True, some of the productivity gains in chip making will be captured by workers in the form of wage increases so that the full productivity increase will not translate into an immediate cost advantage for the firm. But consider certain secondary effects; wage increases for the makers of the ersatz chip may or may not be a direct factor in wage negotiations at the old-line firms; but other wage increases earned by other workers in other progressive sector firms will be factors in bargaining. If the workers in the old-line potato chip plant achieve parity with bakery workers, auto workers, or teamsters, the effect is the same. Their wages will increase more or less in line with general productivity increases in firms similar to the maker of ersatz chips; but the old-line firm will not have the productivity gains of the ersatz-chip maker to offset these costs. Thus, with or without the entrance of the ersatz chip, the old-line chip operation would probably have a prospect of increasing labor cost; with the ersatz chip on the market as a near competitor, the cost pressure is excruciating.

Or take another example, a technological improvement such as integrated circuitry for control designs that results in the substitution of monolithic solid-state devices for control devices using older electronic techniques. First, the change alters internal cost relationships to expose less-favored components as targets for cost cutting. The resulting pressures are felt as bargaining incentives, and inducements to create new technological substitutes and extinguish activities that lag in apparent progressivity. Surely such responses to altering technology and costs are the ways in which a flexible economy maintains and improves its overall efficiency in production. What then can be wrong or destructive in the process?

The issue turns on whether the efficiency inducements lead to a broadening of the society's economic base or whether the primary effect of such inducements is to increase the initial advantages held by work force, management, and ownership interests within the dominant progressive sector enterprises. In the present industrial environment the latter effect appears to dominate—that is, the job defining and labor-market impacts of the progressive sector are such that the lion's share of the benefits from productivity increase and economic growth are sequestered within the progressive sector. It must be recognized that the sector itself is a major part of the economy and that growth and productivity increase in the sector by sheer statistical weight give the appearance of general growth; but the appearance of general growth is deceiving if another major part of the population is excluded from the process. The deception is particularly dangerous if policies undertaken for the ostensible purpose of encouraging general growth and improving general welfare only feed sectorally unbalanced growth. Of course, the deception is cruelest where the express purpose of growth policy is reduction of poverty.

Job- and Labor-Market Implications

To deal with this type of problem we must examine some ways in which the meanings of "jobs" and "labor market" in an advanced industrial economy deviate from the usual understandings. Lester Thurow catches the essence of the contemporary occupation-technology structure in his most recent work.[3] Focusing on the fact that machines, advanced industrial processes, and organizations are literally and figuratively rigid in their work-force requirements with the number of buttons, handles, and control nodes dictating the number and types of jobs, he concludes that the pattern of compensation will be determined without reference to the potential substitution of a labor type for another since the machine does not offer such options. As Thurow sees it, relative wage differentials will tend to be constant over time and the entire wage pattern, if it alters at all, will tend to shift in unison. Shifts need not have a convincing economic rationale: they may reflect tradition, or past bargaining strengths, or bias (as where particular jobs in the pattern are defined as "women's work," "black's work," or "blue collar"). Under these conditions, the causal links between specific individual differentials and relative productivities become blurred. In contemporary industry, productivity increases may only be identifiable over divisions or other large segments of an operation and such productivity increases provide a basis for compensation improvements only for the pattern as a whole.

The labor market is transformed. The occupation structure is itself effectively insulated from external market control, being delimited by firm personnel policy and the pace and direction of firm expansion. There are markets of sorts at entry levels, and traditional labor markets for certain skill categories and types of operatives; yet the overall picture is one in which organizational charts and administrative policies define internal

occupational structures which are ultimately realized through the technological development of the enterprise. Viewing this phenomenon from
the perspective of a labor economist, Thurow argues convincingly that the
replacement of the market by administratively determined occupation
structures has undermined one of the most powerful justifications of
capitalism: that simple productivity determines distribution.

However, Thurow did not examine some of the other general implications of the replacement of the labor market. Paradoxically, the productivity factor reenters as an influence on distribution over long-term periods
of development through the medium of enterprise control of the technology itself. This control establishes the scale of operations of the progressive sector and, through direct cost pressures, reduces the scale of other
industrial activities and the employment associated with them. However,
there is no solace for system apologists in this; since the development path
so generated is itself insulated from effective market control.

Implication of Enterprise Control

Thus far, we have described rather loosely a number of patterns in
the operations and technological development of major enterprises. To set
the stage for the broader analysis, let us review the patterns and examine
some of their systemwide implications. The beginning point is the association of educated and skilled personnel with productivity change. On
first examination this appears to be a technical phenomenon based on the
rather obvious knowledge foundations of technological advance that would
seem to hold for all advanced, industrial systems regardless of ideology.
However, within a managerial capitalist system, there are additional developmental and distribution implications since this educated work force,
to a significant extent, translates into the technostructure factor and the
skilled personnel structure beyond the entry level. The compensation received by these groupings will reflect monopoly rents in a stagnant economy augmented by general productivity increases in a growth economy.
Observed returns to education will, to a significant extent, reflect both of
these patterns. Our focus is on the productivity component of these returns and the presumption here is that this component will amount to a
disproportionate share of economywide productivity increase.

The major industrial firms play a critical role in the process. A number of major firms will be prime generators of new technology but even

the less inventive major enterprises can be the passive beneficiaries of advances developed elsewhere but designed to fit their style of operation. In effect, market position converts itself into an effective and superior claim against the future growth of the whole.

The system, as described, implies positive observable relationships between the general rate of growth, rates of technical progress, improvements in technostructure compensation, and returns to education. If the rate of technical progress were given from outside the system and the scale of opportunities for the progressive sector work force were fixed, distribution would be completely determined and there would be little scope for policy. However, the relationships are, to a considerable extent, reciprocal: the rate of technical progress depends significantly upon firm behaviors, while the opportunity structure is set by the choice of production scale and capital intensity.

This last factor is central for determining actual distribution and the path of economic development. We will see that the present pattern of technological choices fixes the scale of progressive industries below what is required to accelerate the assimilation of major groups of the population into the critical mainstream of the economy. In addition, the choices raise barriers against job creation for groups of workers at the margin of employability and entry into the mainstream. These groups face double hazards for a corrolary development is competitive pressures on activities which lack the productivity cushion to match the advancing wage structures in the industrial core. The technically stagnant activities will be extinguished with time; and, under the conditions postulated, there will be no compensatory creation of jobs for the afflicted work force. This process is the source of general dualism. Its modification is the problem for policy.

The system just described is in most respects consistent with the facts of contemporary industry once one strips away the naive preconceptions inherent in the view of the modern firm as an automaton that reacts passively to prices and pressures from the external world. But it is one thing to describe a particular style of enterprise behavior; it is quite another to show how that pattern can be consistent with a sustainable path of development for the system as a whole. This takes us to a set of "economist's questions." Can individual and corporate saving out of incomes generated in progressive sector firms finance the needed investments—and, if so, under what conditions? And under what conditions will purchasing power grow in pace with the growth in product?

SUSTAINABLE GROWTH FOR THE
ECONOMY AS A WHOLE

Earlier, we considered some determinants of productivity change and technical progress as they might be generated by the operations of individual enterprises or firms. Economic growth, however, is a comprehensive process that involves a good deal more than the simple compilation of technical requirements for expanding output. At a minimum, the entire economy or substantial sectors must adjust in such a way that the output finds a market. Furthermore, the conditions of sale for the output must meet enough of the prior expectations of producers so that managers do not become frustrated (or bankrupted) by results from pursuing aggressive growth-directed activities. In brief, the growth of purchasing power must parallel the growth of output and sustain efforts aimed at increasing productivity.

Yet, as we have seen, there are many varieties of technical change that can appear as advantageous to the individual enterprise. Of these, some lead to an expansion of both output and employment; but there is no guarantee that the job specifications of a particular technique of production will match the job needs of the labor force; that the capital requirements can be financed; or that the compensation received by the employed labor force will provide the required purchasing power. One way around this formidable list of problems is to assume their nonexistence, and this expedient has become a convention in many theoretical studies of growth. Unfortunately, this scheme has also become the intellectual foundation for discussions of actual policy.

In such a scheme a constant rate of technical change is assumed to occur year in and year out. The changes are assumed to be forecasted perfectly and the additional capital investment required always matches the new saving generated by income increases. Since saving and investment occur on schedule, the work force remains fully employed and working with the proper amount of capital. In one version of this type of abstract system, the number of machines and the value of output grow continuously at the same proportional rate against a labor force of fixed size. The apparent productivity of workers improves while capital investment is carried out so as to maintain full employment of this work force (and increase its real wage). Capitalists are satisfied with the outcomes, meaning that their prior investments turn out to have been validated by events, and they have every expectation that future profitability will meet the targets they set today.[4]

As misleading and oversimplified as this picture is, it seems to provide a fair approximation of what has occurred in the U.S. economy within the progressive sector during periods of active growth such as that of the 1960s. But it is dangerously misleading where it seems to suggest that a bit of the right sort of stimulation will liberate the latent energies of the production system and that once liberated the system is intrinsically capable of maintaining itself on the growth track, with purchasing power continually keeping up with production and enough saving generated to buy the needed machines.

The danger is in a presumption that today's growth is equivalent to that of earlier periods in which a developmental transformation of the society occurred and the progressive sector grew both in unit productivity and in its scale of operations, resulting in both increased incomes for a class of individual workers and expansion of the class. Such broad expansion corresponds to the myths of growth and social mobility. However, as we have seen, the reality today is that the enterprise concerns may determine a qualitatively different situation in which growth and the favorable effects of growth are limited only to a subsector of the system and a relatively narrow population. In that case, growth is sustainable and can be initiated by standard policy but growth forces operate only within the progressive sector compartment. What is it then that permits enterprise behavior to shape the present tendency towards compartmentalization? There appear to be at least four main factors.

First, there is technological style: firms within the progressive sector create the techniques, machine designs, and patterns of organization which become the next generation of technology. The designs are oriented to the existing work force in the progressive sector and are biased towards providing more capital for the existing work force rather than expanding the employment base of the sector. The techniques are designed so that there may be no financial incentive to increase investment beyond that needed to employ a fixed or declining labor force. This, of course, is something other than an inescapable trend. The analytical appendix will show that even the most exaggerated enterprise-determined technological styles can be consistent with sustainable growth for the progressive sector in isolation; but this is not the main issue. Technology is in principle a characteristic which is within the domain of management and planning.[5] There need not be automatic acceptance of a technological style that in effect rejects the claim of major groups to participate in the economy.

The second mechanism involves a form of political inertia. At the present time a large portion of the society is attached to advanced industry and progressive activities, and there is little inducement to expand or broaden the scale of the domestic progressive sector. The incentive to develop has surely declined from past eras when the base of industrialization was relatively small. Since the economy can appear to be successful just on the basis of the record of the progressive sector, it is easy enough to find rationalizations for why certain groups do not share in its success or why they should wait for benefits to trickle down. With no imperative need to broaden the economic base in an advanced economy, there is neither broad social awareness of the problem nor political pressure on industry to mobilize for its solution.

Third, there is the relationship between technological progress and growth. The overall rate of technological progress and productivity increase may be great enough to create an impression of advance but not so great as to break through a growth-rate threshold above which developmental expansion takes place. There are many elements which interact to influence the long-term, or what is frequently termed the "natural," rate of technical change and very little is known about the response of the natural rate to direct subsidies or to an environment of particularly favorable expectations. For example, we do not know—and perhaps cannot know—the exact functional relationship between dollar grants to pure mathematical research in universities and annual rates of productivity increase in the computer industry; we can only note that unusually high growth rates have tended to be associated with heightened pure research activity. But this does not mean that emphasis on pure research in and of itself brings growth, since the benefits from the research may not accrue within the economy producing the research.*

Specifically, it is not clear how growth interacts with "disembodied change"—a productivity increase that cannot be specifically attributed to any particular factor of production. Managerial improvements and organizational efficiencies fit the picture; as does the type of improvement generated by the agricultural schools (or the fertilizer companies). Generally, improvements in this category would derive from programs in technical institutions and would be enhanced by favorable growth expectations. It is possible that a relatively small number of service research institutions can have a profound general impact.

There is better understanding of "embodied change"—the potential

---

* It has been claimed that the United Kingdom has been unable to capture in its economy technological advances which have been initiated by its research establishment.

for productivity increase wrapped up in a particular machine design; e.g., the latest computer generation. A favorable growth environment encourages capital investment in the newest designs and design development itself. Specific grants to technology firms and such standard inducements as investment credits, depreciation write-off incentives, and the like all help in reaching the growth threshold.

Again, as has been stressed repeatedly, education and skill development are at the center of the interactive process and are perhaps the factors which most drive the system once the threshold is reached. A case can be made that the natural rate of growth in the U.S. was reduced by the deflection of resources away from research and technological development. Military adventures and foreign extensions by multinational firms drained productivity in a few key fields and, by implication, reduced the potential rate of growth for the progressive sector so that the developmental threshold for the entire system was not reached.

The fourth and final reason for compartmentalization, that cost pressures from the progressive sector tend to extinguish the developmental process, will be the subject of the next four chapters. Briefly noted, the key issues are the direct stifling effects of cost on education, public services, and a range of other private activities, along with the indirect effects of these pressures on labor force status and distribution.

The preceding discussion implies the possibility of controlling the components of the natural rate of growth and (with control over aggregate demand as a major facilitating factor) driving the system over the developmental threshold. Thus Japan appears to have pulled itself onto a growth path with a significantly higher performance and developmental standard than we have accomplished. The rapid turnover and modernization of capital, a frequently observed operating characteristic of the Japanese economy, suggests support of the embodiment element to growth and the integration of the capital-goods industries into a rational forward-planning system. Basic and applied research have burgeoned and the industrial sector has broadened and drawn larger and larger proportions of the population into its activities. Similar elements are to a qualitative degree disappearing in the U.S. so that the progressive sector grows at a faster or slower rate depending upon the stimulation of the moment. But the progressive sector has ceased to be a developmental force.

On this view there are two significant dimensions to policy and policy failure. The first dimension concerns fostering and supporting the established patterns of the progressive sector subsystem without any thought of interfering to change these patterns. The second involves attempts to influence the entire economy by expanding the scope of the subsystem. It can be argued that the policy failure of the 1960s involved the latter dimension. The attempt to resolve the poverty problem through growth enhancing policy was an appropriately motivated but ill-formulated intervention. Growth was strongly established and apparently sustainable within the core of the economy; however, the core remained closed and did not extend itself into the life-space of the poor. On the other hand, the current policy debacle involves failure along the first dimension: the growth process itself has been checked and even the core of the economy lacks coherence. In other words, the problem of the moment is twofold: first, to reestablish growth dynamics within the now stagnant "progressive" sector and then alter its predispositions toward compartmentalization so as to extend and broaden its range.

4

The Unbalanced Effects

of Growth

I n the foreground of our picture of the U.S. economy is the progressive sector, a complex of activities which are associated either directly or indirectly with market-dominating firms and which are characterized by patterns of investment, product development, research, and management that result in significant technical change and productivity increase. The progressive sector is essentially oriented toward growth; but given the haphazard nature of stabilization policies in the U.S. economy, the actual rate of growth for the sector as a whole may vary from one year to another. The propensity to encourage growth and productivity change will also vary from enterprise to enterprise within the sector. For example, firms at the leading edge of the semi-conductor industry have registered amazing increases in productivity, while other firms have been more passive as generators of technological advance and have received less spectacular gains—secondhand, as it were. Regardless of these variations, the resemblances among these firms, particularly in those characteristics which foster adaptation to change and to prospects of growth, set the sector in bold relief against the background activity (and inactivity) which exhibits negligible productivity change.[1] We have already seen how certain enterprise behaviors within the progressive sector tend to promote technical styles which strongly favor the sector itself and we will examine variations on these phenomena again and again during the course of the book. The issue for now is somewhat different and concerns the manner in which the growth of the progressive sector generates trends in wages, prices, and costs that tend to inhibit, if not extinguish, activities within the background economy. This effect may be the single main cause of compartmentalization and dualism. Ordinarily one thinks of economic differentials as gaps which will be bridged or filled by market action and other calculating responses by economic man. The phenomena we will be examining now exacerbate the divisions between progressive-sector foreground activities and the stagnant background, yet by distorting cost relationships, destroy the incentive to bridge the sectors through market adjustments.

WAGES, COSTS, AND PRICES

Trends and pressures on wages, costs, and prices are triggered by the direct effects of technical change on costs of producing ordinary commodities in the progressive sector. Intuition is a sound guide in this case and it tells us that favorable technical change leading to higher output per worker will reduce direct costs for a given volume of production. These lower costs permit the progressive-sector enterprise a number of adaptations: product prices could be cut in parallel with the drop in production costs; or price levels could be maintained so that with workers receiving the same wage as before, profits would rise; or workers' compensation could increase in line with the productivity increase. In the last instance, the wage paid the individual worker would increase, but since he or she is producing proportionately more, the dollar outlay by the firm for each unit produced would be virtually unchanged. In this case prices could remain what they were before the technical change, but the real wage or purchasing power of workers in the industry would increase. In practice, different combinations of these effects will be exhibited at different times. For example, in the case of semi-conductor devices, price cuts are frequent phenomena as the principal manufacturers jockey for market positions and are blessed (or cursed, as some in the industry might claim) by extraordinary productivity increase. In long-established industries (such as steel making) where the basic product is fixed in form, markets are oligopolistic in structure and unions are powerful; sharing out of productivity gains among workers, administrators, and profit claimants is more likely to be the case. The pattern of adaptation will shift according to general business conditions; according to relative strengths in bargaining; and, in some instances, according to the preexisting structure of employment among production workers, nonproduction workers, technical employees, and managers. The exact pattern need not concern us now; the point is simply that in some combinations the unit costs of production will fall or the average incomes of personnel attached to the sector will rise.

These trends will press against the economic viability of firms in the background economy and/or the status of workers attached to them. There are many possible effects and combinations of effects, but the substance of what happens within the stagnant sector can be comprehended by examining the prospects for worker standards of living and employment and firm viability in two exemplar cases. The first case applies to firms in which the workers lack the political and bargaining power to raise their wages; in the second case, wages rise more or less in parallel with wage increases in the progressive sector. In both instances we will be considering the position of firms which produce items that are comparable to and compete with items also produced in the progressive sector.

In the first case, where wages in a particular stagnant-sector industry remain constant, firms in the industry could survive in competition with firms in the progressive sector that gave up productivity gains to their workers. Since we have assumed that wages are fixed in stagnant firms, the total labor costs of producing a unit would stay constant and prices could stay in line with the prices of products from the progressive sector. Workers, however, would suffer continuous worsening of their relative positions compared with workers attached to progressive activities. But note that the stagnant firm can compete only if its relative prices hold constant. If the progressive activity passes on any part of the productivity increase to the consumer in the form of lower prices, the stagnant activity loses ground and must cut back its operations and work force. Actually, the expectation is for job attrition to occur sporadically. There will be leads and lags in price-cutting and wage-setting, and some years will be better than others for the stagnant activity. However, the general long-term pressures for shrinkage of the size of activity and increasing relative poverty are inevitable and irreversible because many in the labor force now associated with the stagnant sector are unemployable in the main stream of the economy and there are no effective forces to expedite a transition. When a stagnant sector job is closed out, it is not replaced by an equivalent opportunity for the displaced worker.

In the second case we allow for the possibility that pressures in the labor market can force up wages for workers in a particular stagnant activity (or, as is more realistic, minimum wages rise). The immediate outcome must be an increase in the total labor costs of the activity since there is no offsetting productivity increase. Sooner or later this must mean price increases for the activity relative to goods, services, and activities in the progressive sector and, in most cases, the quantity demanded of the product of stagnant-sector activity will fall off and, except for the sheltered few, unemployment will worsen.

The processes described above might be benign if technical change turned out to mean no more than the improvement of techniques that replace degrading activities. What if, for example, technical change could mean the replacement of back-breaking, pick-and-shovel techniques by techniques using backhoes, power shovels, or bulldozers? This turns out to be an instructive process to examine in some detail. Suppose that the manual worker earned $2.50 per hour before the change, and a backhoe operator $5.00 per hour. Suppose further that in a particular operation—digging irrigation ditches and loading dirt into dump trucks—both techniques begin by operating at identical total costs per cubic foot of earth moved. In this situation, both techniques could coexist, since a contractor is basically indifferent as to how a job gets done so long as it is accomplished at least cost. It is obvious that there is little room for improvement either in wielding picks and shovels or in maintaining them; the technology is stagnant or frozen. Opportunities for improving the machine-using technique are not exhausted, however. New designs, new machine configurations or accessories, improved manufacturing techniques and materials are possible, and each such change would represent a movement in favor of the machine technique and the machine operator. Say the technical change amounted to a 3 percent per annum increase in the apparent productivity of the machine operator. A wage increase of 3 percent could be given to the machine operator without worsening the cost position of the machine operation. If the relative wage increase were less, the machine operation would drive the pick and shovel gang out of competition. The effect might not be abrupt, but the unskilled day worker would find greater difficulty in finding work and, as time passed, fewer and fewer days spent on the job.

At first glance it would appear that the extinction of grunt labor is an entirely desirable trend, and so it might be. There are, however, some questions to consider before registering this case as an example of technical progress, with emphasis on the "progress." We must ask what other employment activities will arise for the manual worker; whether he will become the backhoe operator and participate in the technical progress, whether he will find employment in some other sector, or whether he or his dependents will find it increasingly difficult to find active employment of any sort. The phenomenon of hard-core poverty is very much tied to the last potentiality; unbalanced growth extinguishes stagnant-sector job opportunities, but there is no effective mechanism that leads spontaneously to simultaneous creation of job opportunities in mainstream activities. Arguments of this sort are not uncommon. They arise in discussions of "technological unemployment," "automation," or "laborsaving bias." The generalization we apply to these cases is the following: *The extinction of low-level stagnant-sector activities results in diminished employment possibilities for an entire stratum of workers.* Because of skill or educational deficiencies, these workers are ineligible for employment in the technically oriented mainstream activities that displace the old-line jobs.

This is essentially an historical process which affects different activities in different ways and at different times. In agriculture, the pattern has been continuous and most dramatic with the flow of new technology inevitably oriented to the progressive, capital-intensive operations. As David has shown, the outcome of the process is the extinction of opportunities for a major class of farm laborers.[2] In industry the pattern is more subtle, since the major multidivision firm has the ability to shift its internal loci of production and impacts will fall at different points along intricate production chains. For example, production is shifted from an East Coast city to an industrial park in the Southwest. The workforce implications may very well be a net reduction in jobs for semiskilled operators within the firm, but split unevenly between the two locations. It may also result in the extinction of opportunities in labor intensive supplier firms and the cost pressures of unbalanced growth on labor-intensive competitors. These impacts, of course, are difficult to identify directly, but the outcomes of the process—the exacerbation of dualistic divisions in the work force—are observable.

Additional inferential and indirect evidence for the strength of the mechanism can be found in the qualitatively important case where high-level, high-status work forces are enmeshed with stagnant technology. Let us consider, for example, the cost and production economics of live performances in music, theater, dance, opera, and other media. A rough measure of "production" for such activities is audience size, and an accompanying measure of productivity might be the ratio of audience size to the number of persons involved in producing the activity. How then does one raise the productivity of a string quartet in concert?[3] None of the answers—perform in the Astrodome, take out the second violin and play as a trio (a 25 percent productivity increase), or play faster—carry much artistic appeal. But aside from these measures and a few others that make a bit more sense (improve the ticket distribution system, eliminate ushers), there is very little that can be done to make live performance technically progressive without destroying the intimacy, immediacy, and directness which are the essence of the aesthetic experience itself. This fact of technical stagnation generates a depressing economic prognosis for the performing arts. Successful performers, being skilled, talented, and highly educated, bargain for a wage at least comparable to that earned in technically progressive production activities. This means that over time their compensation goes up while their productivity stays nearly constant, which in turn implies that the costs of putting on a performance increase with time, and the cost of a ticket must increase as well. The process is inevitable. If performing arts are to attract talent, they must pay a wage comparable to that paid in the progressive sectors; and this must lead to performance costs increasing unchecked so that the relative position of these activities steadily deteriorates.

However, there is more to the dilemma of artistic activities than just this direct effect: nearly every stagnant-technology, live-performance activity has a counterpart activity in which progressive technology is the rule. Against concert hall performances there are recordings; against the small studio jazz group there is the rock concert; against the Broadway play, the motion picture. In some of these instances, one sees the development of a valid and valuable artistic medium; in others, the technically progressive version is an inferior copy.* In some cases, the existence of a near substitute (i.e., recordings) provides artists with supplementary (or primary) income; in other instances (e.g., ballet), there are few adjacent sources of high-level incomes to support the basic activity. However, regardless of the quality of the substitute and the existence of income alternatives, the end result is the same: the live activity suffers in economic competition. The evidence for this trend is clear enough in box office patterns and a diminishing number of new productions. Bowen and Baumol clearly show this, as well as the necessity of subsidies, if live performance activities are to survive at all.[4]

Whether subsidized or forced to rely on the market, the performing arts are faced with a disadvantage that grows with time. They can be sus-

---

* The electronic media (rock concerts, electronic synthesizers, recorded performances, etc.) represent the development of a valid esthetic experience, but one distinct from live performance. This is not the place to debate artistic values, but clearly, a strong case can be made for electronic music and motion pictures as significant media in their own right.

tained only if the society exhibits unusual willingness to foot the bill; e.g., a 10 percent increase in per capita disposable income and a proportionate increase in performance costs must be matched by a willingness to spend 10 percent more money on performing arts without getting any more actual performances.

EDUCATION AND GOVERNMENTAL SERVICES

This picture of the plight of the performing arts provides a "scientific" explanation for what is ostensibly an esthetic phenomenon. In addition, it contributes insights into the political economy and budgetary politics of education and a number of "critical" government services. The cost dynamics of growth are perverse when activities such as education, which contribute most to growth and social transformation, are those that are hurt most by the cost pressures consequent to growth. Understanding of these mechanisms is essential if we are to undo some of the damage done by unthinking, knee-jerk reactions to the cost accountant's figures.

At a superficial level of analysis, the educational process appears to be a simple activity in which "production" can be measured by the number of degrees issued or students serviced in one way or another; while productivity can be measured in terms of the ratio of student outputs to faculty inputs—e.g., the student/staff ratio or the size of the average class. However, the classroom teacher is, in his or her way, a live performer, and again an unlikely source of significant "productivity" gains in an institution operating at some reasonable level of the student/staff ratio within a moderately up-to-date physical plant. Can the instructor talk faster in lectures; or should the small class, section, or seminar be turned into a large lecture; or should teaching machines be brought into the system? Each of these expedients (however beloved they may be in the offices of administrators) foreshadows deterioration in the quality of the educational process and decay in the effectiveness of the operation. Here we face a striking dilemma: education is a primary source of economic growth; but the fact of growth makes education appear to be an inefficient, archaic activity, largely lacking in the technical progress which characterizes mainstream activities. Caught in this dilemma, but not understanding it, educational administrators and government officials view education as a perniciously backward and ineffective endeavor. Reacting to cost figures, they force budgetary stringency on the actual operations despite the intrinsic and inevitable nature of the economic pressures. Such administrative reactions eventually cut into the effectiveness of the process itself. Whether paid by the student or the taxpayer, the tuition bill must go up; and, perversely, the faster the economy grows, the greater will be the cost pressure.*

The pressures which are now being felt in education also exist in many other areas of government. Virtually any service that relies heavily on direct client contact (social welfare, counseling, medical services) or on labor-intensive services (police, criminal-justice systems at all levels) will be faced with similar cost patterns and trends.† Notably, many of these activities are services provided to the poor that are essential to transformation of their position. In effect, unbalanced growth causes cost disadvantages that make these services increasingly expensive.

In contrast, the governmental activities which stand up best under growth forces are those which rely heavily on the computer or other industrial hardware. These activities gain from the general productivity growth of the economy and therefore sit in a favorable position in budgetary determinations. Most governmental program allocations are made according to a budgetary system that tends to denominate programs in terms of their *dollar* rather than *real* scale.[5] If all activities increased their budgets in proportion to last year's dollar allocation, stagnant activities hit by unit-cost increases amounting to more than this end up declining in real program size, while the progressive activities are able to increase their real impact. The actual data tend to support this contention: costs for a pupil-day in school have increased at a *compound interest* rate of some 6.7 percent during the period 1947 to 1967, with unit costs for police and hospital services rising still more rapidly.[6] The data on actual production of real services are ambiguous, but there do not appear to have been any technological changes to provide significant offsets to this deteriorating cost position.

Of course, this is an oversimplified view of cost and budgetary factors. The stagnant activity may have other claims to budget resources and a political base that gives it power in negotiations and the ability to claim exemption from the adverse cost position. However, the stagnant activity must fight an uphill battle against budgetary claimants more favored by

* Data on this phenomenon need not be rehashed. Most readers will have had some experience with rapidly increasing tuition bills. A doubling or trebling of institutional charges with no relaxation of budgetary pressure has been the characteristic pattern in academia over the past fifteen years.

† Medical services are a special case, marked by the existence of strong monopolistic controls over the supply of services and trained personnel.

technology; and when performance evaluations are made, the stagnant activity always shows up as inefficient and ineffective in comparison.

That is why education, like other social services that require direct personal contact, will continue to be hard pressed, continuously fighting just to maintain existing services. A deterioration in the quality and types of services offered will always appear as an expedient. The productivity arguments for increases in class size and the use of machine surrogates might overwhelm "educational" arguments for personal contact and the contact of minds. In many cases, productivity arguments will win out; in some cases the changes will not be deleterious and in fact might be valuable—there is always merit in forcing a reevaluation of basic objectives and performance. But in many other instances the victory will be one based on impressions made by "hard numbers" in conflict with "soft ideals," and the changes will adversely affect educational quality.

University teachers are already aware of a chain of decisions that can stretch over years. First, class size is taken as an "advisory" measure of productivity; then, low-enrollment courses are cut. As class sizes in the remaining sections grow, the argument is heard that there is no difference between a class of 50 and a class of 500. Soon this argument wins out and teachers move to large lecture halls; from there the step to closed circuit television is an obvious one; and at this point comes the evaluation document stating that the educational process has no discernible effect on the intellectual development of students. This type of pattern can be projected onto a wide range of governmental activities, from the cop on the beat to the actively involved caseworker.

The argument suggests that education and the critical social services are most affected during periods of intense growth, when the discrepancies between the progressive sector and the stagnant high-level fields are strongest. They are also subject to pressures of different sorts during periods of slow-down, since the budgetary sources on which they depend are highly sensitive to conventional labor-market slack and the client groups they service are under particular peril where the trend in capital accumulation is biased toward labor-saving. (This group can be hurt regardless of the macroeconomic outlook.) The experience of the recent past is suggestive. The evidence is accumulating that the 1970s mixture of inflation, repressed growth, high interest rates, high unemployment, and inflexible tax structures has resulted in severe deterioration of the position of transformational activities. The situation is, of course, difficult to analyze since so many elements in the society are forced to operate in a crisis mode—"out-of-equilibrium" or "off-the-schedule," as it were. What seems to be happening is that the pressures of imbalance build up during the periods of growth or near growth, but the monitoring agencies in the system are unobservant and forgiving when the general outlook is favorable and optimism reigns. The cost cutters and the fiscally responsible have their day in the slack period when there are no optimistic general forecasts to relieve the threat of specific crisis.

Paradoxically, while public institutions are put under heavy strain at their existing level of operations and are also called upon to act as the employer of last resort, no similar requirements are imposed upon the major progressive-sector enterprises. This is suggested in the most recent experience of macroeconomic distress. The progressive-sector firms reduced their overall rate of growth, but still retained their basic orientation toward the use of technology within their internal operations. Their overall demand for a high-level work force slackened, but their internal organization towards adoption of capital-intensive productivity-enhancing technique did not appreciably change in quality (although, as we will see, there are other important qualitative behavioral changes to consider). In short, although the progressive sector is not operating with anticipations of high growth, its basic dynamics continue independent of the requirements of the larger system—thus placing the burden of accommodation on public activities.

Perhaps it is unrealistic to expect the widespread adoption of criteria that would properly weight the social contribution of activities such as education, but it is sheer folly to accept the signals of the marketplace if this leads to the destruction of important social institutions.

It is clear that the formal budgetary systems and budgetary conventions on productivity measurements call for destruction and dissolution of institutions on the criterion of fiscal integrity. This fact alone should cause questions as to the propriety of the evaluative systems themselves. The definitive response to proponents of tight fiscal standards comes from an unexpected source, Mao Tse Tung:

... while a good or a bad financial policy affects the economy, it is the economy that determines finance. Without a well-based economy it is impossible to solve financial difficulties, and without a growing economy it is impossible to attain financial sufficiency. . . . Financial difficulties can be overcome only by down-to-earth and effective economic development. To neglect economic development and the opening up of sources of finance, and instead to hope for the solution of financial difficulties by curtailing indispensable expenditures, is a conservative notion which cannot solve any problems.[7]

PART TWO

WHO GETS THE GAINS?

5

Education and Income

in a Growth Economy

WE have described education as the factor which makes possible technical progress and growth. But, as we have also seen, in an environment of "unbalanced growth" an activity such as education can be penalized in budgetary terms by the very growth that it creates. Over time these interactions in an unplanned system tend to inhibit growth, particularly the mythical sort of growth in which the pie is supposed to grow in order to provide a large slice for redistribution. The projection of decay in the growth impulse is obviously controversial and the phenomena involved require close examination and study. There are other reasons for controversy as well. In particular, the analysis of educational choice presented here differs substantively from the standard treatment of the problem—that which derives from the concept of "human capital" as refined by Becker and Blaug.[1]

THE HUMAN-CAPITAL APPROACH TO EDUCATION

According to conventional applications of the human-capital approach, education and skill development are looked at as ways of augmenting the basic productive capabilities of a worker. Implicitly, the human-capital analysis starts with the notion of a "minimal" man, a worker with the minimum basic education and minimum package of skills. The economic effect of higher levels of education, then, is that of raising a worker's potential productivity above the minimum productivity of this "minimal" man. If compensation is based on the productivity factor, then (excluding short-term unforeseen oversupplies) the educated worker should command a wage premium over the uneducated worker. In addition (presuming that the educated worker can find a line of work where the augmented skills pay off), the gain from education will be realized in the tangible form of a higher paycheck for the individual and higher expected lifetime income for those in a particular generation who have this level of education. The analysis may or may not take into account the joys of the activity itself. Let me simply note that economists who work on this problem would not like to have as colleagues or as students in their own classrooms the calculating individuals they describe.

If the payoff to education can be identified as the increment to lifetime income, then investment in education can be identified as the sum of direct outlays (tuition, books, and materials) and indirect costs (income which might have been earned during the period of education). In the same way that a firm calculates the returns to investment in physical capital or a security holder calculates yield on stocks and bonds, one can calculate the apparent rate of return to an investment in education by finding a discount rate that equates the amount spent to the value of the future gains. For example, suppose that a particular school system pays teachers with a master's degree $1,000 a year above the salary paid to teachers with no more than the baccalaureate. Suppose further that a master's degree requires $3,000 in tuition and fees, and that a beginning teacher gives up $7,000 in income and benefits to obtain the degree. This sets the investment amount at $10,000 and the annual return at approximately $1,000. Assuming a career of thirty years, a standard financial calculation shows that the compound interest rate of return for investing in the degree comes out to be approximately 9 percent.* Carrying the financial reasoning further, the "investment in education" would be taken on if the outlay of $10,000 could be raised at an interest cost of less than 9 percent and if there were no strikingly superior uses of the funds. Accord-

---

* Mathematical tables show that 75¢ grows to $1.00 in five years at a compound interest rate of 6 percent. We then say that the present value of $1.00 five years from now is 75¢ at 6 percent. Similarly, the present value of $1.00 in five years is 78¢ at 5 percent, or 71¢ at 7 percent. Where the outlays stretch over some period of time, or occur sporadically over the individual's lifetime, the only practical approach is to calculate present values at some appropriate discount rate. The educational choice, then, involves comparison between present values for benefit-outlay streams generated by different educational options.

ing to the human-capital approach, an actual human being need not go through all the calculations and make all the projections and determinations. It is sufficient that some of the economic burdens and potential benefits be recognized and brought into reflections on the decision.

If enough individuals act in this way, it should be possible to generalize on the investment returns to society from education. Through statistical analysis in large survey or census samples, groups of like individuals—some with, some without the higher level of education—can be isolated along with differences in income between these groups.* Rates of return actually realized can then be estimated for the typical investment amounts needed to obtain the higher degree. Studies along this line appear frequently and they used to demonstrate that human-capital investments pay off at least as well as conventional investments in machine capital.

The interesting questions arise when it comes to identifying the source of the payoff. The individuals, parents, and career counselors see the payoff in financial terms; but the links to real activity and growth still have to be established. In many cases, the educational payoff represents straightforward productivity advantages (as in the case of a degree in a technical subject where directly usable skills are acquired). However, in other instances, the payoff may represent special sources of gain only indirectly tied to productivity factors (as where the degree represents a way of legitimating preexisting abilities or a ticket of entry into restricted professions). But we will gloss over these important considerations, and concentrate directly on isolating the relationship between educational development and economic growth.

EDUCATION AND GROWTH

As has been stressed in the preceding chapters, many of the most advanced industrial activities in the economy require highly educated work forces, supervisory staff, research staff, and management.[2] There are indeed a great number of associations between educational level and the state of technology. We have already examined a few such patterns: the need for a highly trained staff to operate computer based technology; the need for

---

* In these instances, one might cover a variety of different types of master's degrees: M.B.A.s, M.A.s, M.P.A.s, etc. In the extended sample, income differences would, of course, not be simple mechanical consequences of a rigid salary schedule as in the text example.

a trained research staff to originate such technology; the need for responsible individuals where extremely complex and expensive equipment is used; the need for imaginative individuals on the shop floor to discover new applications and potentialities; and the need for technically-oriented supervisory and managerial personnel to evaluate and install new techniques.

Along with these technically imposed requirements, there are also administrative factors to consider: a high-level technological base requires continuing staff capable of sophisticated planning, forecasting, and control. This in turn creates a need for significant expertise at all supervisory and managerial levels. Finally, it should be noted that a technically-oriented management and research and development staff sets up management initiatives with a life of their own. If there is any validity at all to Galbraith's notion of a technostructure, this staff will create and attract to itself advanced technology, frequently of a sort that requires further employment for itself.[3] Where there is a choice, the technostructure will tend to choose those options that offer the greatest scope and potentiality for technical virtuosity and growth. Even though, as Galbraith argues, employment patterns that emphasize growth and stress on techniques for their own sake may be pursued past the point of profitability.*

These tendencies result in a causal association between education and progressive technology and between the productivity gains of the progressive sector and the compensation of those employed in that sector. This in turn implies that growth is an important source of the returns that are observed to flow to the educated work force.

Intricate and interactive causation is included in this view of productivity. Education may make a worker more productive in the sense that he or she can dig twice as long a ditch as can an uneducated worker. This is the simple "labor augmentation" view. However, our "growth interpretation" goes beyond this in defining education as the means whereby the worker attaches to a process favored by technical change. In this structure, the existence of an educated work force is a precondition for growth, whether the technical change appears spontaneously from outside the firm operating the process (as when a new generation of computers is installed in a user firm), or whether the firm itself plays some part in generating the change (as when its own research group develops a new computer application).

It must be emphasized that while this picture deviates significantly

---

* In Galbraith's view, technostructure-controlled firms would attempt to grow beyond the point of profit maximization and would tend to use sophisticated techniques even where a technique employing low-level labor might be the approach of choice under profit maximization.

from standard theory, it clashes less with what seem to be the major facts or trends. Because of the natural lag of empirical work behind theoretical propositions, there can only be a limited amount of direct evidence in support of the specific mechanisms advanced here. Nevertheless, the story told here is consistent with what indirect evidence there is. In any case, we do not claim that we have presented the whole story, only that it provides a reasonable mirror of reality and an antidote against misperceptions of the growth process that follow from primary reliance on the augmentation concept.

Unbalanced Growth and the Returns to Education

We have identified two possible sources of financial returns from education: simple labor augmentation and attachment to the growth core of the economy. Let us suppose that the two sources are separable for purposes of analysis: the simple augmentation effect as today's wage differential between two job categories, and the growth effects as the expected rate of increase in income within a given job category beginning with the base salary at the moment of entry and ending with the expected retirement check. To be realistic, this should count all relevant components: base wage and salary, promotional increments, profits, profit-sharing, advantageous retirement benefits, and secondary income.

The base for comparison is the pattern of expected lifetime income for a worker in low-level, stagnant-sector activities. For unskilled physical labor, peak salary does not rise much above the starting salary, which approximates the minimum wage, and there is a severe drop-off in later years. On the down side, earnings could drop to the level of unemployment benefits or relief. This is a realistic prospect for many, considering the high chance of unemployment for workers in stagnant sectors of the economy. On the up side there are a few Horatio Alger possibilities: finding a sheltered position linked to the progressive sector, increasing family income through moonlighting and pooling income from jobs held by several family members. (There is also, of course, the classic opportunity of major criminal activity—which, incidentally, has raised its educational requirements.)

In the progressive sector, income opportunities for an "educated worker," besides being more lucrative, are also more varied. For an individual who does not continue to postgraduate education, the income stream starts four years after matriculation at an entry-level salary which is usually higher than the comparable wage in the stagnant sector and which increases from there more or less in parallel with the assumed productivity growth of the sector as a whole. In brief, it is reasonable to project an average situation in which the stream of income and benefits starts at a level above the stagnant-sector wage and increases exponentially to retirement.

Against these income prospects we have the burdens of the "direct costs" of education, the tuition bill, and the "indirect costs," primarily the foregone income or wages that would have been earned in the stagnant sector. This by construction will be the same for someone starting school today or a younger sibling who matriculates five or ten years in the future. However, the cost of tuition can be expected to increase over time because education is a "live" service that must pay the progressive-sector wage (the unbalanced growth argument). These trends interact in complicated ways to produce significant differences in the decision setting as it will be perceived at different times by prospective matriculants of differing background, resources, and status. There are coherent patterns, however, and at this point we can make good use of the financial calculations of the human-capital decision model.

The Individual Decision

Suppose that at the present time four years of "education" are required to prepare for progressive-sector employment. Suppose further that the student gives up immediate income of $4,000 per year to go into the educational program, and that the tuition bill is $2,000 to start but increases at an average rate of 3 percent per year in accordance with the unbalanced growth prediction. Let us further suppose that at the time education begins the minimum entry wage in the progressive sector is $6,000. This wage is expected to grow (after allowing for inflation) at an average annual rate of 3 percent (projected salary increases, promotional increments, etc.) for a working lifetime after four years of college of forty-four years. Taking discounted values of the benefit stream and outlay amounts, we discover that net present value is zero at an interest rate of approximately 14 percent, positive at lower rates, and negative at higher rates; i.e., the prospect resembles an investment which appears to be returning 14 percent.[4] A few additional considerations will put these figures into context. Suppose the tuition bill were increased; this would amount to increasing the amount of the (negative) outlay component and reducing the rate of return. Suppose education required a fifth year; this would add outlays and reduce benefits by shortening the working lifetime and again the impact would reduce the rate of return.* On similar logic, a lower growth rate in incomes would lower rates of return, but would somewhat ease the tuition effect; while redistribution that favors the stagnant sector alternative would reduce the prospective gains from education by narrowing the expected income differential. These factors can be influenced by policy, either for individuals or for broad groups; thus, there is every reason to say that the conditions for educational choice are system-determined. The social implications of various choice positions are our next concern.

THE DICHOTOMOUS DISTRIBUTION

As we have seen, the economic component of the educational decision is ultimately a choice between progressive sector and stagnant sector lifetime income streams. In effect, according to fairly reasonable sample data, the decision amounts to a commitment to invest a total of upwards of $24,000 in direct and indirect outlays over a four-year period in order to earn a 14 percent rate of return. Is that a reasonable venture? The answer is different for individuals or families of different class backgrounds.

It is a truism that the poor have few material resources, little ability to handle substantial commitments, and face high finance costs. This suggests there may be two rates of interest governing the educational decision: a relatively low rate for those families who have already made it into the progressive sector; and a relatively high rate for the children of the poor—or what amounts to the same thing, total inability to foot even a small part of the educational bill. Only the group with access to the relatively low rate will invest in education, and accordingly the distribution of population between these individuals and the relatively poor will remain frozen for the immediate future. The social barrier thus can be portrayed as a financial one.

The barrier itself is felt as one or a combination of the following factors. In the first place, the poor, especially if they are close to a sub-

* One area in which little is known or there is little convincing conjecture concerns the effects of historically high interest rates and inflation rates on the educational choice. In later sections we will consider dampened growth expectations as the topical and relevant contemporary case; but it is not at all clear if this is the best way to describe the current economic environment.

sistence standard of living, may totally lack funds to finance education. Moreover, external financing of human capital investments is subject to institutionalized biases against lending to the families of the poor. (This situation is exacerbated where current family income is accepted as the criterion for credit worthiness. It is improved where loan programs are subsidized and subjected to a means test.) The interest rate paid by the poor is implicitly influenced by a large "risk premium" which, after all, reflects the social reality. Even if the poor complete their education, lower social status or cultural background reduces the likelihood of eventual economic success. And, of course, the risk of noncompletion weighs heavily on the poor. If the degree is not completed, the loan obligation persists even though the income stream originally projected does not materialize.

All this, of course, is very abstract. A more realistic portrayal would show variety within any class of matriculants corresponding to various subcategories of the middle classes, various educational and intellectual traditions associated with different socioeconomic and demographic groupings and, of course, various levels of attainment in scholastic aptitude. These factors are important in determining how a particular age cohort of students will affiliate with different schools and professions. Many interesting and familiar patterns are involved here: the return of children of alumni and alumnae to alma mater, the ascent to the Ivy League of children of municipal college graduates, and the first-time matriculants from particular families and social groupings. We will look at some of these patterns in the following chapters.

INTERIM CONCLUSIONS AND PRACTICAL CONSIDERATIONS

Our main conclusion has been that the educational choice tends to segregate individuals into two qualitatively different groups which correspond to divisions in the structure of the economy itself. The financially motivated educational decision sustains the division, so it is essential to examine this mechanism with care. Of course, the human-capital model may be more illuminating as an empirical scheme with which to relate some portion of present income differentials to past investment in education and skill development than as a metaphor with which to describe the contemporary decision. There will be a few instances in which something close to explicit rate of return comparisons occurs; but for the most part, students and their parents react to signals of a different sort.

Many (including those with extraordinary talent) will be well away from the margin of choice. This is certainly the case in the more affluent families where higher education is never an issue; college is a foregone conclusion and the only question concerns the particular career path to be followed. At the opposite extreme, the problem for many of the hard-core poor is survival in the streets, achievement of simple literacy, and avoidance of addiction. Here the question of higher education does not arise and the choice is effectively "made" by the time the child reaches the teenage years. In the typical New York City slum junior high school, it is rare for more than one or two children in a class of thirty to be open to the possibility of pursuing an academic line at the high-school level.

The area of meaningful choice, then, is for groups between these extremes. One must note here the importance of institutional and local patterns. For example, consider a company town in Ohio where the typical expectation is for sons to follow fathers in blue collar ratings, for daughters to work in the shops or in the company front office for a few years before marriage. Possibly a very few exceptional students (and of course, the children of the top executives) break away to the state university, to out-of-state schools, or to the big city. Now, open a state university branch within easy commuting distance, and the choice widens. Within a few years, college, junior college, or technical school becomes a meaningful option for a major portion of the graduating high-school class and education begins to be seen as a means of entry to new lines of work that are qualitatively different from the traditional ones.

Similar choice situations apply to municipal colleges, extension schools, junior colleges, agricultural schools, and special institutions like the Negro colleges of the South. To the limited extent that economic costs and consequences are perceived, the above financial decision scheme would seem to be a reasonable approximation.

The Current Crisis in Higher Education

One way to examine the workings of an economic mechanism is to see how it performs when the larger system in which it operates is clearly working badly. Take the current "crisis in higher education." The primary symptoms of this crisis are some half million or more unfilled or "poorly filled" places in universities and colleges, along with severe cost and budgetary pressures within universities which were staffed and structured in accord with previous growth projections. The disruptive effects on the scholarly and creative life of the country have been enormous. What caused the crisis?

The end of selective service and miscalculations of the baby boom partially explain the excess supply of educational vacancies. But that is not the whole story. As repeated comment has it, "There are also second thoughts on the (payoff) and returns to education."

Why the second thoughts and revaluations of education? The obvious answer (in terms of the arguments presented here) is that the retardation of national growth has diminished to a significant extent the anticipated flow of benefits from education, and has also reduced the financial resources of many at the margin of choice. And in fact, evidence based upon extrapolations of current salary levels and job availabilities supports this. Thus during a time of stagnation the perceptions of shrinking resources and scarce jobs combine with depressed anticipations for the future leading to abrupt worsening in the apparent financial returns from investment in education. Some of the unbalanced-growth pressure may seem to relax as the national growth rate drops, but this effect will be swamped by the downgrading of expectations. It is a good guess as well that the effects will be felt most strongly by the poor.

The overall picture is an unhappy one: growth intensifies cost pressures on the educational system, but stagnation leads to rapid erosion of the base of prospective matriculants and precipitates a crisis. This is a deadly syndrome; the "revaluations and second thoughts" provoked by the crisis serve no useful purposes. The financial signals are cries for cuts and stringency, but education is one of the critical ingredients in a successful growth policy. Retard growth by inhibiting other elements of the process, and the payoff to education itself is reduced. Constrict the educational system in reaction to the financial signals, and prospects for future transformational growth are killed. In short, the market controls which govern the development of the educational system fail as an adaptive mechanism.

6

Freezing the Income
Distribution

Accoriding to the view of education, technical advance, and distribution presented here, "economic growth" is entirely consistent with social stagnation. In fact, to many observers tendencies toward social divisions seem to be most intense at the moment of strongest growth as during the Sixties. True, we know from recent experience that economic stagnation can only worsen the immediate fiscal problems of educational institutions, diminish personal anticipations, and make assimilation through education an uneconomic proposition for marginal groups; but what we do not know is whether or how tendencies toward social stagnation can be reversed within a growth economy. The process of assimilation through education is complex, as is the general growth-productivity mechanism. Thus we will have to examine the terms of the educational decision more closely and in a way that projects the positions of later generations to determine if time and growth can alter the relative position of the hard-core poor and the structure of incentives they face.

THE OUTLOOK FOR FUTURE GENERATIONS

The financial barrier facing the calculating individual is the metaphorical equivalent of the social and institutional barriers of the real world. For the present generation of hard-core poor these barriers are solid. But can the barriers break down with the passage of time? In terms of the human capital decision, will the figures alter so that the educational choice will become worthwhile for individuals in some later generation? To answer this question, we must project the basic trends of cost and advantage, and then recalculate break-even conditions for financing education as they would appear to each succeeding generation at the threshold of education. Thus we look at a succession of projected present values: the first for a seventeen-year-old in 1979, the next for a seventeen-year-old coming of age in 1980, the next for a seventeen-year-old coming of age in 1981, and so forth. We call these projected present values "contemporary values" and ask if contemporary value will ever turn from negative to positive for a representative individual within the population of the hard-core poor.

There is at first a glimmer of hope. The educational trade-off may improve with the passage of time simply as a mechanical consequence of the compound interest aspect of growth. True, according to the unbalanced-growth cost argument, the tuition component of educational outlay will increase with time. Thus, seventeen-year-olds ten years from today will face a much higher tuition bill than that faced by today's high school graduates, just as today's graduates face a higher bill than the graduates of ten years ago. However, the benefits stemming from progressive sector income will also be larger if growth is sustained. Calculations indicate that if the educational period is of standard length, and the working lifetime is about what it is now (so that there is enough time for the income benefits to offset the inflated tuition bill), contemporary value for the poor will begin to improve.[1]

The issue can be restated in the following way: on present standards, the education route to full assimilation of the poor into the core of the economy is ruled out by the economics of private choice; are the trends of the system such that the terms of choice will change to favor assimilation for a later generation? If so, we have found a natural and spontaneous solution to the problem of income–class disparities and confirmation of the belief that a growing modern industrial society tends to extend its benefits broadly. Unfortunately, this may be a false hope.*

---

* Some readers may feel that the argument is moving toward the tearing apart of specially constructed straw men. But for many economists, questions of educational policy must be expressible and resolvable in terms of the human-capital model, and this sets the framework for debate. By the conventions of the discipline the economics of private choice are an essential datum in an organized analysis of social choice. This orientation, however artificial it may appear, is necessary. We are treating the progressive sector core of the economy as a closed growth subsystem, and the choice mechanism is one of the factors that tends to encapsulate it.

Incentives to break down the dichotomization of the system depend upon whether (or to what extent) "contemporary value" changes over time. Recall the figures introduced in the previous chapter: progressive-sector income of $6,000 and a growth rate of 3 percent; depressed-sector income of $4,000. The tuition bill in the initial period was $2,000, implying an internal rate of return to education of 14 percent. Now suppose we extrapolate growth trends for five years and recalculate the terms of the investment decision. The rate of return would increase from 14 to 16 percent after this delay and would increase to 18 percent after a delay of ten years and to 20 percent after twenty years. (Delays of forty, fifty, and seventy years would correspond to rates of 25, 30, and 40 percent respectively.) These figures mean that a family facing financial costs of 20 percent would find the present value of educational investment to be negative today but favorable for the next generation of children twenty years hence; contemporary value becomes positive at that time.

Thus a possibility for transformation exists, but the prospects are less than encouraging. Other trends interfere with the picture and are such as to make spontaneous remedies and bootstrap transformation of the poor more and more a remote possibility. This is a critical point; in previous years and generations, spontaneous forces led to increases in the demand for education as an economic proposition and corresponding increases in the number of places within the system. Opportunity has been a dominating motif in the society. The proposition suggested here, however, is that under current conditions and trends, opportunities and optimism for social transformation will be seriously restricted.

INHIBITING FACTORS

The Tuition Barrier

The financial model oversimplifies by reducing the educational decision to one involving simple comparison of present values (or of rates of return to costs of finance). There can be a great deal of difference between a prospect offering a 15 percent rate of return on a $10,000 investment and one offering a 15 percent rate of return on a $20,000 investment. For most of us, the absolute dollar amount that has to be committed makes a difference. Tuition trends impelled by unbalanced growth imply a steadily increasing level of expenditures in absolute terms (above effects attributable to general inflation). The dollar amount that has to be financed increases exponentially and this absolute financial barrier offsets to a significant extent improvements in the rate of return itself. To point this up, note that the figures used in the numerical example are completely out of date and actually pertain to the educational choice circa 1970. Realistic current figures for the direct cost and opportunity cost components are slightly less than double those given, reflecting both pure inflation and unbalanced growth effects. The financial requirement for the full (private) costs of four years of college therefore ranges between $25,000 and $40,000, depending upon individual circumstances. Even for those individuals whose income and wealth have increased in step with the tuition bill, the greatly increased dollar requirements may represent a qualitative increase in obstruction.

Interruptions of Growth

It follows that if growth is the engine for improvements in contemporary value, cessation of growth delays the process. The stagnation of the seventies is a case in point; the education-transformation process is essentially on hold. In terms of our numerical example, if there had been substantial real growth over the period, the current figures would not simply be approximately double those of five years ago; progressive-sector income (indexed by starting salaries for college graduates) would be higher still by an additional 10 to 20 percent and the financial advantage of higher education would be generally viewed as favorable. The full impact of the hiatus in growth has not been assessed. The deteriorated career outlook of today's degree recipients is of itself a potential source of further stagnation in general growth. The combined effects on younger students further down the pipeline are likely to be profound. In other words, if growth is interrupted or viewed to a significant extent as interruptable, the tendency towards improved contemporary value can be significantly retarded. National surveys of individual "ladder of success" anticipations have been taken in 1964, 1974, and 1975.[2] It is not surprising that individuals throughout the society now rank themselves lower down on the success ladder than did individuals in 1974 or 1964. What is extremely disquieting, however, is a general pessimism in which individuals see little chance of moving up rungs over the years to come. In the previous polls (taken in years of growth), individuals projected substantial improvements in their personal status. Such deteriorated anticipations must link directly to views on opportunities through education.

Length of Study ... Higher Degrees

With the passage of time and with growth, certain other trends will establish themselves; and on balance these trends will tend to retard redistribution through the education mechanism. First, it is likely that the growth process will lead to a number of changes in tastes and in the conventional institutions of the labor market. The work day or week will be continuously reduced and the retirement age lowered within the progressive sectors while money incomes will increase at a lower rate than the actual rate of productivity increase. The effect that this trend may have on the investment incentives of the poor is problematical. Will they comprehend and react to a complex package of income and leisure time as they might react to the "invisible equivalent" in dollar terms? *

My own predilection is not to take this effect too seriously, but the argument provides a useful prelude to one of greater potential significance. The taste for leisure may operate as a willingness to grant one's children more years in school and more years in nonwork "life experience." The taste may, in effect, be institutionalized as increased degree and educational requirements for particular progressive-sector activities. We need not elaborate the mechanisms that have led to degree escalation. The point is that this trend could adversely restrict the children of the present poor.

The number of years devoted to education is critical here. An increase in the schooling period has a double-barreled impact, adding significance to the tuition and cost components in the equation and reducing the period over which income benefits accrue. This effect is easily illustrated with numerical calculations. If we use the figures of the earlier example for comparison, increasing the study period from four to six years would result in a drop of internal rate of return from 14 to 12 percent. Delays for assimilation would increase from five to seventeen years at a 16 percent discount rate, from ten to thirty-five years at 18 percent, from twenty to fifty years at 20 percent.[3] Again the point is not whether the additional years of education result in real productivity gain, but that a tendency toward a longer educational period results in a higher barrier and reduced potentiality for social transformation. If an M.B.A. is a prerequisite for

---

* If the taste for leisure is only learned after one has already tasted material prosperity, the class distribution may remain frozen; the rich, reckoning income equivalents to leisure in their value computations will continue to invest in education, while the poor, basing values only on tangible pecuniary elements, will still not find the educational commitment worthwhile (as the dollar payout is below its potential, while the period of compounding is reduced).

entry into the major industries, and the B.A. is only a degree taken in transit, as it were, the dichotomous distribution freezes hard.*

Part-Time Study

Part-time study has long been an avenue for social and economic mobility among the urban poor. Yet this road to economic mobility is particularly damaged by the whipsaw effects of degree escalation.⁴ The part-timer will have missed many lines of promotion and advancement by the time of graduation and will have faced excruciating strains in pursuing a double career; tendencies toward degree escalation or cost inflation are very powerful and destructive for this class of students, who at the very best of times totter close to the margin of choice.†

The Dilemma in Income Redistribution

Our analysis distinguishes between simple income redistribution and social transformation. The former concept is static in nature and connotes a momentary alteration in the distribution of dollar claims. The latter concept is dynamic in nature and connotes the creation of a continuing and permanent claim to participate in the progressive sector and draw income from it—whether the claim is attributable to an alteration in productivity, an improved political or bargaining position, or a better credential. As stated here, the dualism and dichotomization phenomena apply primarily to the hardening of barriers to transformation. A dilemma is emerging, however, since policies to ameliorate the symptoms of poverty of the moment can conflict with programs aimed at expediting the transformation. Misperceptions abound on this point, along with a stock of knee-jerk prejudices retained from past controversies over the main interventions: welfare, social security, minimum wages, "poverty policies," medical finance, food subsidies, and significant components of other major programs.

---

* The rate at which contemporary value can improve with time is sensitive to the length of the educational period. Rough calculations show that if the educational period reaches one-third of the entire working lifetime, there will be no contemporary value improvement and hence no improving opportunity for the poor. The critical ratio is reached now in certain medical specialties and a few academic fields. On the logic here, these areas would not on their own become vehicles for social transformation. Extraordinary subsidies would be required to break this pattern.

† Generally, the part-time college student begins study after one or more of the following: a period of military service, a period of part-time secondary school education, a period (sometimes of quite a few years) outside of school. There will also be sporadic breaks in the period of schooling once it has begun.

In later chapters we will examine approaches that give maximum scope to the forces of transformation; for the moment, however, we will take a first look at a mechanism wherein increases in stagnant-sector base income, whether from wages or welfare, can damp the spontaneous transformation.

The nature of the dilemma is exposed when we examine the matter in terms of the individual or family calculation of the value of education. In this context, increases in the base income of the working poor in stagnant activities have two effects: the sacrifice of present income for the period of education is greater and the differential from later progressive-sector employment is reduced. These effects lead to reduced present values for educational investment. They also retard the process of contemporary value improvement and any spontaneous breakdown of the dualism phenomena. However, there are complexities. A likely side effect would be an improvement in the financial position of the poor that would help to break down the dollar barrier of the tuition bill. On the other hand, growth of poverty class income implies transfers from progressive-sector income recipients, so that it is possible that the incentive to invest within the fortunate class will be further eroded. To cut the knot it is necessary to make transformation policy and social planning explicit; and some ways to do this are discussed in succeeding chapters.

The issue of the moment, however, is to complete the dissection of the private-choice mechanism. The claim is that the private mechanism alone is incapable of accomplishing the implied social decisions on redistribution and attainable growth. The unfortunate practical consequence of redistributive altruism through conventional transfer programs can be restriction of the education/skill base of the progressive sector, leading to a situation in which the growth rate of the economy as a whole might slip toward zero. The default case of malevolence in transfer policy is preposterous, keeping the poor in poverty until the relative position of their children has deteriorated so far that contemporary value perforce improves or there is no choice but to step in with crash remedies.

I have intentionally put things in this convoluted form in order to give emphasis to the dilemma. Education is a vehicle for social transformation and effective redistribution as well as a primary source of growth. The decision to go on to a particular level of education is traditionally within the private domain, but direct private costs for education and the number of places in educational institutions are subject to social and political influences. The growth issue is also in the public or social domain but is unappreciated and misperceived in politics, nor are appropriate instruments available at the level of operating agencies. The impetus to develop along this dimension is lacking; largely because, as a matter of history, the private domain took care of this line of development in a quite satisfactory way. In the early years of industrialization and growth, the inducement to go on to further education was high, the social transformation aspect was apparent, and the realized growth and productivity gains more than validated anticipations. My argument now is that in a more mature economy the inducements for transformation through the education mechanism are blurred by an affluence which provides the means for redistribution through conventional pecuniary means (differential tax rates, wage subsidies, or transfers). Relying exclusively on the latter can lead to a dramatic deterioration of the growth impetus which brought the system to where it is. It should be clear from previous discussions that I am hardly opposed to the idea of redistributive transfer *per se*, nor do I wish to provide ammunition for those who locate the source of our problems in the "generosity" of the welfare system. The issue is that of managing altruism so as to eliminate interferences between education, transfer, and social-transformation programs, on the one hand, and effective growth policy on the other. However, before seeing how this can be done, it is important to understand why individual educational institutions will not be the instruments of constructive development.

Educational Finance

In the sort of budgetary environment in which schools, colleges, and universities operate, the unbalanced growth cost pressures force internal changes that seem in all cases to be antagonistic to the transformation process. Because of the need for compensatory programs and special support, students drawn from the lower social classes are frequently the most costly to service and are hardly viewed as sources of tuition revenue (or benefactions). Thus, although an educational institution may for a time adopt the transformation idea, it is more likely to suffer second thoughts when it evaluates its efforts in the face of budgetary pressures that may imperil its traditional functioning. This is, of course, a condensed description of New York City's experience with open enrollment at the college level. The costs of the program (as originally formulated) were found to be extremely high; to more traditional academicians, the impact of the program appeared to be the destruction of intellectual values; and the prospects of further intensification of budgetary pressure were depressing to administrators.

As has become clear, budgetary prospects are even more unpromising in the face of deteriorating growth anticipations. The institution's cost structure carries within it mandated cost elements based on recent growth, but the relative rates of return and job opportunities are seen as diminishing by the prospective students. (Using the figures of the example we have been following, a rate of return of approximately 14 percent in the face of 3 percent national productivity growth falls off to 8 or 9 percent if expected national growth itself drops off to 2 percent.) As well as depressing individuals' anticipations, the deteriorating situation is seen by public authorities as a collapse of the rationale for transformational education.

CONCLUSIONS

All this suggests a specific conclusion: so long as the key decisions are made at the level of the individual, the family, and the single educational institution, or by public agencies emulating the private choice, the decisions will be biased against educational transformation. From this it can be argued that unless one is content with the implied freezing of the income distribution, control over the process must be a system-wide or national concern. This concern implies that educational finance be linked to the broad saving behavior of the economy; and since saving must also finance ordinary capital formation, a delicate interplay between machine-capital and human-capital results. In general, it will be true that an increase in the proportionate scale of education will require an accommodating adjustment of machine-capital in the system. It is critically important that these adjustments result in the creation of the appropriate number of high-level jobs. This would require that the way in which technical change influences the labor intensity of production techniques, and thus the number of such jobs, also be a subject for social control and planning. The problem itself dictates that these matters be part of explicit policy. Obviously, such policy would go well beyond what is traditionally taken to be the field of permissible intervention.

The terms of educational choice have changed substantially in the past few years. The earlier ethnic minorities and major socioeconomic groupings who have in the past stepped upwards through education did so in a period when the base figures for educational outlays were reasonably close to prevailing wage levels, both in stagnant and in progressive activities. This order-of-magnitude equivalence meant that a threshold of wealth had not been exceeded, and there could be a sensitive reaction to changing opportunities and to the availability of educational outlets. The basic career patterns were foreseen and prepared for and adjustments were relatively smooth. The pace and rate of transformation in recent years has appeared to be unstable and without the backing of consensus views as to what constitutes reasonable progress in career sequences and social-class mobility. We focus on these matters in the following chapter, which is concerned with the past history of the transformation process and a planning approach to foster its continuance.

PART THREE

TAILORED GROWTH

7

Planned Social

Transformation

THE economic stagnation that we have experienced in recent years represents a break in one of the most durable trends in American social history—a hundred-year record of steady increases in the proportion of the population receiving postsecondary education and the successful assimilation of this population into mainstream industrial and service activities. The statistics are impressive: in 1900, 4 percent of the 18- to 21-year-olds were in institutions of higher learning; the percentage was 33 percent in 1958, and is estimated now to be stabilized in the neighborhood of 40 percent (exclusive of special vocational and training programs).[1] The increase is even more impressive if we note that the proportions grew during a period when the overall population doubled and that the proportions going on to postgraduate education grew steeply as well. What many commentators have found difficult to comprehend is that until quite recently this increase had not been accompanied by a deterioration in the quality of the student body. They are bound to be profoundly disturbed by the recommendation here that the trend of increase in the proportion educated should be vigorously reestablished.

ACADEMIC STANDARDS IN AN EXPANDING EDUCATION SYSTEM

Havighurst has noted a preponderance of instances in which established schools and universities have increased their cutoff points for admission with no loss in enrollment.[2] In effect, Harvard and Yale greatly reduced their numbers of gentlemen's "C" students, while less prestigious schools attracted student bodies that were in many ways equivalent to those at Harvard and Yale a generation earlier. Although the formerly low-ranking institutions and the new universities, colleges, and junior colleges undoubtedly picked up a larger share of the less gifted students in the population, many of these schools nonetheless attained a respectable standard. But this is hardly a uniform trend. In the past few years, for example, there has been a break in this pattern with indications of deterioration in the apparent quality of the student body. This may mean that the bottom of the barrel has been reached or that the rate of expansion of higher education has been too rapid. It might also mean that the cost factors have begun to bite on preparatory institutions and corroded quality there.

To be sure, assessments of comparative student and institutional quality rely on subjective judgments, impressions, nostalgic recollections, and imprecise criteria; but there is some hard evidence on this matter as well. Up until the mid-1960s, median scores and distributional parameters of widely administered examinations such as the Scholastic Aptitude Test (SAT) indicated no decline in the quality of the prospective student body (or more properly, that proportion of the student body that sits for this examination). In fact, the contrary was true, and the indicators of average quality actually improved during the period of greatest growth in enrollments.*

Taking another point of perspective, it has been noted that post-secondary enrollment of children of higher socioeconomic status ("upper middle" and "high" family income) increased to over 90 percent in recent years, whereas the college bound proportion in these groups in the 1920s amounted to approximately 30 percent. Two possible explanations for these statistics are worth considering: that children of families of high

---

* The decline in SAT average scores beginning in the mid to late 1960s (paradoxically, as enrollment growth began to slow) is now the subject of detailed and extensive statistical analysis.

socioeconomic status may be that much more intelligent than the rest of the population; and a considerably more optimistic explanation concerning the outcome of educational expansion.

The issue turns on the way in which the entire population orients itself to a particular set of educational expectations and aspirations. It is most helpful if we can distinguish between a "steady state" in which successive generations carry roughly identical expectations into the education decision and "transitory states" in which the expectations and aspirations at the time of the decision differ from those held in earlier formative years.

On this reasoning, the ways in which children are prepared to go on in education, the way in which society provides places in educational institutions and the way in which the job market opens up for graduates of these places are all interlocking elements. Where the expectation of higher education exists for the children of a particular grouping, the children are prepared for the step at all points—in the home, in the choice of schools, and in expected performance in the classroom. And when the time comes for graduation or advancement, a significant number of children in the grouping will have the requisite preparation and credentials. On the other hand, where the anticipations are unfavorable, preparation and performance will match.

An illustration may help to clarify matters. Let us say that because of discrimination in the educational system and in job markets and because of the economic consequences of past discrimination, only one percent of age cohorts in a particular socioeconomic grouping have tended to go on to higher education. Focusing on a particular "vintage" of students in this category, "steady state" reasoning suggests that if we could look forward in time to the entry of graduates into the labor force, we would find that the number of opportunities matched the supply of new entrants. Similarly, looking back through time, we would have found that the number of students in academic streams and college preparatory programs within this vintage cohort matched the expected number of places in higher education. This pattern would have been visible still further back in the history of this cohort at the elementary and preschool levels as well.

If we compare this grouping to one in which a far higher proportion, say 40 percent, goes on to higher education, we would expect to see appropriately higher proportions of the latter group in academically oriented streams and in ultimate positions with educational and professional associations. Given the interlocking anticipations and actions we would be unable to state whether it is the expectation of superior post-graduate opportunities that leads to the academic orientation in early years or whether it is this academic orientation that gives the grouping its superior preparation for entrance into the higher education stream.

In contrast, the critical transitional case is one in which opportunities suddenly change and the expectation of gains from higher education is born close to the actual time of matriculation. The period of preparation in academic training and through family and community influence will have been compressed and the required scholastic aptitudes less than fully developed. This is a natural consequence of the inertia (or vicious-cycle aspect) of the previous steady state.

What this seems to suggest is that an expansion of the entire higher-educational system must be looked at primarily as a transition toward a new steady state. In some instances the transition will be smooth, as in the case of a socioeconomic grouping in which college aspirations are developed well in advance of the actual time of admission. For other groupings, the aspirations and opportunities will not have been anticipated and preparation will be rushed at best.

One must recall the many American novels detailing the procession of generations up through the social classes, each generation achieving one higher level of educational attainment supported by the aspirations and sacrifices of the preceding generation. *Studs Lonigan, Augie March, A Tree Grows in Brooklyn, The Invisible Man, Marjorie Morningstar,* and *Portnoy's Complaint* form an eclectic sampler, but the list can be expanded through literally thousands of genre pieces and nearly that many "great American novels." Throughout we have a picture of preparation through generations for the moment of advancement, an image of the process of waiting for the moment of what we defined in the preceding chapters as "favorable contemporary value."

A clear implication of these considerations is that scholarly ability is to a significant extent a derived characteristic which is influenced by anticipational states and historical economic processes. Perhaps there is some "innate ability" or "I.Q." which occurs in some genetically determined distribution; but it is also widely known that measured or tested I.Q. is subject to significant influence from environmental or developmental factors. Controversy abounds and expertise in this area is quite limited and probably incapable of projecting just how high the proportion of potential college students might be; but the success of previous educational expansion in this country and elsewhere suggests that the pool of unexploited talent and ability is not yet exhausted; that innate intelligence appropriately culti-

vated can support a higher level of formal education and a higher proportion of the population at that level than is commonly believed possible.

For the sake of comprehensiveness, we should examine contrary arguments: (1) that the pool of innate talent had already accumulated into
the upper socioeconomic categories so that the high proportion of post-
secondary education in these groups reflects the higher proportion of
basic talent within them; or (2) that the poor are identifiable with racial
minorities, and that a Jensenist or similar assessment applies to them.
It is not yet possible to test either hypothesis in a definitive fashion. One
simply should note that either could have been advanced with parallel
supporting arguments fifty years ago as justification for not allowing an
increase in educational places. The course of events has established that
such a construction would have been unwarranted.

One comes to similar conclusions in evaluating the educational expansion in England that resulted in the formation of "new universities" and
enlargement of existing institutions. The prevailing opinion of my colleagues at the University of Cambridge was that there had been no visible
deterioration in the quality of the student body there and that centers such
as Sussex and Essex had attained or even exceeded the Oxbridge and London standards.

PLANS TO PROVIDE OPPORTUNITIES

Where does one go from here? The preceding arguments imply that the
ultimate innate-ability constraint on educational expansion may not yet
have been reached. They also suggest that the process of advancement
must be coherent and integrated with previous preparation and with
forward anticipations concerning the labor markets.*

The planning problem is formidable. The educational system determines the supply side (the number of graduates entering the labor market); what remains to be seen is whether the demand side (the number
of significant opportunities) is controllable, so that the development-
broadening approach could be thought of as a realistic possibility. The
answers are conjectural and, I fear, must be considered the shakiest elements in the entire formulation. What is involved here is a reversal of the

* Again it is surprising that "open enrollment" and "new university" programs
like those in the City University of New York have had even a slight amount of success, given that they were introduced with virtually no preparation of the prospective
student body and no development of an ultimate labor market for graduates.

usual way of thinking about "manpower" planning.* And, as is so often the case when one poses a "different sort" of approach, there is little in the way of data and experience available to support it.

Let us look closely at the problem. It is common practice to develop manpower requirements to fit a projected production objective. The process involves working backwards from a production target to man-power requirements that support the objective. To obtain these figures, it is therefore necessary to extrapolate rates of productivity change and the bias of technology towards capital- or labor-intensity.[3] These charac-teristics allow the planner to estimate the number and particular cate-gories of labor needed, and it is a simple conceptual step to go from final labor force requirements to requirements for intermediate supporting labor (educators to staff the schools needed to build the final labor force skill mix) and workers in the service (tertiary) activities compatible with the projected level of overall income and output. The projections are then developed within the constraints of the demographic structure of the society, certain obvious process limitations, and restrictions on maximal rates of construction, retraining, and the like.

In practice, the elements of a manpower-projection plan might be very simple (for example, projected faculty to student ratios could be used to estimate the need for educators); but a complete system that offers some detail would be computationally massive. In the ordinary course of events, the planning scheme would be designed as a mathematical model which could be used for a relatively small number of simulations of pos-sible futures under the plan, to generate information on the feasibility of the initial objective and on likely bottlenecks in critical work-force cate-gories. For example, it might be found that the initial output target fixed for a date twenty years hence was too high. A slightly lower output target might be found to be reasonable; however, to reach that target, a substantial increase in the number of technicians with two or more years of education beyond the high school level would be needed. Such information would be used to institute plans for, let us say, new junior college construction and a program of vocational education.

Various experiments are commonly performed with such manpower

---

* Up to this point in the book I have tried to avoid terms for the work force that carry sex identification. However, there is no convenient synonym for "manpower" or "manpower planning" which in a common usage relates to the development of a labor force to meet a prescribed production objective. I will use the term on this re-stricted understanding, but with apologies to all readers. Slightly later in the text, the term "work force priority planning" will be introduced to cover a suggested modification of the "manpower" approach.

planning systems. For example, the model system might also be run with trial values so as to discover sensitivity to errors in initial projections or in subsequent management. In certain restricted cases, the system could be used to develop "optimal" plans which would take into account the costs in terms of consumable output of the resources flowing into capital formation and into the educational program.

There are several varieties of manpower plans on this logic, and manpower programs are run with more or less comprehensiveness and more or less technical sophistication. However the common element in most if not all such systems is that the logical orientation of the system is that of calculating manpower requirements to fit the material target. My contention is that standard manpower systems contain sufficient information to reverse the logical orientation: to instead stipulate a work force goal (a skill and educational level of the population) and calculate the output required to support the standards of living implied by this socioeconomic structure. On this reasoning, the inverted plan (which we will henceforth label "work-force–priority" in contrast to "manpower") would begin with a stipulated work-force objective, say that of increasing to 55 percent the proportion receiving postsecondary education. After preliminary calculations of the transitional build-up of teachers and educators required to support this overall level of education (the same calculation that is made in conventional manpower planning), the next determination would be calculation of the standards of living required to support the projected educational and class distribution and, incidentally, to justify the implied investment in human capital. *Given these projections, the key determination would be that of structuring sectoral development and public expenditures to generate jobs that would support the output level and be consistent with the projected work-force pool.* The crucial factors to control would be the rate of gross productivity increase and the extent to which technical developments are biased towards saving labor. This, however, takes us into waters that are for the most part uncharted, and some further conjectures as to the production process are required.

There are many potential productive techniques, but engineering and economic decisions made at an early stage of the design process determine what technique is chosen for development, what will be its final operating characteristics, and, whether these characteristics reflect the generation of pollution or the generation of jobs. It is natural to ask if planned influence over such characteristics and the production process is anything but a vague hope. There are several lines to consider. First, we should recognize that nearly every type of bias in technical change is system-determined, e.g., an endogenous factor influenced by economic decisions concerning expectations of costs, prices, wage rates, and labor supply.[4] To the extent that this is so and machine designs are not immutably determined by gods of invention, there is an opportunity for influence via commercial incentives and, of course, by direct stipulation of engineering requirements. One should also note that reliable forecasts of work force availability could themselves be an instrument that would influence design.

The second avenue of influence is through the sectoral emphasis given to expenditure programs and public employment.[5] There is obviously a considerable difference between the work force requirements of a high-technology activity such as the space program and a program of urban housing construction; therefore the weights given such activities represent a significant guiding force. In fact, even finer control is possible. The difference in work force requirements of the space and housing programs could be accentuated or diminished through contract requirements in the latter. For example, the urban housing program could be set up to explore new construction systems and would therefore call heavily on highly skilled technical, design, and production personnel, or it could emphasize conventional construction methods and call on a pool of skilled and semiskilled workers. The particular line chosen would also carry with it an implied rate of productivity increase (which can be estimated from past experience) so that the sector's contribution to the overall rate of technical change and manpower utilization might in principle be controllable.

The final line of influence is perhaps the most obvious and involves control over the resources flowing to the research and development establishment itself. One should note, though, that this is an area that is imperfectly understood. Does the productivity payoff come from pure or mission-oriented research? Should resources be directed to educational institutions, research organizations, or research branches of industrial firms? Does it pay to build redundancy into the research system and support several approaches to the same problem, or is it better policy to fix on a single approach from the start? [6]

We must proceed without definitive answers to these questions, yet it seems fair to suggest that a setting of anticipated economic growth in conjunction with formal support to a broad range of research establishments can lead to an increase in the overall rate of technical progress and provide direct and incidental employment to a large pool of educated workers. A case can be made that the greatly reduced support given to education, research, and related activities in recent years has significantly damaged the U.S. position as a generator of technology and technical change. It is a reasonable premise that in the immediate future, at least, one could greatly increase the flow of resources to these areas and feel confident that the payoff would be favorable. It would be even more favorable if the missions of applied research were oriented to the design of methods, systems, and techniques that would carry forward the work-force objectives (e.g., by building work-force–skill requirements into a contract for the design of an urban transportation system in just the same way that safety, noise level, pollution level and affirmative-action standards are already employed).

These conjectures constitute the intuitive case for a programmatic approach that gives priority to an explicit structural socioeconomic objective rather than system derived manpower requirements. There is little in the way of previous empirical work for guidance, and there are still many conceptual problems to be solved as to the properties of inverted manpower programs.[7] Yet I believe one can proceed with the motif as a rationale for policy.

It would be an error to categorize the work-force–priority approach as a particularly unusual or arcane policy instrument; it is, after all, a direct extension of an established planning procedure for less developed countries. Nevertheless, a fairly extensive search of the recent planning and manpower literatures failed to turn up any materials that came close to developing this style of analysis for the U.S. labor market. Although I may very well have missed some citations on this matter, it is clear, at least, that work-force–priority planning is not a recognized theme within the manpower field. I was reluctant to publish on this issue except that I did find one citation that also deplored the lack of attention given to thinking in the work-force–priority style; and most growth economists (and undergraduate students) who have worked through the argument with me have accepted the basic reasoning and policy relevance of the approach. The citation below shows something of the significance of the issue.

. . . What are the various techniques—factor combinations and methods of application—by which a given public service can be produced and delivered? It is remarkable, said [Professor Bennet] Harrison, that not even the most technically qualified participants in the seminar [on public-service employment and manpower planning] had ever raised the question, "an oversight which would be unforgiveable and inexcusable in a discussion about employment generated by the production of physical goods. Undergraduates in the economics principles course are taught to ask such a question before they are taught almost anything else. . . .

. . . What are the alternative manpower requirements associated with the production of any particular level of service output . . . how much labor is used to produce X units of service by "process" (method) 1? by process 2? by process 3? More importantly, what are the skill distributions of these derived manpower requirements? [8]

EDUCATION AND THE POLITICS OF EXPEDIENCE

The earlier discussion of educational "quality" suggests that there is still considerable room left for expansion of the supply of educated personnel. The discussion (and assertions) on the conversion of "manpower planning" into "work-force–priority planning" further suggests that a significant expansion of the trained work force could be more than accommodated within the economy. Combined, these suggestions cover both the supply and demand sides of the market for skilled personnel and amount to a general proposition that further developmental broadening may be viable as an avenue of growth. The developmental-broadening approach takes on additional merit first, as it would be favorable to creating a climate for growth, and second, as it generally could be selectively focused on supporting such sectors as education and research which are most subject to the dualistic-imbalance syndrome. This is, of course, a qualitative and intuitive proposition that is several steps removed from operational usefulness. One would like to know at the very least how fast one could proceed with educational expansion and how one should structure the expansion across academic disciplines, vocational disciplines, and, of course, students' interests. It goes beyond the scope of this book to deal with the latter part of the operational problem; instead we will concentrate attention on the former—the issue of "how fast?" *

* As an example of the sort of problem I am avoiding, consider the following: An expansion of 30 percent in the university population is projected. On simple extrapolation, this implies 30 percent more teaching hours in English literature and inferentially a 30 percent expansion in the number of courses on the Victorian novel and scholars with that interest. If academics are expected to preserve an interest in research as well as teaching, does the expansion in education carry over into attached scholarly research, or would an assessment be made that sufficient resources are already devoted to research into major and minor Victorians (and that an extension to the miniscule Victorians would be unwarranted)? As stated, the problem is ludicrous; but it might not appear so at a department meeting to decide promotions based on an assessment of scholarly contributions.

The first point to note is that the "how fast" problem seems to be susceptible to the sort of analysis that economists do best.[9] That is, it is a problem of finding the best way to organize resources to meet an objective for a specific timetable. In fact, the problem can be set up so that, in principle, one can derive a family of programs, each corresponding to a specific deadline. In this sort of projection, the elements to consider are the impacts on current production stemming from shifting resources to the educational sector and the impact on future production and technical change of operating with the resulting highly educated work force. Each program in the family of "solutions" would consist of estimates of attainable production of consumption goods and other outputs for each year of the program and a timetable for meeting a distributional objective. The most cursory analysis indicates that developmental broadening would not be bound by personnel shortages and there seems to be a strong potentiality for favorable rates of return, even at some remarkable rates of social mobility. It appears, then, that the answer to the question "how fast?" is: "nearly as fast as you like," or "nearly as fast as the system has expanded in the past." One must listen carefully when there is silence instead of the dog's bark that one expected to hear. Educational expansion has slowed dramatically when there is apparently room for further expansion, educational transformation, and programmable growth to further work-force priorities. Perhaps the real question is not "how fast?" but rather "why so slow?"

The answers to this question are discomforting. Surely the cost pressures stemming from the dualistic-imbalance syndrome have much to do with education's apparent loss of appeal; but there may be more to the matter than just this. In the past, primacy was given to the objective of social advance within the family and tacit endorsement by public institutions of the principle of upward progression of the generations. Nevertheless, there is a flow of opinion against education and educational institutions; and I am personally at a loss as to how to evaluate its significance and how to assess whether it is different in quality or intensity from earlier anti-intellectual, antischool movements. (The first person singular is used extensively in this section since the matter presented is very much undigested personal impression.)

I might not write in this fashion if I had not had the experience of living a year in California, where antischool, antieducation sentiment flows strong and deep. Antagonism toward education was exhibited at all levels: for the early grades, as antagonism to the property tax and in school bond refusals; and at higher levels in policies of the Reagan administration (continued by the Brown administration) that were perceived as outright hatred of the University of California. These attitudes could be interpreted as denial of opportunity to one's children and rejection of the idea of social mobility via education. If this is a correct interpretation and the sentiment is general, one cannot place confidence in the traditional politics that supported education in the past through appeals to personal motivations revolving around economic opportunity or social mobility.[10] If there is a forum in which this issue will be heard, it may be politic to propose educational expansion as a vehicle for general growth rather than as a means to promote social equity or establish a democratic society.[11]

Let us nevertheless look at the case based on equity principles, even if this case may not be sustainable politically. The past record has indicated a steady increase in the proportion of the population advancing in educational status, and the anecdotal and case record suggests that this phenomenon occurs as a regular pattern of advance from generation to generation. There are a number of ways to incorporate such patterns into formal analysis, but it is natural when the context is that of economic growth, to associate intertemporal regularities of this sort with a sort of social contract, a compact between generations based on a "golden rule." The original golden rule of growth was suggested by Phelps and pertained to the rate at which particular generations should invest in machine capital.[12] The rule translated roughly into the principle: "Invest for the next generation as you would have had the previous generation invest for you." There is no way of knowing whether the past pattern of support of educational ambitions corresponded to an implicit golden rule of social mobility, but it is a pleasing thought to imagine that it did. Perhaps one could extrapolate an obligation for the current generation to provide as great a range of opportunities for emerging groups as was provided in the past for it. This would be sufficient rationale for support of educational transformation and there would be no necessity to seek other justification for growth through educational development.

As it stands, though, we must recognize that the economic opportunity objective as a social institution has weakened, and it is no longer possible to rely on the presumption that the mobility imperative will provide a critical foundation of political support for educational programs. This is disappointing, but nevertheless obligatory, and the original proposition on education and developmental broadening must be rephrased. In its new form, it reads as follows:

(1) Further educational expansion need not connote deterioration of the educational system.

(2) A developed labor force could be incorporated into the mainstream economy with suitable work-force–priority planning; however,

(3) There may no longer be a social imperative for developmental broadening, and such an approach may require support as a means of advancing a general economic or growth goal rather than a distributional and ethical requirement.

This retreat toward expedience and toward what some might call political reality is something of an affront to my finer sensibilities. But the acceptance of what goes on within educational institutions has, after all, traditionally been a matter of sufferance based on the productivity of graduates without the institution. The problem now is that the public appreciation of even this justification has diminished. Habermas provides a superb (and sardonic) description of the functions of the modern university within advanced industrial society:

Universities must transmit technically exploitable knowledge. That is, they must meet an industrial society's need for qualified new generations and at the same time be concerned with the expanded reproduction of education itself. In addition, universities must not only transmit technically exploitable knowledge, but also produce it. This includes both information flowing from research into the channels of industrial utilization, armament, and social welfare, and advisory knowledge that enters into strategies of administration, government, and other decision-making powers, such as private enterprises. Thus, through instruction and research the university is immediately connected with functions of the economic process. In addition, however, it assumes at least three further responsibilities.

First, the university has the responsibility of ensuring that its graduates are equipped, no matter how indirectly, with a minimum of qualifications in the area of extrafunctional abilities. In this connection extrafunctional refers to all those attributes and attitudes relevant to the pursuit of a professional career that are not contained per se in professional knowledge and skills. . . .

Second, it belongs to the tasks of the university to transmit, interpret, and develop the cultural tradition of the society. . . .

Third, the university has always fulfilled a task that is not easy to define; today we would say that it forms the political consciousness of its students.[13]

In terms of these functions we can see an efficiency dimension and a political dimension in current attacks on higher education. Among the reactions to growth failure and an apparent excess supply of technically qualified personnel has been erosion of support for education on nominal efficiency grounds. The default on a promised payoff is apparent to state legislators, prospective employers, students, and their parents. The failure to manage the economy so as to validate past promises is less likely to register. The unbalanced growth cost factor only serves to exacerbate the apparent inefficiency of the educational system.

However, the political dimension is equally important. We have examined the educational system in its functional role within the economic infrastructure. Yet clearly the university exists within a broader tradition which may well come into conflict with the transient objectives of the larger society at critical times. Students crystalize their criticisms of the society within the university (incidentally transferring some of their antagonism toward the larger society to the educational institutions which are seemingly integrated to its support). And the larger society tends to regard the university as the wellspring of uncomfortable ideas or the nesting ground of subversive youth. Tension between University and Nation is a natural phenomenon. The university can presumably withstand attacks on the political dimension if it is perceived as performing its economic support functions; it is hamstrung where its efficiency basis is undercut.

8

Control of Technology Within

the Modern Corporation

THE work-force–priority approach outlined in the preceding chapter brings us back to the doors of the major firms. In essence, the planning motif has three basic requirements: first, expansion of the labor force qualified for progressive-sector employment; second, reestablishment of anticipations of general growth so as to renew the processes that generate productivity change; and, third, guidance over the design of new industrial techniques so as to cultivate a predisposition to employ the existing work force. Clearly, to meet the second and third of these conditions, it is necessary to establish a significant degree of control over the activities and propensities of the major firms which have dominating weight in the progressive sector. Of course, these enterprises possess the resources (and probably the inclination) to resist controls to the utmost. The question before us now concerns whether or not it is practicable to effect such control.

To examine this issue we will run through a lengthy list of behaviors and attributes of progressive-sector firms relating to the use of technology, competitive and noncompetitive actions, and susceptibility to influence. Again, the basic picture is one in which the dominant firms and the personnel associated with them form a coherent, self-contained and self-sustaining subeconomy. When left to itself, this subeconomy exhibits certain operating characteristics including particular rates of productivity change within its boundaries and particular patterns of technical adaptation which result in greater or less assimilation of population from the background economy. The point to keep in mind is that these manifestations of progressive-sector activity are not immutable: they are what they are because the subsystem operates within a setting which is determined in large part by government activity and policy interventions. In turn, the style of policy reflects general perceptions or misperceptions as to the functions and behaviors of industry. This is a fairly obvious point that is too often forgotten. We will attempt to refine the perception of the progressive sector in order to discover lines of influence possible with altered styles of policy. Our focus is the enterprise which has achieved dominance through control, command, and management of what is emerging on an historical time scale as the critical factor of production, organized pools of skills and talents. Through guidance, we would hope to alter the "givens," making the rates of subsystem development and assimilation matters for social control.*

Finally, a note to the reader: To help keep matters in perspective and provide a framework for the argument, this chapter is organized in a somewhat unusual way. Critical descriptive statements and propositions on firm behavior are set off from the text. These statements (some of which have been encountered before, some of which are presented for the first time) provide a sketch outline that covers the role of the progressive-sector firm as a source of income generation through growth, and exposes points at which policy leverage might be applied.

THE TECHNOSTRUCTURE FACTOR

The critical role of the major firm in mobilizing the emerging education-skill factor is suggested by the first items in the set of propositions and defining statements.

(1) Technostructure organization (or something that approximates it) is the vehicle for business and commercial employment of the technically skilled work force and those educated in modern management, design, and applied science.

(2) The enterprises adopting this mode of organization are also prime generators or beneficiaries of technical change so that the technostructure factor

---

* Once one proposes generalizations that embrace such entities as General Motors, General Dynamics, General Foods, et al, theory becomes intrinsically political economy. If growth emanates from the activities of General Etcetera, then we must also consider the implications of such growth to power relationships within the society and to politics. Furthermore, it must be recognized that because of their power, the major firms operate with a substantial margin of choice as to their behaviors.

forms a major and significant part of the link between education and favorable productivity change.

(3)   The technostructure firms, by and large, sell their products in markets which are oligopolistic in organization or otherwise noncompetitive. If they do in fact generate technological change or otherwise improve productivity, they can hold onto a far greater proportion of the benefits than can the competitive firm in a competitive industry.*

(4)   Given statements (1) through (3), it follows that the educated staff and skilled work force, which act as a facilitating instrument for the productivity increases, have a significant claim against the firm for a sizable portion of the dollar gains from these increases.

If these claims are in practice made good, the work forces involved are linked to the basic productivity and growth forces of the economy. Their compensation will tend to be above the average and, in an environment of general economic growth, it will grow at (or above) the general output growth rate. In fact, in a 1960s type of economy, progressive-sector compensation from various sources (wage-scale increases, profit sharing, promotion increments) will tend to show exponential increase. An outside observer comparing this phenomenon to the fixed (or slower growing) stagnant-sector wage would be struck by the correlation between education or skill levels and levels of compensation. The observer would very likely explain this association as a return to the education-skill factor as activated by the technostructure mode of organization and would treat the conjunction of technostructure organization and productivity change as a distributional mechanism that seemed to account for the sectoral split in incomes.

Behavior Within the Enterprise

It is one thing to argue in the abstract that the technostructure style can promote a pattern of distribution based upon organized skills as a critical factor of production, it is quite another thing to argue that this pattern would be sustained over time. For this to be, enterprises must be motivated to pursue the line of technical progress and must be rewarded by the actual performance of the system. Furthermore, there is the important question of identifying the mechanisms whereby productivity gains are actually parceled out among claimants against the firm. If, for example, a sizable portion of the benefits are realized as profits

---

* In a hypothetical environment of perfect competition, any firm which develops an advantage because of the increased productivity of its workers will hold that advantage only until imitation by competitors restores cost parity among firms.

and turned over as dividends to a shareowner interest, the resources available to finance growth within the firm are diminished, as would be inducements to work force and management. The list of propositions and defining statements must be extended.[1]

(5)   The technostructure-oriented firm tends to be in a secure financial position and can safely pursue an independent strategic line without fear of creditor restrictions or takeover by an insurgent shareholder interest. If this condition holds, the firm can expand short-term output beyond what it would be if the firm were required to maximize profits.

(6)   The firm could also get away with a lower dividend proportion, retaining more out of earnings to finance internal growth. This policy favors the technostructure interest over the ownership interest. Akin to this would be a tendency to go soft in wage and salary negotiations, allowing a greater share of the firm's potential earnings to be sequestered by the technostructure groupings. It will not be difficult for these internal interests to bargain their claims, particularly since higher management, in effect, sets its own compensation level.

(7)   The internal management and technical interests will be motivated to pursue growth as against profit seeking, so that the above tendencies will be facilitated and reinforced. This involves recognition by managers and staff that their financial, career, and promotion opportunities are enhanced in a firm that adds division after division in pursuit of growth. This self-interest is more readily perceived than the obligation to serve as steward for the shareholder, who, after all, is little more than a magnetic impulse in a data file stored in the computers of a bank corporate-trust department.

(8)   In pursuit of the growth goal, the managers are particularly inclined to follow lines of technical development and technical sophistication. This will mean emphasis on machine processes and on advanced management; together these inclinations will tend to expedite high rates of design improvement and learning.

(9)   The firm will enter into or sponsor research into its own production processes and product development. This will involve considerable expenditure and management and staff emphasis over an extended planning and development period.

(10)   The firm will strive for control over final product markets and will select product lines for further development if they offer the potentiality of such control. One line of control is through need creation via advertising; a second is through linkages with large purchasers (including the government). Control is needed in order to ensure a stable final-product market in the face of the large commitments involved in technology, research, and industrial-system strategies.

Readers familiar with the *New Industrial State* will recognize much of the above as a paraphrase of Galbraith's description of the 1960s dominant firm. I have varied emphasis slightly and put matters into a slightly different logical order, but this was done so that distributional effects and growth-enhancing aspects would come out strongly. The point is to show that the technostructure organization of the major industrial enterprises can explain a particular pattern of distribution and also explain the motive force behind the generation of the technical change that drives the system. This is the key behavioral force in the historical picture of unbalanced growth. In effect, the technical orientation can provide the high rates of productivity change and subsystem growth, while the work force requirements of the technostructure account for the favored position of the educated and skilled.

The Realization of Technical Change

The analysis here rests on a presupposition that the efforts of industrial firms to plan for and control technical change are at least somewhat successful, and that the general state of technology depends upon the activities of industrial firms. However, it is important to note that these firms are not necessarily the source of the changes they promote. There is a good deal of evidence and a strong case for the proposition that the designer-inventor-entrepreneur in a small and competitive business is still the source of significant innovation and technical advance, (noting, of course, that successful innovations make small firms large).[2] There are surely many large corporations and industries in which the innovative intellect has atrophied, and there are very many instances of the small firm pioneering an industry breakthrough. Nevertheless, the large technostructure-styled firm is likely to benefit from technological advances regardless of the source, while the competitive firm is unlikely to have the capital and financial base to fully exploit the flow of innovations.

The American automobile industry is a case in point. Many of the design improvements of the big three automobile producers are derived imitations of speed-shop innovations and foreign practice (radial tires, disc brakes, efficient four- and six-cylinder high-performance engines, front wheel drive, rack-and-pinion steering, and many other features); while many production improvements (automated-boring and precision machinery, computer-controlled assembly, etc.) represent design improvements stemming from suppliers of industrial equipment. A good case can be made that the big three are something less than creative; but it is hard to question their ability to adapt once they are inclined to do so. In other words, the major firms do not have to be highly creative themselves in order to translate inventions made elsewhere in the system into realized productivity change.

This poses an interesting and potentially important question: does government sponsorship of growth which works through the major industrial firms, automatically result in sponsorship of meaningful innovation? If we mean "innovation" in the sense of "invention," "design," or "creativity," as against learning or adaptation, the answer is not all that clear. The innovational focus of the large firm is its own standing operation. It can systematically program research aimed at improving its efficiency, component by component, activity by activity, or division by division; this is the strength of technocratic-bureaucratic organization. Its weaknesses may be in an inertial inability to mobilize firm resources around novel or original developments that do not fit the existing order or flow from its plan. A typical model of bureaucratized research is the large pharmaceutical house's programmed investigation of the "permutation group" of possible variations of a promising organic molecule— beginning with preliminary computer analysis to screen out the subgroups with little commercial potential, followed up by intensive routine analysis of the remaining candidates by dozens of biochemists in dozens of identical laboratories. The hoped-for outgrowth of the process is identification of a small number of molecules which fit the firm's existing production expertise and marketing strengths.

This situation contrasts with classic "venture" development by basement or academic researchers who proceed along an intuitive line on a shoestring budget. However, even after preliminary success in the research stage, a venture to become commercial must, more frequently than not, establish itself as a candidate for adoption (via direct sale, licensing or merger) by the major firm which controls the routes of access to the final market or is itself the market. In other words, both invention and commercial development are part of the growth process. The rewards for this last stage are more often than not gained by the major firm and by its technostructure. But the major firm is not necessarily a support for meaningful innovation. Depending upon circumstances, it may encourage and reward such innovation; or it may, through blocking market access, act as an obstacle to the research function; or, as has been the case in recent years, its orientation may shift away from the development of new techniques and towards the consolidation of its own market position.

Appropriate encouragement of the creative innovative component is ultimately the key to a successful growth policy, but it is an arena of difficult and delicate choices. Therefore, it makes sense to advocate growth that operates in part through major firms and the organized use of education-skill factors; in part through direct encouragement of specific high-technology industries; in part through institutional research; and in part through support of the classic venture, informal creative activity in the basement laboratory or small loft or shop. The large technostructure-oriented firms are undoubtedly important actors in the innovative process, but it would appear to be the height of folly to presume that a single-dimensioned policy to expand aggregate demand and, indirectly, the activities of the progressive-sector firms would necessarily carry momentum into creative invention and design. In other words, we must distinguish the facts of distribution which identify the progressive-sector firm as a facilitating component in the growth process, the facts of power which permit the firm to appropriate for itself a substantial share of the gains from growth, and the facts of innovation which locate the inventive spirit and the ultimate sources of growth and a growth environment in a far broader base.

The Growth Environment

The enterprise behaviors and operations described by Galbraith presumed a favorable innovational climate in a general economic environment of active growth. This was a realistic description of the economy at the time *The New Industrial State* appeared; the United States was well into its unprecedented near decade of continuous advance, and the European and Japanese counterparts of the Galbraithian firm had enjoyed even stronger growth over a longer span of time. The logic of *The New Industrial State* is predicated on growth in the economic system as a whole; so it is worth a moment's pause to ask whether the break in system growth and growth anticipations from 1968 to the present time invalidates the basic construction of an economy driven by progressive-sector activity. A firm may be "Galbraithian," "growth" rather than "profit-oriented," but only as a matter of choice. The options are always open for it to engage in short-term market exploitation on standard lines, or follow the merger route or the line of multinational extension if the technical growth option is unpromising. Given the market power possessed by the major firms, such short-term, profit-seeking behavior is likely to be successful as well, and is the policy of choice when growth anticipations sour. There is more than a suspicion of such shifts in orientation in the recent actions of the major energy firms and in the domestic pricing behavior of Japanese firms in the consumer-goods industries.

The growth-oriented description appears to lack immediate relevance, particularly with the corporate planning departments of the major firms stored away in mothballs and serious attention and time at the board room level given over to the short run, to acquisition prospects, to problems of protecting short-term liquidity, and to the taking of positions in the wildly fluctuating foreign currency exchanges. Yet the prospect of a return to growth must still be considered, and it seems reasonable to expect that the return to growth will be channeled through the enterprises of the progressive sector. Has the now quiescent Galbraithian firm been altered by its exposure to recession and crisis, and will this affect attitudes within it towards technology building and firm and economy planning? This book has no answer to the query except to note that this is a new and dangerous area of economic uncertainty.[3] One now hears the drums beating for recovery and renewed growth, but the major firms still seem to march to the slower pace learned in the long Nixon-Ford recession. Sustained growth is a process wherein prophecies are fulfilled by intensified growth-directed activities of the progressive sector. These activities are largely stalled at the present time, and what we have defined as the growth prospect, or the developmental scenario, requires transforming the scale and range of major firm research and development and investment commitments.

SOCIAL AND POLITICAL IMPLICATIONS OF CORPORATE GROWTH

In strongly advocating growth and, at the same time, linking growth to the technostructure mode, this book may appear to be an apologia for the large firm and a work that explicitly advocates its dominant role and implicitly endorses the social and economic relations that characterize the Galbraithian enterprise. This is very far from the author's purpose in writing and his personal view (which is to consider the contemporary technically oriented enterprise as one of the most dangerous "adverse consequences of growth"). But if one is to control or change or restructure a system (or protect oneself from it), one has to understand its operations and have an accurate picture of its essential causal forces. It should not be surprising that the most distinguished analyses of the modern corporation have emanated from its most severe critics. Marris provides what could be considered a complete handbook for the strategic operation and working finance of a growth-oriented firm; although the title *The Economic Theory of Managerial Capitalism* provides some clue that the author's sentiments lie closer to the neo-Keynesian and neo-Marxian criticisms of Joan Robinson and Cambridge. Similarly, Galbraith, many of the students of the growth-oriented or managerial firm, and many of the writers on the nexus of market structure and innovation are associated with left, progressive, or liberal politics.[4]

From these analyses one can adduce agreement on the following important trends and processes: (1) that further growth within the contemporary model inevitably involves accretions of power to technologically oriented firms; (2) that the planning mechanisms intrinsic to growth involve intimate contact and coordination between firms and government; and (3) that growth requires continued assimilation into the firm of skilled and highly educated work forces. These factors (and related trends) trigger fears of passage towards a corporate state colored variously as syndicalist, authoritarian, bureaucratic, or technocratic. Is it possible to have growth in the economic domain and somehow avoid the adverse social and political consequences at the level of authority and control?

Several social critics have perceived the linkage between growth and educated personnel and have built their prescriptions accordingly. Marcuse, for example, has argued that there is a moment for revolution when the current generation of students assume places of authority within the technostructure; while Reich, in a jejune fantasy, sees in the same moment the potentiality of "greening" the corporate structure.[5] Of course, neither eventuality can be relied on and any change in the style and management of industry will have to come from without.

In brief, there does not seem to be the political initiative to avoid the path of development based upon the large enterprise as the basic unit of organization. To be sure, there are signs that some of the newer technologies may adapt to decentralized industrial organization (for example, both time-sharing utilities and minicomputers encourage fragmented industry); and there are time-honored grounds for believing that many of the *Fortune* 500 are too large for their markets, overlarge in terms of scale diseconomies, and above the size threshold for retarded research effort.[6] But these considerations imply little in the way of immediate relief from the oppressive potentiality of bigness *per se*. A vigorous antitrust effort could dismember some of the very largest firms but would not alter the technostructure orientation of the successor firms and those others retaining their original forms. Footloose decentralization facilitated by radical new technologies is a delightful futurist potentiality and not necessarily a vain hope; but decades of research and experiments in industrial transformation would be needed before we could even test the feasibility of this line of development.

We are left, then, with only one real avenue of ameliorating influence, and that is via the interaction of government and industry.

(11) Technostructure operations are in their own terms adapted to long-term massive programs. Such programs may include within their missions the design and development of new technologies at the frontier of applied science. [This is a poorly masked indirect way to describe Department of Defense (DoD) or space (NASA) projects.]

(12) The accomplishment rate for speculative, high-technology projects is high, although cost overruns appear to be endemic.

(13) The firm technostructure blends well with its counterpart bureaucratic structure in the contracting agency or department; problems of coordination and resource allocation being handled at the government level.

(14) The major government-coordinated project will exhibit productivity increases of standard type in physical processes (taking into account the likelihood that cost overruns were anticipated but not publicly budgeted).

(15) The program or mission approach is well adapted to satisfying extremely complex project requirements and constraints. These can cover both technical objectives (performance characteristics, environmental restrictions) and social stipulations (affirmative action guidelines).

(16) Many of the most effective high-technology firms are of moderate size. Through guidelines on the letting of subcontracts, mission authorities can encourage diffusion of economic power away from the prime contractor. An "antitrust" component can be built into the design to encourage enterprises which are below the senility threshold.

Items (11) through (16) represent a tongue-in-cheek description of the military-industrial complex. However, the same language and wording could be used to describe a decentralized planning system operating in major industries employing high-technology modes of production. This is far from the planning system one would pick given free choice in the matter, but it is at least a way to preempt passage to some of the fiercer authoritarian systems (either public or private).*

One need hardly underline the fact that a constellation of bureaucratic-technocratic-congressional power centers is a far cry from democratic socialism or responsive social planning, but it is probably a step that has to be taken before one can reasonably and realistically consider the

* The points to consider are these: that a growth technology policy can operate in a number of program areas, the DoD-NASA orientation of the past notwithstanding; or, if the program management is aligned to departments and agencies rather than the office of the President, one would expect to see bureaucratic and congressional power centers develop and possibly (given post-Watergate sentiment) a check to presidential power.

legislative problem of founding new political institutions to guide the economic domains. The only things one can really say in favor of this modestly transformed industrial system are the following: that with a reasonable choice of program emphasis (candidate projects are discussed in later chapters) interproject competition could work out to be a viable transitional substitute for responsive politics; tendencies toward augmented presidential power and uncontrolled private economic power would be checked; effort could be directed toward significant social problem areas (with suitable project choice); and the extent and qualitative direction of technical change would be put (in part, at least) under social guidance. Again, it should be stressed that this line of inquiry into institution building is forced upon us. Unless we opt to break the path of technology-enterprise development by continuing to encourage economic recession—in which case the cartel and market exploitation are resurrected—we are forced to consider accommodation with industry; and this inevitably means explicit guidance and coordinated planning, given that market forces have lost their effectiveness.[7]

GUIDANCE OVER TECHNICAL CHANGE

It is now time for return to a major theme of the book, influence over the characteristics of technical change. The final items in the list of technostructure propositions and defining statements introduce the topic.

(17)   Where the primary operations of the enterprise are in the private sector, want creation to secure a market becomes endemic.

(18)   Technostructure control over the style and form of machine designs involves preselection according to criteria of technical sophistication and adaptability to the firm's own work force structure. This amounts to private control over the bias of technical change toward labor or capital use.

(19)   The presumed lack of substitutability between the skilled and unskilled work forces in progressive-sector activities implies that the relative scale of the progressive sector and the extent of bias toward labor saving in its production are together important determinants of the income distribution for the society as a whole.

These statements paint a picture in which the choices over what to produce, how to produce it, and whom to employ in order to produce according to plan are all controlled by the strategic concerns of the technostructure. Leaving aside the question of what final products will be selected for development and marketing, our concern is with the selection of tech-

niques of production, control over the design of new techniques, choice of
the quality of work force to operate the technique, and choice of the intensity of operation. All of these decisions relate to the economist's analytical category of "induced bias in technical change." In abstract analyses
which presume competitive markets, the issue is that of discovering the
extent to which changing wage rates (or wage rates relative to costs of
capital) cause adjustments in selection of techniques and alterations in
machine design or in use patterns.[8] There is no need to inject ourselves
into controversies over what might induce bias in a competitive or near
competitive situation; the point is that if there is any tendency towards
saving labor in an abstract competitive world, it can be amplified in a
Galbraithian world where "technical virtuosity" [9] and delight in machine
capital are part of the value structure. There is no direct evidence on
the extent to which this effect may operate (a statistical comparison of
what is with *what might have been* is beyond econometric method), but
induction suggests that it may be a strong reinforcement to sectoral
dichotomization.

One can only note that where job security is an obligation placed on
the firm (as in the large Japanese enterprise), the firm is encouraged to
work for productivity increases while retaining its work force. This represents a successful adaptation to the bias problem. The issue of control over system bias is functionally in the social domain, since workers
laid off by labor-saving bias, as well as underproduction, become charges
of the society as a whole; and there is no guarantee that a path of
development involving induced unemployment is in any way efficient in
comparison to a path in which the labor force is retained (and frequently
upgraded). Control over bias is an obvious concern that should be prominent in policy but is not. There is no denying the practical difficulties in
analysis, let alone policy design. If labor intensity and skill bias are problems deriving from the domestic operations and technical style of the
progressive-sector firm, its international operations (if it is also a multinational corporation) can both exacerbate the problem and insulate the firm
from effective control.[10]

We can look at the multinational phenomenon as a development that
is consistent with and perhaps contributing to the hiatus in real domestic growth. It appears that the organizational structure and planning
strength of the firm have been heavily applied to obtaining entry to established foreign oligopolist markets (via takeover of existing firms). This of
course leads to expansion of the enterprise but not to real growth. In addition, where the enterprise is engaged in reorganizing production for its own

domestic market, as where a nominal U.S. enterprise produces on an "export platform" in Southeast Asia or South America, it tends to use older technology; so again there is no upgrading of the leading edge of technique. Both of these tendencies represent a break with the "classic" Galbraithian, growth-enhancing activities in domestic production, and both, of course, reduce domestic employment. Whether multinational extension represents an adoption to deteriorating domestic growth, a long-term structural trend, or a new phase of economic imperialism, it has serious inhibitory effects on the domestic production system.

CAVEATS AND QUALIFICATIONS

The path towards social transformation as outlined in this and earlier chapters might be taken as a naive construction based upon a rather simple-minded instrumental view of policy and guidance: e.g., "Transformation requires an environment of growth, growth emanates from the progressive sector; hence light a fire under the dominant firms, cultivate technical change where necessary, and start up the process." A few major caveats have already been offered, namely the formidable barriers to transformation through education and the equally formidable problem of managing the progressive-sector firms—at least to the point of influencing the quality of technical change so as to effect the required high-level employment. However, the long list of defining and descriptive characteristics should suggest a greatly extended list of additional caveats and qualifications. The control problem is extraordinarily complex; guidance of the dominant firm involves influencing a choice which is made from a Chinese menu of options: Market exploitation or growth? Growth via active promotion of technique? Via passive accommodation of change from outside? Via the acquisition route? Via the multinational route? Some other path?

The appropriate choice for a particular firm will be further conditioned by what it perceives to be the advantage of pursuing a particular style. Yet the perceived payoff to a particular style or strategy will depend to a considerable extent on present and anticipated states of the economy and, of course, whether the economy operates in relative stagnation or relative boom will very much depend on the activities of progressive-sector firms as a class. Once (and if) a growth process of any sort is initiated, new perils emerge. Tendencies to overborrow and indulge in speculative financing are classic symptoms of the boom mentality which, at least in the United States, becomes endemic when the indices are rising. The dangers are amplified by the multilayered structure of claims and contingent requirements which characterize this, the "most developed" financial system.[11] If the experience of the 1960s is any guide, the financial structures which the progressive sector and its banking and financial partners concoct for themselves during episodes of growth pose threats of illiquidity, collapse, and crisis, were the growth to show any signs of slackening. Since the growth processes are in fact unmanaged, and since the financial community seems able to evaluate its own profligate behavior only after it is too late to do anything about the consequences of the behavior, credit crunches, financial overreaction, and abrupt halts are literally built into the system.

The expansion phase is likely to be marked by undue emphasis on investment for its own sake rather than as part of a coherent plan for growth. To be counted among the most dangerous general misperceptions is a common view that investment generally, and machine building specifically, are synonymous with growth. Acts of investment, when attuned to work force requirements and to the installation of improving technology, have powerful growth effects; but during the typical expansion phase these considerations can go by the board as resources are trapped in "the big project," in undefined expansion, and the host of creations, fantasies, and monuments which can be characterized as unproductive use of capital.[12]

PART FOUR

THE ORPHANS OF
GROWTH

9

The Poor in the Background

In the beginning of the book, hard-core poverty was identified as the critical social phenomenon of our times. Little more on the matter was said at the time, as the narrative shifted to examination of the active components of the economy. In fact, the problem of social transformation was viewed more from the perspective of the affluent social strata than from that of the poor. There is a reason for ordering things this way. The strong forces in the economy emanate from the activities of what has been labeled the progressive sector; and by default the condition of the poor essentially depends upon the range of the progressive sector and the extent to which this sector excludes or permits the participation of the poor. As we have seen, the strong forces and trends seem to have been building the exclusionary barriers higher and cementing the dualistic structure of the system as a whole. The time has come, however, to shift perspective and examine the barriers from below.

Although the issue of poverty has been successfully sidestepped in conventional politics (if not covered up), the fact of poverty remains; and there is every indication that failure to resolve the poverty problem in the United States would be a turning point of historical significance. The signs are far from optimistic. On the basis of present trends, we cannot dismiss projections of a stagnant economy coupled to a garrison state drawn up on racial and class lines (this, after all, is the pragmatic consequence of the dualism phenomenon). Nor can we have any confidence that the issues, once (again) exposed, can be neatly and effectively resolved by standard politics and policies. The problem is one of political economy in the broadest sense. The analysis must cover technical explanations, the sociological dimension, and the political setting of both the problem and attempts to resolve it.

The technical description given thus far portrays poverty as the image in income and class distribution of the fundamentally unbalanced production basis of U.S. economic growth. This analysis suggests why policies based on conventional manpower or stabilization reasoning have thus far failed to crack the problem of entrenched poverty. The analysis also points the way towards policy solutions but we have seen reasons to back away a bit and tread with caution. When we come to consider vicious cycle intergenerational patterns, self-perpetuating poverty subcultures, and the discriminatory dimensions of U.S. poverty, the limitations of a purely economic orientation and approach become obvious. Economic analysis can suggest orders of magnitude for the resources needed to overcome the problem and can help screen out policies that are likely to be inappropriate or ineffective; but the solutions themselves will not be mechanical. There is no neat multiplier formula that automatically guarantees success so long as a few simple rules of functional finance are followed.

A history of ineffective policy is itself part of the syndrome. It is necessary to determine: (1) why academic and government based analysis failed for so long to discover the poverty problem and to uncover facts which should have been obvious to others besides the actual poor; and (2) what it was in practical politics and policy making that allowed the problem to persist even though it is abundantly clear that the resources and means to alleviate widespread poverty were and are readily available.

SOME FACTS ON DUALISTIC POVERTY

It is well known that the extent of poverty is only partially reflected in the standard indices of economic activity. For example, unemployment rates can run three to four times higher for the high-school dropout than for the graduate; or for the black twenty-five-year old than for the age group as a whole.[1] However, these and similar patterns in the published unemployment data may actually understate the true situation. There is ample side evidence that the published data only count those who are recently out of a job and actively searching for a new position. Those whose unemployment benefits have run out and those who have never even found the first job are frequently excluded from the standard indices.[2] Indications are that nearly half of working age adults in certain critical groupings are barred from anything but sporadic and haphazard employment.

The Concept of Subemployment

In recent years there have been a number of attempts to find a labor market index that bears a close relationship to the dualistic poverty phenomenon. Studies carried out (among others) by Levitan and Taggart at the George Washington University Center for Manpower Policy Studies and by Vietorisz, Giblin, and Mier at the Research Center for Economic Planning have been directed at deriving measures of "subemployment," a concept which attempts to capture the extent to which a lack of "good" jobs in the core of the economy forces workers into unemployment, part-time jobs, and substandard jobs. The concept embodies the view that a "good" job provides earnings which are adequate to support a reasonable standard of living and that it is a social responsibility to provide such jobs.[3] There are necessarily subjective elements in a subemployment measure (beginning with the problem of defining a "reasonable minimum standard of living"). Nevertheless, subemployment measures have been computed on a variety of constructions and assumptions and the concept is now becoming operational. For example, in a study comparing subemployment measures for a specific Detroit Census Employment Survey district, subemployment rates of from 30 to 54 percent (for a range of statistical procedures) were calculated for an income threshold of $5,000, whereas standard unemployment surveys in the same district estimated the rate as 10 percent.[4] If the earnings adequacy threshold is brought up to the $8500 level (close to the usual definition of a "minimal decent living standard" for an urban family of four) the subemployment rates are calculated to be at least 50 percent and perhaps as high as 80 percent. These figures apply to a district that was singled out for its poverty, but it should be stressed that the subemployment measure is not identical to a measure of poverty incidence. Subemployment is based on a population of labor-force eligibles and measures the extent to which this population is inadequately employed. It is entirely possible to have a population of "welfare poor" who would register extreme poverty but relatively low subemployment since very few in the group could be classified as eligible for work or able to work.

Pilot studies indicate subemployment rates in other urban districts comparable to those in the Detroit sample, while unpublished empirical work by the author indicates that the work experience, past and present, of the subemployed is tied very heavily to private activities employing stagnant technology and to low-level jobs in subfederal government.[5] Levitan and Taggart, in applying their variants of the subemployment measure to national samples and to some time-series data, have found that the subemployment rate is significantly less sensitive to changes in economic activity than the unemployment rate and that subemployment rates are disproportionately high among the identified minority groupings.[6]

Deep urban unemployment and associated subemployment seems to continue regardless of the trends and variations in overall production levels. It is as if there were two distinct economies within the national boundaries: one economy, the progressive sector, highly sensitive to policy control on conventional Keynesian lines; the second subeconomy in a state of permanent depression. Those associated with the second economy face a continuing threat of unemployment and inadequate income and are, in effect, a qualitatively distinct (and lower) caste. The insensitivity of this group to standard Keynesian employment policy has been studied directly by Aaron and others who have shown that manipulations of aggregate demand have virtually no influence on employment in critical groups of working-age poor.[7] Case studies by Harrison, Harrison, and Vietorisz and other dual-market theorists verify much the same patterns within the microcosm of the ghetto economy.[8]

The Ghetto Economy

The ghetto economy is not a scaled down and a poorer version of the mainstream economy, but a qualitatively distinct system that is effectively insulated from the core of the larger economy. It is effectively integrated around subemployment, low-level opportunities in stagnant activities, and certain characteristic activities such as "the hustle." It offers its own unique surrogate opportunities to the ghetto resident. A few quotes from the literature on poverty-dualism will spotlight some of the distinguishing aspects of this subsystem.[9]

First we have the marginal quality of firms and industries associated with the subeconomy.

The lack of economic power which characterizes peripheral firms (as reflected, for example, in the relatively high elasticity of their output demand curves) also makes it impossible for them to raise wages and other input costs without eroding profit margins, often to the shut-down point. Finally, the low wages found in the secondary labor market are partly the result of the relative simplicity of the technologies in secondary industries. . . .

This, of course, is the unbalanced-growth, cost-pressure phenomenon as perceived from within the stagnant subsector. Job security similarly decays.

While the primary labor market is characterized by a mutual employer-employee "taste" for stability, both firms and workers in the secondary labor market seem to benefit from unstable work-force behavior.

As might be expected, the work force tends to take on many of the peripheral qualities of the industry itself.

Some groups exhibit what seems to be pathological instability in holding jobs. Changing from one low-paying, unpleasant job to another, often several times a year, is the typical pattern of some workers. The resulting unemployment can hardly be said to be the outcome of a normal process of career advancement. . . . where primary employers and employees interact in an institutional setting characterized by high productivity, non-poverty level wages and high work-force stability, the firms and work forces in the secondary labor market tend to organize themselves into production systems displaying low productivity, poverty level wages and low stability (high turnover). It is important to observe that this contrast between the primary and secondary labor markets takes place in the dimension of *jobs*, i.e., specific industry-occupation combinations, and *not* in the simple dimensions of either industry alone or occupation alone.

Existing manpower and "economic opportunity" programs have done little to change the fundamental inessentiality of the sector.

The training programs of the federal government have taken on the basic attributes of the peripheral stratum of the economy: low "wages" and low stability. Cumulative figures from 1968 through January, 1970 show that, of 84,703 actual hires in the National Alliance of Businessmen's Job Opportunities in the Business Sector program (initiated by Lyndon Johnson and Henry Ford II), 50,225 quit or were laid off. The high implicit quit rate is not surprising; jobs in the NAB-JOBS program paid low wages, the core employers participating in the program often segregated their "hard-core" workers from the "mainstream" force, and layoffs were (as indicated) highly probable. In fact, one steel firm reported to an investigating Congressional committee that, since layoffs are "an inherent part of the American economy," it used part of the Manpower Administration subsidies "in counseling for anticipated layoffs."

In effect, the "perceived" opportunities lie entirely out of the mainstream of economic activity. Criminal activities and "hustling" attract the major portion of available energy.

The young people interviewed had little hope of significant increases in (legal) earnings, because they saw so little chance of an occupational breakthrough. At best, they expected marginal employment at wages which would allow them to "get by". . . .
Hustling was often regarded as a logical and rational option. The market

for gambling, numbers, prostitution, and narcotics is large and highly profitable, and the possibility of "being on one's own" competes powerfully with the opportunities available in the regulated middle-class world.

Criminal activities and the possible handicap of an arrest record did not seem to present problems for these Harlem youth. . . . No great social stigma accompanies arrest, so far as the immediate neighborhood is concerned. Job opportunities are already limited by other barriers, so that the effect of an arrest record is not considered important. The probability of being apprehended is considered relatively small. And the penalty for a particular offense, if one is caught, can be calculated with reasonable accuracy.

These are the most dramatic cases. But debased circumstances and personal tragedies are also to be found among the working poor, those on the margin of the ghetto economy and yet on the verge of entry into mainstream activities. For them the relationship between conditions in the stagnant subeconomy and the economy as a whole appears to be perversely asymmetrical. Layoffs during long periods of business slowdown increase the numbers of the poor; but when new jobs appear, new entrants (for the most part from already established groupings) take the place of cyclically displaced workers in the upturns. A place in the mainstream economy once lost may be lost for all time. This lesson has been learned by many minority-group employees who won their first places through affirmative action only to discover that they were the first to be fired in the economic slowdown.

Dichotomous Income Distributions

The picture of a strong discontinuity between the poor and the rest of the economy is completed by Lee Soltow's unusual and imaginative analysis of empirical income distributions.[10] Soltow studied the relationship between incomes received by adjacent groups along the income distribution spectrum. In his terminology, an economic "incentive" is implied by the magnitude of income differentials—say from the forty-ninth to the fiftieth percentile or from the seventy-ninth to the eightieth. The larger the differential the greater, one would say, is the inducement to attempt an upward move. The incentive concept makes a great deal of intuitive sense. Clearly if there were perfect equality of income, there would be no income differentials and therefore no income incentives in the system. Given the fact of inequality, Soltow looked for regularities that would imply some degree of parity for people at different positions in the income spectrum. He felt in particular that an unequal distribution might exhibit the regularity of "constant incentive." In this situation, the relative advantage of moving to the fiftieth percentile from the forty-ninth percentile would be the same as moving to the eightieth from the seventy-ninth percentile.

Examining the data, Soltow found that from the "poverty line" upwards the actual income distribution fits a constant-incentive theoretical distribution quite closely; however, this regime of constant incentives does not extend to poverty incomes. (Needless to say, the poverty incomes were far lower than those which would be predicted by the constant-incentive rule which seems to work for the upper-income groups.) Further analysis showed that the constant-incentive regime for the upper-income groups remained unchanged with the passage of time,[11] suggesting a pattern of stability in the economic forces that determined upper-income compensation—this despite a near doubling of the average compensation during the period studied. This suggests an established income structure for the progressive sector that preserves its characteristics through periods of growth; a situation bearing a striking resemblance to the equilibrium wage structure so beloved in the writings of economists. Clearly, dualism is exhibited in a wage-income structure for the poor that is totally out of synchronization with the equilibrium implied for the rest of the society.

Soltow's results crystalize the dualism view in terms of statistics of the income distribution. They provide a direct challenge to the standard view of market-oriented economists that dualistic structure is not really a fundamental characteristic, that poverty is just a lower position on a continuum of incomes. At the very least, Soltow's results make it difficult to argue that the poor are coddled by the welfare state and lack a strong economic incentive to get out of poverty.

Dualistic Poverty as a Syndrome

These are just a few of the symptoms and surface social manifestations of U.S. poverty.[12] The basic view taken in this book, however, is that these symptoms reflect deeper structural phenomena that resemble in many ways the dualism of the archetypical less-developed economy. The difference is that the underdeveloped country regards the transformation of the stagnant and primitive majority grouping as a high-priority, if not the primary, economic goal. Within the advanced country, policy is oriented to the already dominant progressive activity, and the political and social imperative to improve the position of the poor is lacking. A substantial majority sees itself as successfully linked to the success states and status paths of the system, and it is all too easy to assume that upward economic mobility is still the rule.

STANDARD AND NONSTANDARD VIEWS ON POLICY

A striking characteristic of dualistic poverty is that the poor are no longer "exploited workers" or "wage slaves" as the poor could reasonably be described in the nineteenth-century industrial world. To be exploited one has to work (or in Marxist terms, only those who labor create the surplus that the industrialists expropriate). The present-day poor are in a more desperate position than this. They are essentially irrelevant, even expendable within the system as it is developing. The growth projections of the major industries can exclude Harlem as a market, as a source of labor, and even as a base for a reserve army.

This is a damning condemnation—far more so, in its way, than the familiar exploitation criticisms—and it is essential to confront its implications. Correct solutions depend upon facing up to the truth, however uncomfortable—there have already been too many generations permanently damaged by chronic policy failures: the failure to analyze poverty at a fundamental level, the failure to listen to the obvious cries of distress, and the failure to design any but the most simplistic remedies. A solution to the poverty problem may involve a shaking up of styles of thought, objectives, techniques, and theory at least equivalent to that experienced as the Keynesian solution to the problem of depression.[13] It is certainly worth recalling certain aspects of that earlier shock to comfortable thought in order to search out some guiding patterns.

Policy Objectives

On the question of objectives and the apparent "irrelevance" of the poor under present arrangements, we must recall that the Keynesian renovation of policy analysis was accompanied by a change in attitudes that made the unemployed "relevant" and maintenance of employment an obligation of the state. The "relevance" point is important; until comparatively recently, unemployment was considered an unavoidable consequence of pursuing "responsible" policies, for the most part, policies oriented to stabilizing the nation's international position.[14] In effect, the economic position of the unemployed industrial worker did not count in policy planning or politics. Evidence of this social blindness stares at one from the literature of the time. And it is still not clear whether the eventual recognition of the employment objective should be interpreted as an accommodation to changing political realities or as a humane realization. An analogous obligation to extend the scope of economic policy to cover all individuals within the society is now emerging in an analogous situation. We will take this obligation as a necessary precondition for further discourse, ignoring whether for various individuals the obligation expresses a humane attitude, a charitable act, a political accommodation, or an attempt to preempt a feared insurrection.

Incomplete Theory

The second parallel to be drawn from the period of the Keynesian revolution is that it is not enough to simply regret the condition of individuals in a neglected class, it is necessary to be able to explain how the economy determines their condition. After all, the reasoning of economists has some influence on policy. What is explainable is a subject for policy; what is not explainable is ignored. Pre-Keynesian reasoning treated unemployment as an aberration in an otherwise well-functioning market system: the result of imperfections, artificial rigidities, and the deplorable resistance of workers to cuts in their wages. When a particular logical order is established as the referent, it is natural (at least for many economists) to focus on the behavior of the perfect system—leaving the neglected aspects, aberrations, and failures of the "perfect theoretical system" to the footnotes. Placing the problem of employment determination in the foreground of theoretical study was an essential feature of the Keynesian revolution and no writer since Keynes, regardless of ideological orientation, can return to the earlier restricted field of discourse and expect to be taken seriously. Carrying the analogy forward to the case of poverty, the parallel statement is that the poor and their condition *must* be an essential aspect of the analysis. The problem of poverty is not a footnote to the study of unemployment.

Poverty cannot be cured overnight with a stroke of the legislator's pen or a fiscal or monetary finesse. To understand and develop meaningful policy one must have an explanation of causes in which the distributional and class phenomena are prominent and in which the time it takes for policy to work on the phenomena is directly considered. This means explicit study of impacts on dualistic structure and subemployment at the same level of detail now standard for studies of unemployment. The lessons of past policy failures are clear. Unless we consciously adopt frameworks which allow explicit portrayals of distributional class phenomena, it will be futile to expect coherent poverty policy. Because it is easy and convenient to relate fiscal policy to employment impacts, dualism impacts are neglected. Similarly, because it is easy to describe long-term trends in terms of processes involving capital accumulation and technological change, dualism transitions are ignored. The key is to work towards formats that specify poverty dualism explicitly and explain its determination within a policy period uniquely suited to the transformation processes involved.

The Policy Period

One of Keynes' major contributions was to change the perception of time in economic analysis. Although not without either antecedents or ambiguity, the "Keynesian short run" (corresponding roughly to the policy period in which a political leadership interested in holding power had better generate results) was a brilliant theoretical stroke and one that adjusted the abstract period of economic processes to the demands of pragmatic policies. Analysis of poverty-class phenomena also requires chronological reorientation. The Keynesian short run is already too short (as is without question the short run period appropriate to individual markets), while the horizons of growth projections are too long. The immediacy of the social problem in conjunction with the need to operate on such long-term characteristics as the orientation and bias of technological change call for a compromise period of analysis. The minimum time needed would seem to be at least the better part of a two-term Presidential stay in office, while a full generation might be required to see the process well under way. What we will come to see as satisfactory solutions require transitional investment (in both physical and human capital) to extend the range of the progressive technology to the presently backward population. With the transition completed, one can return to notions of growth over indefinitely long horizons or concentrate on stabilization problems within the Keynesian policy period.

Data Development

The Keynesian analogy also extends into the organization and availability of data. The Keynesian revolution was advanced by the simultaneous development of comprehensive national accounts.[15] It is clear that we actually know very little about the condition of the poor and the incidence of technological change (in fact, many of the assertions made in this book are presently untestable, since there are no data to correspond to many of the constructions and categories introduced here). If policy is to be at all effective, new data concepts and data sources are required. As noted earlier, the standard indicators of economic activity, employment, and income are virtually irrelevant to stagnant sector conditions. A few cogent measures, such as subemployment rates and labor-force–participation rates have emerged in the past decade, though they have been purposely suppressed by past administrations. Complete and accurate measurements of stagnant sector conditions and adequate measurement of socioeconomic transitions are lacking; nevertheless, there is perhaps enough in the way of crude measures and indicators to have some idea of how policy is working.

Policy Innovation

The final point of the analogy is that we should be alert to the development of sharp policy instruments specifically oriented to the poverty problem. The Keynesian developments included a new orientation toward the use of the government budget as a stabilizing instrument, and the Keynesian literature specialized in studies of cycle damping and employment effects influenced by fiscal adjustments. If the analogy still holds as a guide, a new line of policy should emerge to serve as a rallying point for politics and as a focus for developing pragmatic analysis. Actually, there now appear to be too many rather than too few proposals and there is confusion rather than coherence within the policy domain. The list of policy categories in past "wars against poverty" suggest this confusion ("manpower," "public assistance," "housing integration," "headstarts in early education," "medical assistance," "open enrollment," "economic opportunity," "black capitalism," etc.). Perhaps larger classifications such as human capital or "development" fit over these subclassifications, but still the focus is blurred. This book argues for stronger and simpler notions in the area of poverty policy: specifically that every program and policy measure must be tested for its contribution to the transformation of stagnant activities and the stagnant sector population.

REORIENTATION OF POLICY

We have extended the notion of the poverty syndrome so as to include policy makers and policy analysts as part of the problem. This may be belaboring the obvious, but all the signs seem to indicate blindness with regard to constructive renovations in antipoverty policy and a predisposition toward obsolete formulations. Relief plus stabilization policy (other approaches are considered but not funded) are by default the primary antipoverty policies, even though dualistic considerations and recent experience show the ineffectiveness of both.

Relief policy, as presently constituted, derives from an essentially static view of economic processes. According to the traditional preconception, the target for assistance is a population which is effectively out of the labor force: the indigent elderly, the seriously disabled, and minors in single-parent households. However, with dualistic unemployment and unemployability, there is a far larger population at the same level of economic distress as the classic relief case. Admittedly, this population has spilled over into the relief categories and, to some extent, the relief categories have been redefined to include this population. Nevertheless, these adaptations have been unfruitful as social policy and were doomed to be so. There is overwhelming political resistance to funding that might begin to cover the needs of the broadly defined population of the poor; and the static minimal support that relief offers is entirely inappropriate to a group of labor-force age that is either barred from or unprepared for entry into progressive-sector activities. There also is little reason for optimism in plans for welfare reform; current proposals for reform (either of the negative tax or guaranteed income varieties) seem designed to create a revolving door between welfare and stagnant-sector activities, perhaps lowering welfare costs in a few instances, but hardly likely to facilitate social transformation.

General macroeconomic stabilization and growth policies are ineffective because of the low sensitivity of stagnant-sector employment to changes in aggregate demand. The basic dichotomy in the income and class distribution has persisted, and this dichotomization has been coupled with unparalleled crises within the cities and within education. Macroeconomic growth has produced a sporadically growing pie, but slices for the hungriest population have not been cut.[16]

Given the ineffectiveness of existing techniques, what then should be our approach to policy? We are led by the unbalanced-distribution scheme to categorize the necessary policy as "an integrated design to effect social transformation." This is obviously overly vague and it will be helpful to separate out a few distinct components of the approach, taking existing policy as our starting point.

Relief and Transfers

By default, relief has been the main (and failing) element in current antipoverty policy. In rethinking the relief program, two main objectives should be kept in mind: financing the humane sustenance of the poor and providing an incentive and control structure that will expedite transformations. The moralism is unexceptionable, but the economics are bad, since there is bound to be a clash between transformational programs and the basic disincentive of a high level of sustenance. There is a way out, however. First of all, the incentives must do more than perpetuate the revolving door between relief and low-level laboring; instead, the incentives must leapfrog the stagnant-sector activities and reach directly toward progressive-sector employment. Second, there must be considerable use of nonprice controls—this involves a complete break with the "reform" literature which advocates no-questions-asked programs of the negative-tax type to replace the administrative restrictions that typify conventional categorical relief.

My reasoning on this verges on the Byzantine, but I think it captures a good part of the politics as well as the economics of welfare policy. The imperfect matching of finances with needs has resulted in the regional distortions and the often criticized general oppressiveness of the present system. But oiling a system resembling the present one with money and better approximating needs with resources could reduce the oppressiveness of welfare administration in general and its geographic bias in particular, while retaining mechanisms that could direct the individual case to and through a transition process. This projection reads like the sort of panacea that has failed before and the question remains as to why we should not bypass the extant welfare institutions and move directly to individual negative-tax grants that in effect provide a guaranteed minimum income on a no-obligation basis.

The virtue of negative taxation is that it can bring income relief to a population of wage earners who have heretofore not been candidates for public assistance. This group is presumably also the group most sensitive to incentives affecting labor force participation, and most of the negative taxation plans are drawn up with relatively low floor incomes and low marginal tax rates on earned income to generate the desired work incentives. But one incentive problem that has not been widely discussed is that human-resource development programs would have to bid for recipients of negative taxation, thus raising the cost of these more fundamental remedial programs. Individual participation in such programs can more easily be fostered within a welfare category that permits some retention of earned income, that obligates participation in transformation programs, and that gears benefits to needs during the period of transition. This is obviously the critical point if a developmental approach is to be followed. Transitional programs in education or skill development have primacy and must be supported by the transfer programs; they cannot be in competition with them.

The argument boils down to a view that, if the amount to be transferred is relatively small (a doubling of present transfers could still be classed as a relatively small program, given the size of poverty gaps), then the amount to be transferred will be most effectively utilized through controlled transfers determined on a case-by-case basis. A means test would remain as a way of rationing funds, but it need not be an oppressive instrument. Above all, transfers must be viewed as they affect the inducement to engage in personal human-capital investment or to participate in social programs. The central point is that, for most types of technological change, such investments are necessary if general growth is to take place and individuals are to lift themselves from underclass status. Thus, it is conceivable that higher levels of transfers without accompanying subsidized human capital investment can lower the growth of the economy well below socially optimal levels, with the recipient population persisting for generations in a chronically unproductive and primitive position. This is surely the most critical problem area. Present relief arrangements and proposed negative-tax systems are government-supported adjuncts to low-paid, low-productivity employment. Relief, in effect, operates as part of the dualistic economic structure in which there is virtually no interchange between the mainstream economic activities and the technologically stagnant activities which typically engage the relief clientele. The issue is to find a way to leapfrog the stagnant sector in opening up employment opportunities, and this in turn requires carefully controlled and structured long-term programs of training and schooling. Negative taxation is not likely to encourage active participation in such programs by the critical population (although, of course, it would provide unencumbered support to those who require no direct incentives). A case-by-case approach might, the poormaster tradition notwithstanding.

Urban Renovation

Along with the dependency crisis associated with relief, the ghettoization phenomenon, the concentration of poverty within a key group of cities, is one of the critical trends of our times and it follows that there must be an urban component and focus in a constructive antipoverty effort. There are two sides to such a policy. One is essentially restorative, aimed at eliminating the anti-urban bias in the entire structure of federal and subfederal finances so that the process of urban decay because of inadequate funds can be checked, if not reversed. The second is reconstructive and involves operating on the city's economic base to improve its linkages with progressive-sector activities. These matters are important and controversial enough to merit separate development in a separate chapter, and Chapter Ten deals with policy questions in the context of a picture of the urban economy, depicting unbalanced-growth impacts on distribution, finances, and the structure of business activities. Conventional "job creation" programs are not the answer. The preservation of stagnant-sector jobs or the concocting of new stagnant-sector service opportunities can, at best, result in a few sheltered positions tracked toward obsolescence.

Transformational Programs

Given the preconditions of restructured welfare and urban finances, any real diminution of poverty requires explicit planning for growth and social transformation. Two steps are required for such a program. The first step is that of establishing the principle of managed macroeconomic growth; the second, that of structuring manpower, educational, and production programs so as to advance the transformational objectives. Later chapters describe a few general designs and assess those few specific programs for which we have some relevant experience. This will bring us to the periphery of economic analysis; the principle of managed growth is far from established as a norm in American politics and the programs themselves involve excursions far from the domain of conventional economic policy.

The reader should be able to anticipate some of the main arguments and themes which will run through these chapters. The key point (and really the only source of optimism in the matter) is the "noncompetitive" impact of educational transformations. To the extent that the unbalanced-growth description captures reality, widening the progressive sector to include more of the present poor will not impose significant burdens on the rest of the society. To the contrary, much of the burden of the present transfer system is likely to evaporate. Nevertheless, the proposed policies, however rational and promising, skirt the edges of political feasibility for the United States and involve far greater integration of manpower and industrial-development programming than has been attempted here before. With this in mind, what is proposed here is minimal compared to the social innovations facilitating growth that have been installed in Japan and the Scandinavian nations. My proposals primarily involve altering benchmarks and standards so that the selection of programs is sensitive to transformational potentialities; for despite the essential simplicity of the approach and apparent acceptability on an economist's standard, it goes against the ingrained policy habits of this country and the current trend toward de-educating the population. The following examples may clarify the abstract notion of "sensitivity toward transformational potentialities."

Public-sector employment is an obvious field in which job opportunities for the poor can be expanded and is widely regarded as such. Significant recent thinking on the subject appears in a volume edited by Sheppard, Harrison, and Spring and devoted to public sector employment as a policy strategy. Although the volume devotes major sympathetic attention to the dualism characterization of poverty; only a late reflection turns toward the possibility of altering technology to fit the labor force characteristics of subemployed workers to advance the social objective of encouraging mobility into mainstream activities.[17] In other words, the conventional static orientation towards labor-market issues obscures explicit consideration of dynamic transformation, even in a conference group predisposed toward such a view.

On another front, T. Vietorisz has advocated a policy of raising substantially the minimum wage.[18] This is explicit dynamic transformational policy. The higher minimum wage would undoubtedly cause immediate unemployment, but it would force industry to upgrade technology and thus, when and if the new machines are installed, increase worker productivity (in effect, validating the higher wage after the fact). The approach focuses on subemployment as an aspect of the stagnant-sector syndrome (where workers earning less than the amount needed to sustain a poverty-line existence are classified as subemployed). Upgrading jobs would transform the physical conditions of production; some of the workers previously subemployed would find jobs under the new production regime, while others necessarily would become unemployed in the conventional sense. Vietorisz recognizes that the minimum-wage attack would have to be coordinated with a manpower system that would be involved in technological forecasting and extensive information-gathering and transmittal functions. Public-service employment could be an important supplement to the system, but Vietorisz prefers to emphasize that the business sector has an implicit responsibility to provide meaningful employment to the entire labor force. He stops short of developing the goals of macroeconomic policy that will be required to drive the system to absorb the labor force slack and assist in social transformation, but his approach comes very close to what is advocated here.

The contrast between his approach and the "workfare" approach advocated in some formats for relief is obvious but merits comment. Under the "workfare" of the Nixon administration and its resurrection in Carter's proposed "reforms," welfare recipients can be required to accept a job regardless of the level of compensation with the relief authority making up the difference. The approach seems designed to support the most outmoded and least productive technologies and offers no transformational possibilities for the work force involved.

Summing Up

The portrayal of the poverty phenomena in the preceding sections may have seemed a simple recapitulation of familiar materials: discrimination, labor-market imperfections, and ghettoization have all been considered in the literature; and policy to eliminate these characteristics is hardly novel. But the traditional reforms derive from a static view of labor markets and the industrial system and do not capture the underlying trends and widening discrepancies of a growing economy. We have seen, for example, how reform in public assistance has done nothing to reduce dependency over generations, while standard job creation and labor-market policies do little to break workers out of the stagnant sector. Policies must be considered for their full systemic implications and explicit planning is a necessity.

10

Urban Decay Within

a Growing Economy

$\mathbf{T}$HIS chapter carries the analysis of poverty into a description of how the social, economic, and fiscal pressures of unbalanced growth intensify over time within the cities. The concern here is with a process whereby industrial dualism leads to a concentration of poverty within the cities. The initial concentration, when coupled with a lack of resiliency in the structures, rules, and institutions of public finance, leads to further accumulation and concentration of the poor and additional cost pressures on services. Thus, the resources of urban centers are overwhelmed. With the inevitable curtailment of real services, the traditional "melting pot" social-transformation capacity of the city is vitiated.

THE FUNCTIONING OF A CITY

The life of a functioning city exists in two interpenetrating domains, the human and the economic.[1] The human domain, largely intangible, consists of the possibilities for meaningful interaction implicit in sheer concentration of population and the supporting presence of institutions and traditions that have grown out of past, present, and potential interactions. Great cities—Rome, Vienna, New York, Paris, London, Amsterdam, and perhaps a few others—are made so by the richness, depth and variety of the interactions and associations they offer. The peaks of greatness are reached when these potentialities are coupled with a sense of progress, advance, and transformation.* This abstract description is as valid for commercial life as it is for artistic life; in fact, the two lines of development may not be separable. The pattern extends into many personal and social areas. Although perhaps a romanticized fiction, the archetype great city is taken as offering social mobility, meaningful opportunities, and impersonal objective evaluations of individual claims for advancement. A reputation in the "Big Apple" is a reputation that counts, and, of course, everything is up to date in Kansas City.

A rich variety of human types is, in effect, an image of a wide range of economic activity. Artistic and intellectual vitality depends upon the availability of an affluent and leisured minority of patrons and sizable general audiences. Both, in turn, depend upon commercial vitality; while to complete the pattern of feedback and organic function, commercial vitality is in very large part dependent upon personnel drawn from an active and mobile population. Similarly, the city's potential for effecting social transformation is dependent on the existence of a wide range of employment opportunities. As the traditional image would have it, migrants are attracted in and move (in a statistical sense) up the rungs of the economic and social ladder, keeping a step ahead of newcomers pressing closely behind. The economy of the city must create new opportunities, industries, commerce, and activities to match the pressures and requirements of a changing human domain.

However, human vitality and commercial viability go hand in hand with health in the public finances. The population requires social services, protection, education, transportation, and health care; while the ongoing commercial activities require supporting public facilities and institutions. The bill for these amenities must be paid; the whole package of services is supported by taxation assessed directly or indirectly on incomes of residents and on the commercial activities of the locale. (In the Federal system these basic fiscal resources are, of course, supplemented by flows to and from other levels of government.) The financial balance can be precarious; taxes can be escaped by footloose industries and calculating individuals while the flow of intergovernmental revenues is under the control of higher levels of government generally unsympathetic to urban interests. In this situation interconnections between the human and economic domains tend to be worked out in the financial balance between public requirements and revenues. As we will discover, the pressures of

---

* A touch of decadence may also be an ingredient.

dualistic imbalance can be acute here and the life of major urban centers is imperiled.

Fiscal breakdown is a long process, however, and critical signs and symptoms can appear prior to the ultimate crisis, literal bankruptcy. The symptoms of concern here would be ones indicating that the city was losing its ability to facilitate social transformation, that class lines were hardening (the ghettoization phenomena), and that accompanying social problems such as crime and educational decay were driving out key population groupings. To parallel these symptoms in the human domain, the economic structure would appear to be losing its regenerative capacity. New industries and capacities would not develop to replace the ones that die or move and the scope of opportunities and potentialities would be significantly reduced.

On this line of thinking, the black, Puerto Rican, and Asian migration into Northern cities is not of itself an unhealthy event; their migration is only the latest of a succession of waves. We should instead focus on why the economic system failed to provide them with the meaningful employment and economic opportunities received by their predecessors. (The cities actually appear to have gone further in this direction than the system as a whole.) In terms of symptoms, one notes that the diminished ability to assimilate and transform migrants is an aspect of a syndrome of aggravated financial pressures, increased service burdens, and diminished revenue-generating capacity. A more threatening sign, however, is the apparent loss of the vital ability to generate new activities. This characteristic involves some ephemeral notions, but it can perhaps be brought out by examples and indirect reasoning.[2]

A city such as Detroit, with its single-industry concentration, is characterized by a relatively homogeneous manpower pool (which New Yorkers would say tends to imply a relatively shallow urban life). If the automobile industry were to be legislated out of existence, the ability of the city to survive would depend upon the fortuitous emergence of major new industries with manpower needs in very close correspondence to those of the auto manufacturers. In a city such as New York, a decade or so ago, with its heterogenous industrial and commercial mix and associated range of labor-force attributes and intellectual resources, one would like to think that almost any industry could be lost—even such standbys as finance, garment manufacturing, or shipping—and the human resources and amenities would call in viable replacements. The issue could be put another way: if New York City's development stemmed historically from its status as a port, with commerce and finance building on this base, would elimination of the port activity cause the whole structure to topple? It is clear that many cities (Newark for one) lack regenerative ability; and one can wonder if any American city at the present time retains it.

The author's private signal in this matter centers around a relatively in-conspicuous event—the demise of New York's Cafe Figaro. Virtually all of the many strands of Greenwich Village life from the beat to the hip eras were tied together in this one coffee shop. Distinguished professionals, sophisticates, and hopefuls in photography, cinema, writing, chess, bridge, economics (yes), soft drugs, sex, and other recreations made the Figaro as habitués (avoiding the Saturday night dating scene which, to be honest, paid the bills). Many other establishments from honky-tonks to ethnic handicraft shops grew up around the Figaro and obviously depended upon it. Crowds thronged in the area and land values rose accordingly. Figaro's landlord attempted to triple the rent, figuring that since this was the busiest corner in the city, the space was an obvious choice for one of the more obnoxious chain eateries. Figaro was forced to close. The habitués scattered or emigrated, and no replacement ever devel-oped. The *New York Times* ventured to guess at the cost to the country's in-tellectual life. There is no happy aftermath. Even the replacement stores went broke, along with a fair portion of the neighborhood. The point, of course, is not that one particular institution went under as a victim of New York City's insane real estate practices; this is part of the game. The disturbing fact is that the City appeared to have lost its capacity to regenerate viable copies of vital institutions. A breaking point had seemingly been reached for the binding force of urban amenities—or so it seemed in this one instance.*

PRESSURES ON URBAN FINANCES

With the above unhappy thought to reflect upon, we can go on to look more carefully at what in the economic domain could force the city towards a more visible crisis threshold, the financial breaking point. The forces that directly operate on the city budget derive from the underlying demographic and production structure of the locality, the comparative position of this structure *vis a vis* the rest of the system, and the effective-ness of the fiscal system in capturing revenues from ongoing activities. Putting matters concretely, we are dealing with the economic forces that influence the tax rate in a particular city (this rate being the result of

---

* I wrote this paragraph in a moment of rage some years back. The Cafe Figaro remained closed for seven years until in a happy after aftermath—actually occurring at the most intense moment at the City's fiscal crisis—a complete reversal occurred and Figaro reopened, meticulously restored, even to the bearded economist at the corner table. The restoration has been an extravagant social success and a financial bonanza. The event is noteworthy not only for what it suggests about the dangers in overconfident analysis by participant observers.

separate trends in expenditures and underlying incomes). The tax rate in the city must be considered against rates outside of the city, for such comparisons are likely to determine who locates where. The locational decision in turn determines the class and production structure of the city; which, coming full circle, is an important determinant of the tax rate. We will find that the division of production between stagnant and progressive-sector activities is critical here, and that the fiscal position of the city becomes a special case of dualistic imbalance.*

In essence, the city is viewed against a set of trends operating in the economy as a whole. These trends add up to a pattern: (1) The real wages of those in the mainstream private industry, particularly those requiring educated manpower, increase steadily over time. (2) Another major segment of the economy stays at a stagnant (poverty) wage level. (3) Real wages in education and a number of other areas of government service increase in pace with those in the leading private activities. (4) The unit cost of government services and education increases relative to all other goods due to the general lack of productivity offsets in this class of activity.

Our concern is with how the adverse components of these forces can concentrate within a geographic subsystem, the city. To begin, we classify the functional distribution of the population in terms of three proportions: the *progressive proportion*, consisting of the percent of the labor force in progressive, private activities; the *service proportion*, the percent of the labor force in municipal government; and the *stagnant proportion*, the percent in stagnant private employment or unemployed.

The existing industrial structure of the location is described as the ratio of private progressive-sector labor activity to private stagnant-sector labor activity, or inactivity. This ratio can be stated as *progressive proportion* over *stagnant proportion*. The industrial structure can reflect an historical accident or a conscious development program. We note only that the pressures of space and a natural urban orientation toward using concentrated manpower may have biased prior development away from the capital-heavy industries now associated with the growth impulse.

The municipal-workers variable, *service proportion*, is given the very specific meaning of the labor requirement needed to generate a standard bundle of local government services. The costs of this labor requirement make up a major part of the expenditure budget and, as we have seen, these costs tend to increase exponentially. The burden of financing this

---

* The Appendix Part Five gives a formal translation of this argument in economist's terminology.

budget falls ultimately on the taxpayer; so to identify the effect of cost pressure one must compare the burden to the personal incomes that underlie the tax base.

The total personal income of the city is the weighted sum of stagnant- and progressive-sector incomes. We have seen that the service costs will grow exponentially. However, because a proportion (*stagnant proportion*) of the population will be at the stagnant wage, we can project that the income level will grow less rapidly. Therefore the tax rate must increase unless the locality can tax beyond its own population of residents. In short, the city is in a "looking-glass" world in which it has to run at an increasing rate just to stay in place. In fact, since the cost pressure results from the wage-cost component, good times and better-than-average growth elsewhere in the system will exacerbate the pressure.

We know intuitively that localities with a more favorable underlying incomes-and-activities mix will be better able to withstand the cost trends. So, to complete the picture we need to be able to compare tax rates among cities and between cities and the suburbs. To make this evaluation, let us invent a typical bedroom suburb named Prime. Prime is intended to be representative of the single-class suburbs that compete with the city for middle-class residents, and it is favored by an initial endowment of industries and/or residency mix that makes its proportion of population attached to private progressive activities far higher than that in the city. (Two-acre residential zoning and a ban on multifamily dwellings easily establish such an advantage.) Suppose Prime requires the same level of services as the city. Cost pressures will be felt in both the city and in Prime, but if the class structure in the two locations does not change, Prime will have a substantial advantage in relative tax rates since it can more easily cover its expenditure burden—in effect spreading it over the high proportion of its residents earning the progressive-sector wage. Thus, the ratio of tax rates will be inversely proportionate to the ratio of higher-income residents. In fact, it can be shown that as the trends work themselves out, Prime's tax rate will become a small proportion of that in the city—equal, in fact, to the ratio of the city's upper-income residency proportion to that in Prime. That is, in comparison with a city where 20 percent of the population is in the progressive sector and 8 percent is in municipal employment, Prime's tax rate could fall to 28 percent of the city's.[3] (It should be noted that discrepencies of approximately this size have been exposed in a number of studies of the property-tax base for local school finance.)

Turning the argument and perspective around, we see that the smaller the city's residential proportion of progressive-sector and service workers, the worse its relative position will become. This is hardly a surprising conclusion to urbanists; its significance stems from the fact that it derives *entirely* from the initial pattern of industrial location and general trends in macroeconomic growth. That is, the primary causes of "urban crises" are inevitable and historical rather than attributable, say, to "mismanagement" or budgetary indiscretions. A further implication of the analysis is that the position worsens most rapidly when macroeconomic growth is at its highest; a perverse result as it stands but, nevertheless, one that is supported by the evidence of recent events. Budgetary pressures on municipal governments have been strongest when wage gains in the progressive private-sector force pattern increases for municipal workers and when buoyant expectations of social transformation generate increased demand for social services. During growth periods the pressures amount to the slow but steady strangulation of services. New York City's attempt to relieve the pressure by borrowing to meet increasing operating expense came unstuck during a period of general financial stringency, but the city's salary structure and the debt burden itself were built up during the peak growth years of the late 1960s.[4]

WHERE TO LOCATE

The actual urban situation is significantly more complicated than has been suggested so far and we must consider factors that may alter the pattern of location. In fact, the disadvantages of the city can worsen further since there is the possibility of an exodus out of the city to form new suburbs on the Prime model. The decision to locate, where the choice is between living in the city or in places like Prime, is not accidental but depends upon an evaluation of the packages of burdens and benefits offered by each prospective site for living.[5]

In general, the desire of higher-income persons (who are included in the *progressive* and *service* groups) to locate within the city rather than in Prime depends upon a number of indices of economic well-being and social comfort. The short list includes relative tax rates, rent-equivalent living costs, safety, governmental benefits of particular interest to the upper-income group, and other locational amenities. Common sense suggests that increases in the benefits and cuts in the burdens will encourage settlement in the city; that is, an increase in the suburban tax rate relative to that in the city will encourage the middle and higher classes to remain in the city, as would an increase in the relative amenities of the cities (e.g., the muggers moved to Manhasset).

Of particular interest is the relationship between movements of the upper-income population and the tax index. Clearly, a fall in Prime's tax rate relative to that in the city triggers a movement to Prime but this, in turn, could accelerate the deterioration of the relative tax position as the tax base shrinks in the city with the exodus. The pattern is familiar to all present and recent city dwellers. The key question is whether there are checks to the process so that the exodus ceases before the entire population is lost. This will depend upon whether or not the pull of amenities is great enough to support what we might call a "locational equilibrium": a position in which the population desiring to remain in the locale can support the associated tax burden. In effect, the proportion of the higher income population that wishes to settle in the locale depends upon the relative tax rate; but the tax rate in turn depends upon the proportion of this population that has established residency. The "equilibrium" is a point of mutual consistency. At a point away from equilibrium, pressures will mount for changes, either in the migration pattern or in tax rates.

A highly volatile situation is possible wherein a small divergence from equilibrium could trigger dramatic movements towards a single-class city, (i.e., a worsened tax position and out-migration or an improved tax position and massive in-migration). This case corresponds to the population clusters of the West Coast metropolitan areas, for example, the small residential cities along the east bank of San Francisco Bay, or the Los Angeles suburbs. These locations are essentially undifferentiated except in the tax/service package they offer; hence, they are vulnerable to any real or signalled alteration in the residency pattern in terms of income, class, or race.* A stable variegated class structure seems to depend upon a situation in which some "hard-core" city lovers among upper-income groups would remain in the city even in the face of an extreme disadvantage in tax rates. Because of this favorable propensity—associated, perhaps, with cultural amenities or strong inducements for progressive industry loca-

---

* The archetypical transforming city evoked in the elegiac introduction to this chapter was founded on my perception of New York and other major Eastern cities. Because of its class and demographic homogeneity, the individual small Western city lacks transformational potential. However, metropolitan areas such as the East Bay taken as a whole may function as a full urban complex.

tion—the locational equilibrium would be "stable" in this sense. A number of the older major cities of the East Coast, the Midwest, and the far West correspond to this stable case.

Finally, there can be a situation in which only complete ghettoization can occur; the city lacks regenerative capacity and because of a lack of strong amenities is intrinsically incapable of sustaining any significant upper-income population.

POLICIES AND POLICY ADJUSTMENTS

The processes described thus far have placed government in a neutral role; but it is clear that an active administration can accelerate or retard the basic trends through alterations in expenditure emphasis and in tax structure. The changing incomes distribution and the associated budgetary pressures have their effects on the demand for services and on expenditure mix within the city. Two trends seem of particular importance where the initial tendency is toward the exodus of the upper-income groups. First, public-assistance expenditures will mount (relevant to the extent that these programs require local finance) and intensify the difficulty of financing services and merit goods. Second, the burden on education will be acute; particularly if we consider education to be one of the critical means of social transformation. Making matters even worse, the middle- and lower-middle-class groups most likely to provide educators to the system have undoubtedly moved to Prime and have taken themselves out of the city as taxpayers.

The budgetary pressures can work themselves out in a compromise of needs, reflecting the willingness and ability of the jurisdiction to tax itself or otherwise attract and obtain financing. The abstract tax measures for the model city and Prime are obviously only approximate representations. One way to readjust to budgetary pressures is to vary the progressivity of the set of taxes that falls basically on income recipients within the jurisdiction. This can be done by varying the progressivity of income-tax schedules, the effective progressivity of property tax, and the weight given to sales taxation. Of course, while a progressive tax structure seems in order if the burden of increasing real costs is to be tied to the progressive sector, we cannot overlook the fact that it is just this sector which is most mobile and (as opinion would have it) most sensitive to locational inducements. Thus, when the city attempts progressive financing of its service burdens, it increases its disadvantage *vis à vis* Prime, which with its one-class structure will be able to offer a better bargain through strictly proportional taxation.

This situation is evocative of a number of current problems, issues, and events in subfederal public finance. Attempts to institute a local progressive income tax (as in New York City) are frustrated by avoidance through exodus and by political pressures to reduce the effective steepness of the schedules. The characteristic response to financial crisis is still the short-term tactical move toward revenue sources such as sales taxes that increase the regressiveness of the overall tax structure. One of the few factors that may tend to retard the deterioration of the city's position is that proportionate taxation will not be achieved in practice: the city has a few more taxing channels than the suburbs while property taxation, the primary fiscal means of the suburbs, may be slow to respond and adjust to pressure.* Of course, Prime will not be without its own financial problems. The absolute level of service costs will be increasing with unbalanced growth, too, and, more likely than not, these trends will not have been anticipated—heated town meetings and frustrated expectations are inevitable.

Once we understand these trends and their impact on fiscal positions, it becomes clear that a full-scale renovation of subfederal finance is necessary. Anything short of a shift to the federal tax base to support the major portion of subfederal expenditures can only be a stopgap without power to check the perverse locational biases of the present system. The only real point for discussion is on techniques for distributing funds to subfederal jurisdictions for expenditures.

This still leaves us with matters of zoning, taxation of commercial property and locational inducements to industry. One suggestion is that a jurisdiction, in planning and projecting its industrial base, should attempt selectivity on lines of potential productivity growth. Unfortunately, it is not so easy to find practical means to this objective, particularly where jurisdictions may end up competing for desirable industries. Increased national locational planning is, of course, an implied solution; but this step seems beyond the present policy consciousness and it is likely that we will still see self-defeating competition among localities. In any case (that is, with either local planning or a national locational policy), there is still a long way to go. The notion of imbalance in the incidence of

---

* Offsetting this is the ability of many suburban areas to form complex and overlapping taxing jurisdictions, e.g., water, school, or fire districts with boundaries distinct from political subdivisions.

technical change suggests pragmatic criteria for categorizing industry types and classifying manpower pools; but the task of statistical analysis and data development to provide the information needed at the practical level still remains. Needless to say, political effects must also be considered. For example, a "Southern strategy" pattern of federal disbursements is a frequent allegation. While it is not at all clear how significant or lasting this manifestation (attributable to focused federal expenditures) may be, or how it may aggravate or offset the underlying production trends, it points to why one must think twice before advocating further scope for national *political* control over locationally sensitive instruments.

Conclusions

To conclude, the description of social problems and remedies in this chapter recapitulates familiar material in the literature of urban economics, economics of poverty, and economics of education. The description presented here establishes a fresh line of interconnection among these subject areas, relates them to underlying conditions of production, and shows how a particular pattern of national growth process may intensify the urban crisis. The present pattern of "solution" through budget cuts and reduced service levels is clearly shown to be no solution at all; the cost pressures must reemerge once general growth is reestablished and the benefits disposed of in the budget cuts may be irretrievably lost.

The major policy conclusions stemming from this line of inquiry are already quite familiar to urbanists. What is new here is the establishment of links between questions of location and issues in national economic policy. We note that the uncomfortable patterns develop out of parallels in industrial configurations and income distributions. This would seem to suggest that practical remedies could be found in systems of commercial zoning, commercial property taxation, and special funding for locating progressive-sector activities. This is a promising line to pursue; but until one can be confident that the N-city game of "locational incentive" has a felicitous solution other than providing tax-abatement windfalls to foot-loose enterprises, or that full-scale national locational planning will be instituted (in other than politically focused forms), it is best to be cautious before projecting details of policy.

PART FIVE

POLICIES
FOR PROGRESS

11

Management
and Mismanagement:
A Polemic Interlude

THE discussions to this point have provided an alert to potential problems in unmanaged growth and a call for a number of constructive policies geared to the intelligent management of a growth economy and the renovation of its distributive mechanisms. However, before one can confront these complex matters in any practical way, it is first necessary to establish growth of some sort, even growth on the old unsatisfactory pattern. In this context, it is disquieting to think that policy mismanagement to date has actually raised doubts as to whether any sort of rudimentary growth can be sustained. With each quarter that slips away, the eventual restoration of growth seems to become that much more problematical. If this is so, the first order of business is to review recent experience to try and discover what went wrong with the economy and the nature of the mismanagement risk.

ECONOMISTS' MISPERCEPTIONS OF THE NATURE OF POLICY

Most academic economists (the author included, until recently) conceived of the economy as a controllable system: one that can be stabilized at a high level of employment with satisfactory price levels and international performance, and with sustainable and controllable growth. This view on policy also subsumes an idealized view of instrumental governance which rests on a conviction that different presidents will conscientiously act "rationally" or "efficiently" although they might differ on certain values—i.e., one president might prefer to trade off some price stability for some growth and higher employment levels, whilst another (for unimpeachable [sic] reasons) might check growth in order to satisfy a preference for a reduced rate of inflation. On this construction, the President's task is to pick the right objective, letting advisors select the appropriate policy steps. In the typical textbook example, a Republican president would stress controls over inflation and maintenance of the value of the dollar; a Democratic president would pick a point that reflects a concern with jobs and employment. The initial background studies made by the idealized advisors would have the function of demonstrating to the President how he or she might best pursue such objectives. The presumption, of course, is that presidential attitudes would reflect coalition and constituency politics (mixed with a bit of personal taste). But for those who hold or held this view, there never was any doubt about whether a president would or would not attempt to reach an optimal position in keeping with this construction of responsive pluralistic political direction. This was the way an economist would look at the matter and there was never any doubt (at least within mainstream writings) that this was also the way the problem would appear to the president as decision maker. (Perhaps after an initial period of orientation.)

The solutions obtained under this construction of policy choice would be described as falling within a range of reasonably stabilized outcomes of the system. Most academicians (again the author included) have felt that the main macroeconomic problems were solved both technically and politically and that Keynes had been vindicated by policy successes in the postwar Western industrial nations. It made sense to cross the business cycle off the list of unsolved problems, cancel courses in economic fluctuations, and remainder the textbooks in these fields.

I am something of a maverick on this particular point, but it seems to me that the Watergate revelations yield important data on the nature of policy choice and that, along with memoirs on conventional management of economic affairs, they suggest the naivete and misperception of the standard "economists' view" of the policy domain, the nature of presidential power, and the extent of their own policy influence. It is too often forgotten that the public's comprehension of policy is limited. For example, past growth policies were understood by many as aspects of national chauvinism, a space race, and a technology race. Economic advance was not understood as a value on its own terms, nor was it understood that growth could obtain independently of chauvinistic goals.

In light of this, the possibilities for either willful or well-intentioned deception of the public are considerable: if ghetto unemployment figures are uncomfortable, stop collecting them; if poverty and lack of growth is the problem, declare war on inflation; if all else fails, reestablish the private right to hold gold. Most of the intelligent lay public lacks a firm grasp of basic macroeconomic mechanisms and can be deceived by plausible claims. They eventually end up without confidence in any statement on economic policy.

The confusion can be intensified by public relations. Consider the efforts to establish inflation as the critical economic problem. Inflation is a highly visible sign of disorder; but it may not be particularly damaging on its own. In fact, on a comparative level, the problem of U.S. inflation was much exaggerated (the U.S. inflation rate has been relatively low compared with inflation rates in the main trading nations). Such public relations are easy to manage. On paper, a 5 percent inflation rate looks every bit as serious as a 5 percent unemployment rate—and, of course, inflation is visible to everyone. It is also fairly easy to give an appearance of concern and activity in an anti-inflationary campaign. The difficulties of the campaign and lack of success in the combat can then be presented as evidence of just how intractable the problem is.

In effect, official critics have their attention preempted. Instead of being able to devote themselves to the real problems of poverty and stagnation, they are obliged to respond to each tactical move in the shadow battle against the publicized problem. The situation is not helped when the main issues are lost in doctrinal disputes. The pronouncements of economists in controversies over smaller technical points often give the impression of total intellectual disorder in the field.*

All of these factors together leave the public without benchmarks for judging policy and, specifically, without the one indispensable critical insight: that a growth economy should be obtainable without excessive strain.

---

* On a related point, despite the policy disarray on international finance, the vast majority of economists were united in their abhorrence of the status quo throughout the 1960s. The sheer noise of their quarrels over the best alternative systems (nearly all alternatives were superior to the crisis-prone status quo) drowned out the basic correctness of the critique itself, left the existing system in command long beyond its useful life, and opened the door to the totally wrongheaded Smithsonian "reforms" and the debacles that followed.

Growth Consciousness

With these qualifications established, we can go on to look at just how the growth forces have been dismantled. The argument builds around the notion of growth "consciousness" and the possibility of discrepancy or conflict between consciousness at the policy level and the operations of the economy at large.

We begin with the notion of "consciousness" to express the complex of attitudes and perceptions that go into: (1) the manner in which government sees its economic responsibilities and powers; (2) the ways in which firms and investors form anticipations; (3) the attitudes held by workers and union leaders in their approach to wage and salary negotiations; and (4) the ways in which economists perceive the functioning of these elements within the system.

It seems useful to start with categorization of three levels or states of consciousness: (I) the pre-Keynesian way of looking at the economy, (II) the "new economics" viewpoint of early editions of Samuelson's *Economics,* and finally (III) a modern growth orientation. In the sections that follow, these consciousness states (labeled Consciousness I, II, and III, or abbreviated C. I, C. II, and C. III) will be looked at with some seriousness and we will perhaps obtain some insights into the "misperception" phenomena introduced in Chapter Two.*

CONSCIOUSNESS AND CONSCIOUSNESS CONFLICT

Levels of Consciousness

Consciousness I is essentially the pre-Keynesian view—economic fundamentalism (in the theological sense). Firms and the public at large are oriented toward the inevitable cycle, attuned to short run extrapolations and reversible short-term positions in both the product and financial markets. A government with this perception is almost completely passive. Constant themes in the official rhetoric are the virtues of enterprise and the dangers of intervention. The verbiage may, in fact, indicate that the mechanics of active stabilization are imperfectly understood. The balanced budget is a norm (that "old-time religion" in the words of a recent

---

* I apologize for the "Greening of America" coloring of the nomenclature; there are emphatically no other associations with Reich.

Treasury Secretary); selective and structure-changing policies are anathema. Perhaps the only allowable policies are: (1) rather coarse monetary policies based on the pre-Keynesian notion that heightened investment activity will follow monetary ease; (2) profit-enhancing tax policies based on the view that the causal chain runs from profitability to investment; and (3) "open-mouth" policy to guide and reassure.

Consciousness II corresponds to the perception of economic policy associated with the "new economics" or an early Keynesian view on stabilization. Government sees the possibility and takes on the responsibility of regulating the economy at or near what it perceives to be the full employment level. Policy becomes moderately active and aggressive. The primitive version of C. II focuses on taking the violent swings out of the cycle, but the more advanced and sophisticated consciousness II sees the cycle as something that can be entirely eliminated so that potential GNP becomes an entirely reasonable target for short-term policy. In fact, under C. II one goes on to think of other targets, such as improving the international position or influencing the rate of growth within the general stabilization goal.

Consciousness II in the business community involves the acceptance of the stabilization principle coupled with corporate planning under the assumption that the stabilization goals will be achieved with some degree of success. On the practical level this means reducing the emphasis given to crisis liquidity, adopting (and believing in) short-term forecasting systems, lengthening the planning period, and engaging in more aggressive financing. Opposition to general Keynesian policies—anathema under C. I—is softened in the C. II business community. Parallel effects are exhibited in the financial markets. Defensive characteristics and liquidity become less important and the tolerance of debt and high earnings multipliers increases.[1]

Consciousness III evolves in an economy governed by C. II thinking, but with a history of some degree of success in macroeconomic stabilization. In this situation it becomes possible to think of qualitative goals such as growth, elimination of poverty, enhancement of public services, and control over the environment. In other words, once one is convinced that it is possible to achieve full employment, the question becomes that of finding the most desirable way of doing so. For example, under C. II one simply accepts that $50 billion in lump-sum spending will generate about 5 million jobs; in an emerging C. III one begins to ask whether the particular pattern of expenditures is likely to generate new technologies or employ critical labor groups. A more developed consciousness would consider and comprehend a far broader list of options in the level and general pattern of expenditures. Although other goals are considered, the dominant motif in C. III is growth (in the idealized form), with specific government policies oriented to achieving a target rate of growth by appropriate inducements to capital formation and to productivity-enhancing technical change.

Analogously, growth consciousness extends to all sectors of the economy. Business firms extend their planning periods and involve themselves in market, production, and product-development strategies that require continuing macroeconomic growth for their validation. Debt financing and retentions in advance of anticipated growth become characteristic behaviors. Similar extrapolations are carried out in the financial markets and growth-stock evaluation becomes the basic analytical tool (in fact, C. III probably developed first within the financial markets and the contrast between C. III and C. II reasoning can best be appreciated by comparing Japanese and American investment newsletters).

Other C. III manifestations can be cited. Among the most important are the acceptance of long-term goals implicit in the expansion of higher education, and the presumption of growth and productivity gains which is carried into the typical wage bargain. The main point, though, is that a coherent pattern of anticipations emerges. The pattern is oriented to expected growth and in fact enhances the chances that the growth target will be achieved.

Consciousness and Economic Structure

We have described three levels of consciousness and, by inference, three corresponding configurations of the economic system: the pre-Keynesian economy, a cycle-prone, boom or bust economy corresponding to C. I; the stabilized economy (but with no particular expansionary dynamics), corresponding to C. II; and the managed growth economy corresponding to C. III. Where the consensus level of consciousness and the actual configuration of the economy correspond we have something akin to a qualitatively distinct system, a particular structure of self-fulfilling prophecies. Consciousness I, combined with an unmanaged economy, not surprisingly, suggests a cycle-prone volatile and unstable system, e.g., the pre-World War II world. Consciousness II, combined with active stabilizing policy, suggests a highly predictable near-full-employment economy, e.g., the U.S. economy during the war years, during the later

Truman administration, and during the first Kennedy-Johnson administration.[2]

The growth economy combined with C. III might also be predictable and manageable so long as there is: (1) some consensus on growth expectations; (2) strategic emphasis on productivity enhancement; (3) moderation in encouragement of capital formation; and (4) avoidance of the grossest forms of speculation. A serious claim can be advanced that the U.S. economy approached such a position in the mid-1960s; for a brief time, at least, the economy made the qualitative jump to a managed growth system with the ruling motif C. III.

Clash Between Consciousness and Structure

We have finally reached the critical point as regards policy failure. The coherence between consciousness, particularly policy consciousness, and the general state of the economy was not sustained and herein lies the cause of many of the nation's economic ills. A brief chronology covering the period since 1960 will help to clarify the matter. Kennedy was quickly educated to a passable C. II level (Walter Heller, his chief economic advisor, writes of Kennedy's typical C. I naiveté when he came to office).[3] He accepted the principle of aggressive stabilization along with policies leading to selective encouragement of strategic technologies. Stabilization was carried forward in the first Johnson years; the tax reforms and the war on poverty were plausible steps toward managed growth; and the prevailing background thinking was oriented to formulating a long-term growth-enhancing program (a dominant theme in Council of Economic Advisors and Joint Economic Committee activities).[4] Concrete manifestations of a C. III economy also appeared, largely in response to the unbroken expansion of the early sixties. Corporate long-term planning became an accepted high-level procedure. The growth orientation (with roots in the mid-1950s) dominated the stock market and the extrapolation of permanent productivity (and inflationary) gains dominated the wage bargain. The educational expansion was at near-peak acceleration and prospects for social transformation of the poor seemed bright.

In 1965, at the very moment that managed growth seemed about to be established, the impetus was lost when the social programs and technology-oriented expenditures were deflected by the war and policy took on a C. II cast.[5] Policy consciousness in government dropped to C. I with Nixon's inauguration. It possibly returned briefly to C. II in 1972 with the need for a cosmetic preelection boomlet. The evidence for unfocused consciousness in the years since abounds.

The list includes: pandering to fundamentalist sentiment with balanced-budget rhetoric, use of monetary and profit incentives to increase investment (as if Keynes had never existed), tightening the financial screws on federally supported research and educational programs, ignoring the growth potential in social transformation of the poor. Finally, one has to note the absence of growth-oriented economists in critical advisory positions within recent administrations. It is not surprising that we have not had a growth policy since there seem to be very few people around the Treasury or the Council attuned to growth reasoning. William Fellner was perhaps the single outstanding exception to a rule exemplified by a Treasury secretary who devoted his first efforts to expediting speculation in gold and a Council that persisted in labelling returns from cyclical lows as "growth."

The conflict between an economy which had operated at or near the C. III level and a new policy regime operating at a very low C. II level (at best) was devastating in its effect. Wage demands which were predicated on an economy growing at a 4 percent real rate generated excruciating inflationary pressures in a slack economy. Of course, C. II corrections based on the presumption of demand pull are futile since they only serve to increase the discrepancy between anticipations and actual real output. Consciousness III reasoning suggests that the real growth rate could have been restored without a disproportionate expansion in money incomes and increased inflation using supply expansion coupled with controls. But these potentialities never intruded into what passed for public debates over policy. The discourse space was preempted by the White House and by the need to reply to specific initiatives seemingly picked for their divisiveness by that source. The key fact obscured is that the growth rate of *potential* manufacturing output slipped from 6 percent in the mid-1960s to less than 2 percent in 1975. Supply expansion at the previously established rate would surely have eliminated any demand-inflation component, leaving ample scope for controls to operate on the administered-price component. Wage-price controls are not inconsistent with a C. III economy, but up to now they have been used only in haphazard and stop-go fashion. In fact, when used grudgingly and indecisively they may destroy confidence as to the possibility of constructive intervention. The Nixonian phases and the rhetoric that accompanied them served to drive the economy back to a C. II orientation at best.

The obliteration of opportunities in critical technical manpower areas and the starving of education and research are also symptomatic of a consciousness crisis. The data show a decline in *real* research and development expenditures, with or without the defense component, through the 1970s. This after nearly two decades of research and development and education expansion with obvious links to macroeconomic growth! Growth requires technical progress, and technical progress is not a completely magical and spontaneous force. The massive dislocations in these areas show how growth capacity has been effectively taken off-line.

THE REESTABLISHMENT OF GROWTH

In the previous sections we have seen that the politics of macropolicy do not provide an imperative for growth, and that the Nixon/Ford administration had taken full advantage of this freedom to mismanage. Yet it is hard to figure out why they did so: agribusiness, oil, and banking could have been helped as much by economic growth as by economic stagnation, if helping these sectors is the purpose of government. The broken plateau in the Dow Jones and Standard & Poors stockmarket indices surely demonstrates that Wall Street or the larger "military-industrial complex" has gained little from this interlude of stagnation. Whether out of ignorance or out of adherence to C. I doctrine, growth confidence was destroyed, and this means that transition paths back to growth must be negotiated with caution.

Why has there been this lack of awareness of growth reasoning at the highest levels? Consider the comment made earlier: that the economists at the highest advisory positions in the Nixon-Ford administration held in common a lack of experience and expertise in growth economics, and that the administration itself seemed to lack any commitment to or understanding of the growth objective. One should ask, then, why there had not been significant external pressures from the opposition or internal pressures from friendly forces, i.e., from business and other influence groups to alter this orientation. A few groups have profited from corrupt activities and from special situations in energy, food, and banking; there has been significant reverse distribution (of smaller real product); but the static Dow Jones average remained and remains to index the general state of the business environment and the presumed welfare of presumed influence groups. One still wonders why the lack of growth has not dominated discussion in the business and financial communities. The dog has not barked for some time and one expects a trained ear to detect a deafening silence.

I have a personal and private view that the style of economics education in the U.S. may be assigned some portion of blame for such missed chances and misperceptions. The fact is that undergraduates and business students nearly everywhere else in the world cut their teeth on policy-oriented growth formulations that most M.B.A.'s and Ph.D.'s in economics here never see. In addition, most are exposed to Marxian, structuralist, and Neo-Keynesian critiques or analyses that encourage the search for alternative ways to view the economy. Growth economics in the U.S. generally deals with topics of mathematical interest, but many steps removed from the policy domain. In the world of affairs, American business, most of the government economic bureaucracies, and all of the media are oriented to C. II versions of economic thinking. Short-term projections relating to forecasting capital-spending, job creation, and the actions of the federal government are the characteristic exercises.

Within the policy domain itself, the two main manifestations of the lower degrees of C. II are on the one hand, willy-nilly endorsement of expenditure programs solely on the basis of employment and job-creation impact, and on the other hand, particular sponsorship of any and all programs which carry the label of investment or capital formation. Examples of the former abound: the ultimate manifestation of half-baked comprehension of the employment criterion being the endorsement of the Neutron-Bomb project because of its favorable job-creation effects. Over-concern with investment *per se*, however, is less easily disclosed.

As far as economic growth is concerned, investment is important if it creates production capacity or the basis for productivity increase. However, the motivation for investment in a capitalistic economy is financial advantage and only a portion of the investment that appears on the national accounts will be productive in the real sense as against the financial sense. The economy is particularly prone to commit resources to unproductive uses during prolonged periods of financial speculation. This was Keynes' insight in his reference to investment as a "bubble" on a sea of "speculative" activity, an insight renewed by Minsky in his latest work.[6] But this insight has by and large been forgotten by several generations of "Keynesians" who, in company with union officials and businessmen, counted the jobs attached to the investment proposal, measured its multiplier impact, and accepted without too many questions the justification of the project itself. After all, a good case can be made for any monumental construction: both the Egyptian pyramids and the Twin

Towers of lower Manhattan created jobs in their building and attracted tourists in their maturity.

In short, the problem with investment is an intrinsic problem of capitalism. There are virtually no avenues of control over even the most blatant capital malformations; no checks over the occasional speculative flight of fancy; no mechanisms to ensure that capital building will enhance technical development; and no broom to sweep up the trail and restructure financial claims and obligations that are left behind following today's and yesterday's acts of misjudged investment. In other words, the stagnation of the moment will not disappear simply with the installation of a new administration with a C. II cast and a degree of optimism; the legacy of the no-growth years remains.

To begin, there is the crude fact of a deteriorating and obsolescing capital stock that may prove to be a serious bottleneck in any attempt to "pull" the economy into growth by brute stimulation of aggregate demand. The facts are known: data on capacity constraints have been appearing on a daily basis in the financial press since early 1976. Particularly notorious is the state of the machine-tool-fabrication industry, where the average age of capital is now greater than it has been at any time since the Depression. The principle danger is that demand stimulation without regard for selective industry impacts will precipitate new rounds of inflation which would, in turn, for political reasons force a policy counterreaction and reinstate the "stop-go" setting.

Another significant negative legacy is the apparent undercutting of U.S. technical leadership [7] except, notably, for industries in the computer complex (mainframes, semiconductors, microprocessors, large-scale circuit integration). The general problem of restoring leadership status to declining industries can be described as falling somewhere on the spectrum between "resuscitation and resurrection." The specific strength of the computer industry is the one saving grace. Many future technologies are likely to be based on microprocessor components and computer-controlled processes (as earlier technologies were based on machine tools). Experience and systems in this area are highly transferable; so that it is conceivable that previously progressive industries may again advance comparatively rapidly once oriented to the potentiality of growth and open to infusions of the new technique. This, however, is conjecture; the immediate fact is that technological development is quiescent in many critical areas, and a substantial rebuilding and restaffing effort would be required to reactivate it if growth on the old pattern were to be pursued.

The final bequest is a significant deterioration in career anticipations and personal aspirations. *The New York Times* survey on "attitudes and aspirations" has shown that a broad sample population expects to advance far more slowly up the "ladder of life" than did counterpart samples in the past; and the change in aspirations seems almost entirely due to experienced deterioration of economic prospects through the early 1970s.[8] The implication of this alteration in growth consciousness (in the sense used earlier) is that workers will be less likely to take career risks, less likely to seek out educational opportunities, and more likely to accept "adequate" jobs (frequently jobs tied to stagnant technologies and service industries). Clearly, this mind set is unconstructive as regards transformational growth.

In short, the policy problems posed by this legacy are considerable. Worse, the problems are not confronted by proposals which are now or have recently been in the legislative hopper. These, for the most part, have carried a C. II flavor, especially the Humphrey-Hawkins "planning" bill and the long list of measures for public service employment, all of which relate to jobs *per se* without regard to their technological base.[9] The transition problems posed by the no-growth bequest are formidable and they can only be mastered with explicit regard for the growth, productivity, and technological setting.

12

A Program for Social
and Technical Advance

T_{HE} previous chapter indicates many
of the political complications that may arise from a general misperception of the basis of growth. Resurrecting growth consciousness will require
caution, advance calculation, and delicate prejudgment. Given the present
stagnation of the economy and the general low level of consciousness on
questions of economic policy, it will be difficult to directly program the
system into growth. Although one might wish to contemplate conscious
explicit growth policy, realities dictate the need to investigate "gradualist"
or indirect means of nursing the economy. To be frank, the variations on
"explicit growth policy" suggested thus far add up to a program of *de
facto* socialization of the investment function; this chapter considers how
that might be achieved either by direct purposeful intervention or by
disguised thrusts amounting to some fair copy of conscious policy.

TWO APPROACHES TO GROWTH

Growth and resurrected growth consciousness could be a by-product of
policy which is explicitly directed toward some other goal (i.e., pursuit
of a national strategic objective, entrance into a space race, or following
up an environmental initiative). The growth pattern that would result
would be similar to that of the 1960s: disproportionate emphasis on a
few leading activities (defense and the space program in the 1960s);

relatively slow acceleration of growth; and a moderate overall growth rate (surely below that achievable in Japan). Since the system would be relatively unmanaged except for the key sectors, it is likely that there would be continued exacerbation of the dualistic-imbalance characteristic. We can label the pattern as *accidental* or *by-product* growth to stress the point that we are not talking about a prearranged and deliberately planned sequence, but rather, growth that indirectly might germinate from a modest reorientation of the White House towards Consciousness II and the acceptance of an appropriate strategic objective.

The best that one can say about this more than likely scenario is that it is politically the easiest to initiate and it may reestablish some semblance of growth expectations and growth consciousness; enough so that comprehensive growth policy would have a foundation on which to build.

An alternate (and more desirable) scenario can be described as the *explicit* or *developmental* managed-growth path. This would include a design to cover macrostabilization, aggressive manpower policy, educational development, encouragement of technical progress, control over the labor-using bias of technical change, redistribution and growth-oriented transfer policy, urban renovation, and environmental responsibility. (This last concern can mean development at a massive scale of new industries, technologies, and energy sources that would be both positive for growth and positive for the planet.)

Management and Control: Indicative Planning

It seems essential for either sequence that some degree of guidance of the "soft planning" or "indicative planning" type be instituted. A key problem for the "by-product" or "accidental" sequence would be reestablishing growth consciousness. Indicative planning means, in effect, designation of a particular medium term forecast as official; the planning is hard or soft according to the degree of commitment assigned to the forecast. Even the softest sort of soft planning supported by conventional macroeconomic controls would expedite the transition. Of course, planning is explicit in the *managed-growth* sequence, and as we will see, soft planning is the most digestible format for an economy and political system such as ours. The administrative transition to an indicative planning system would be relatively easy to negotiate, and the expertise to operate such a system is surely there. In fact, the Carter Administration has been operating a masked soft plan since establishing a set of employment and inflation targets for 1980. Since "planning" per se carries political risks, the effort has been masked to the extent of doing much damage to its effectiveness.

Also we should not forget that the planning power can imply a legal-political threat to the population at large. Explicit power to set objectives and sectoral preferences may be perceived as an intrusion; though it can be argued that the amount of control and restriction needed to implement an indicatively planned growth system can actually be less than in the present system of "reactive" controls (and masked plans that will be revealed as "plans" if they work). Controls (such as supertight money or off-and-on-again wage and price restrictions) are actually "reactive" or "passive" in nature. Since such controls are instituted to check the economy, they have to be strict if they are to be effective. On the other hand, under an active control strategy, one operates to guide, to create a favorable climate of expectations, and to reduce uncertainties. Little in the way of formal control is required once a policy establishes its initial credibility.[1]

The main objective of an explicit indicative-planning system is to establish a consensus forecast of an attainable growth rate and an implicit commitment from the government that policies will be directed toward attaining that growth rate. If the consensus and commitment are accepted generally, then firms, industries, and labor groups can proceed with a degree of certainty as to how their current commitments and contracts will work out in the near future. Given this degree of partial certainty, they can invest, research, or develop aggressively and without too much liquidity anxiety. The system requires a constant exchange of information between the firms and the government's economic authority, both regarding plans and constraints operating on the participants (resource shortages, strikes, bottlenecks, etc.). The exchange of information would be iterative: each side utilizing the information it received to improve its operating plan and then passing on data on revisions of its plan to the other participants, who in turn further refine their positions. Although the informational requirements of such a system are formidable, they are no more severe than the informational requirements in such conventional settings as conflicts over the setting of price controls, regulatory rate setting, attempts to attain variances for wage increases, or even private forecasting. Without going into the many technical questions involved in the construction of an indicative planning system, let us proceed on the assertion that such a system can be instrumental in instituting a consensus of growth prospects, and that such a consensus can be an important ingredient in establishing economy-wide growth consciousness.

There is some magic to this sort of potentiality. For example, in Japanese planning the formal planning apparatus has consistently predicted a rate of growth that has been well below that attained by the economy itself. The "error" in the planners' forecast is not really an inaccuracy, however. The "planned" forecast in annual real growth can be interpreted as a minimum level of achievement that will be guaranteed by the governmental economic authority through the use of standard fiscal and monetary policy. The private sector builds on the foundation figure and on predictions of sectoral emphasis for overall growth. There is some danger that a plan that is consistently short of actual outcomes will come to be taken as "decorative." But if the "minimum commitment" motif is understood, soft planning seems to accomplish a reduction of perceived uncertainty that permits sizable resources to be committed to product research and development, development and installation of the latest vintages of capital equipment (without fear of being trapped by a rush to liquidity in a recession scare), and coherent and confident educational and human capital development.[2]

There are, of course, questions to ask before one endorses such an approach for the U.S. economy. The motif of coordinated development seems unduly supportive of the Galbraithian large firm; and there is a possibility that contact stemming from coordinated forecasting could become a means for cartelization that would, in effect, increase the concentration of industrial power. Given recent experiences with excesses of executive power, one might also wonder whether an indicatively planned economy could be the final step toward centralization of political power in the office of the President.

It is not clear how one should assess those potentialities; techniques of indicative planning could be used either to disrupt cartel discipline or to provide a framework for cartel formation.[3] Which path actually gets taken depends upon whether the basic allegiance of the planning authority is to members of the industries involved or to the public at large. Our experience with regulatory agencies and commissions is not encouraging on this matter.

On the question of executive or presidential power, one line seems fairly secure. The planning-forecasting agency could be set up with the same sort of independent authority as is held by the Federal Reserve system. This would be the most effective antidote to accumulation of White House power, and on balance seems the most desirable approach.

This format or one close to it is followed elsewhere in the world, both in socialist and nonsocialist regimes. Fears of concentrated federal power or conflict with specific developmental programs would be justified were the authority to be placed within a cabinet-level department. The greatest danger, of course, would be that of placing the authority within the office of the President, in or adjacent to the Council of Economic Advisors.

In summary, effective growth requires the reestablishment of growth consciousness and some means of maintaining positive growth anticipations during periods of adaptation and transition. An indicative planned-forecasting mechanism is consistent with decentralized economic organization and the present level of private ownership; it would provide sufficient control to maintain growth consciousness during sectoral transition and would not add significantly to the burden of restrictions currently in force. However, there is no discernible political support for such a system (called by its own name)—aside from some murmuring that big labor would be willing to cede planning control to big business for an asocial contract guaranteeing job security.

Thus, given no assurance that planning can emerge as a conscious solution, we should be prepared to consider growth and growth policy planning—if and when growth comes—as an accidental by-product of policy oriented toward some goal which is not explicitly economic. (The most likely planning system then would be an *ad hoc* facilitating adjunct.) With this caveat in mind, we can examine specific structural and sectoral problems, keeping alert both to potentialities for aggressive planning and to tactics of establishing a defensive and protective stance against adverse side consequences, should accidental development be the operating regime.

CRITICAL PROGRAMS

Education

Previous chapters have shown that there are two aspects of educational policy which must be considered: the inherent budgetary pressures resulting from unbalanced growth and the transformational potentiality of education.

The key *defensive* problem in the years to come will be that of protecting the educational system from further deterioration and insulating it from the tyranny of a misunderstood budget. The cost of a given unit and quality of education will mount during periods of general growth, and the stereotyped budgetary reaction on the part of school boards, state legislators, trustees, and administrators will be to hold the line on such increases. As we have seen, holding the dollar line means cutbacks in the real scale of the system or moving toward the automated classroom and all that that implies.

There is nothing in the existing system to check such tendencies. Each individual administrator sees his or her cost-saving actions as virtuous attempts taken in the name of the taxpayer; and, in the face of what would be perceived as local financial stringency, the system-wide aspects would not be generally assessed. Fighting these tendencies at the level of the local property tax assessor or the local school board is futile; a national (or state at the least) fiscal approach is required; and even here the prospects are disheartening. The system has been allowed to drift into financial crisis, and this development has not even been noted as an uncomfortable state of the union in Presidential New Year's addresses.

Reasonable remedies involve linking educational programs at all levels to general revenue—perhaps through the earmarking of general funds on a rigid formula, either to replace or to supplement the existing revenue sources. It is not at all clear that revenue reform could be accomplished quickly or in a direct fashion; conceivably the changes might be precipitated when taxholder revolts and school bond refusals reach the crisis stage. The public and legislators may come to recognize the problem of dynamic pressure on educational budgets as they came to recognize environmental dangers. It is also possible that adaptations to equalize the fiscal positions of individual school districts may result in full state or federal assumption of school expenditures. However, the prognosis is not bright; and further fiscal pressure and an eventual deterioration of the educational system are likely, given the American propensity to accept fiscal trends as definitive. Mao's warning given earlier is surprisingly current.

Transformational Educational Policy

In contrast to what has been labeled a "defensive policy" of resisting cost pressures is a policy that explicitly recognizes the cost tendencies and also comprehends the transformational, redistributional, and positive growth aspects of education and skill development. Such a policy approach is not without precedent; the United States has moved in this direction before, with emphasis given education after the post-Sputnik shock of recognition, and with the now dormant economic-opportunity program. In both cases the budgetary factor and deflected political attention checked the original initiative. Yet perhaps there can be a return toward transformational educational policy; so let us consider what might be.

Recall that education has been portrayed here as a facilitating factor in growth, not the driving force itself; and this implies a program and policy structure that is surprisingly uncomplicated and free of conjectural elements. The first step in policy would be to establish secure funding for the existing level of educational activity. A number of formulas for finance and for final delivery of funds would work. The fiscal problems are soluble; the critical questions are those of programming the overall educational-manpower effort.

The work-force–priority approach toward educational programming suggested in Chapter Seven actually involves a reversal of the reasoning in conventional manpower planning. The manpower approach proceeds by first setting an economic objective in terms of rates of output growth and types of final products. These output projections are then translated into requirements for intermediate industries, and then the industry projections are translated into personnel requirements specifically broken down into numbers of engineers, scientists, technicians, blue collar workers, etc.

The next stage involves calculating numbers of teachers, social service employees, and other supporting personnel needed to support the final operating manpower mix. Of course, the manpower program also takes into account the existing stock and age structure of workers and develops educational, training and special transitional programs accordingly. Operational plans on this model are commonplace; the more sophisticated versions take into account trends in technology and productivity, and interactions between productivity and work force quality.[4] Numerical projections involve keeping track of the existing work force and its retirement tendencies, working backwards from target output levels through an index of expected productivity change to labor input requirements, and then using student/staff ratios and demographic facts to set educational requirements. In essence, this approach means that production structure is allowed to determine the structure of employment opportunities and, thus, the distribution of economic welfare and class structure. However appropriate this style of planning may have been, there is good reason to argue that it is by now outmoded. Today there are available sufficient means, understanding, and instruments of guidance so that it would be possible to begin with the objective of a desired distribution of worker skills, levels of education, and degree of social mobility, and then (within certain limits of feasibility) tailor the physical economy to fit the social objective (the work-force–priority approach suggested in Chapter Seven). In effect, I am asserting that the social promises implied by higher levels and a broader extent of education could be validated by growth, and that developmental broadening of the economy can itself be a strong source of growth.

The OEO Approach

In looking for programs to handle the transitional problem, we should note that the Economic Opportunity (OEO) designs of the early War on Poverty come close to fitting the requirements for a practicable running system. Again, the buildup of transformational educational programs from early childhood to entrance into the labor market requires, by the very nature of things, the better part of two decades to work itself out. Such a program must be accommodated by appropriate macroeconomic growth policies and must be supported by appropriate guidance of technical research and development. The OEO programs were never tested in terms of this standard (which was their own implied standard), and the social, work-force–priority approach has never really been tried at all. The historical record on the association between unplanned educational expansion and growth (Chapters Six and Seven) should be encouraging as to the favorable potentiality of a planned approach; but to be practical, it must be remembered that the existence of a poverty problem has been systematically covered up for years while the national political mythology equated "economic opportunity" to "boondoggle."

Relief and Transfer Policy

From our examination of the problem of the hard-core poor in earlier chapters, it is clear that the relief system requires fundamental reform in both its funding and its operation. Reason dictates full federal funding, and a consensus seems to be building on this point at least. Negative taxation has wide support among economists—mainly as an abstract principle whereby one can transfer income equitably among a broad population within and outside of the labor force. However, negative taxation is entirely without merit as an instrument for transformation, and it now appears that reasonably humane program parameters imply fiscal burdens which would be unacceptable within the foreseeable political future. I believe that a federally funded extension of the present requirements-based system is best adopted to the interlocking problems of political resistance to relief expenditures, a need for transitional financing linked to programs for social mobility, and a requirement of providing a humane standard of living to those effectively out of the labor force. (The presumption is that once growth forces are reestablished, the core of the hard-core poor can be softened and reduced, and the society can make a step toward a more comprehensive negative-tax system.) There would be little difference in relief programs under either the defensive or active sequences, except that the burden falling on the transfer system would be larger in the first instance. It is, of course, well known that a substantial component of the fiscal burden of the cities would be solved by federalization of relief on almost any formula related to the existing patterns of expenditures.

Critical Industries and Encouragement of Technical Change

The "defensive," indirect-influence sequence presumed that growth forces would be regenerated by expenditures tied to a few industries in which political or national interest was vested. For example, the center of such interest could be the "high technology" industries, and the impetus could be a technology race with Europe and Japan. Tactics in the race would presumably follow the standard pattern of incentive subsidies and special expenditure programs, with concentration directed at influencing the bias of technical change in favor of social priorities.

This is a highly conjectural area, but the actual program tactics could be of standard types: selective tax incentives, special design subsidies, special public employment programs, and, if the planning system has any teeth, requirements for employment (on the affirmative-action model). The text is intentionally vague in not spelling out the details of specific program variants. Concern with the fine points is premature and would deflect attention from the key matter, that of establishing awareness of the need for a particular dynamic *style* of policy and a particular way of analyzing problems in the domain of social economics. The point simply is that *control over work-force characteristics in developing technologies should be seen as legitimate*—just as miles-per-gallon requirements and emission limits are now accepted as appropriate interventions. Once legitimacy is achieved, the details of specific programs will emerge as a matter of course.

The planned-growth approach could take significant steps in encouraging critical industries. As suggested earlier, enormous growth potential is present in urban housing and construction technology, biomedical and medical care delivery fields, mass transportation, fusion energy, and special environmental sciences, e.g., the use of enzymes and bacterial agents. Long-term programs with substantial initial and continuing research components are the designs of choice. Again, the areas of need are obvious and the core ideas for programs are certainly familiar enough to readers of this book. The organizational problems are also within reasonable bounds. The space program (or, for that matter, the Department of Defense) provides handy and instructive [*sic*] models on which to pattern management of high-level strategic industries. Really, all that is needed is active concern with the dynamic pattern of employment and alertness to possibilities of integrating technical requirements with emerging structural characteristics of the work force under transformational social programs.

TECHNICAL DEVELOPMENT

The Example of Less-Developed Countries (LDCs)

The problem of conscious control over the laborsaving bias of technical change has received greatest attention in the technical literatures on labor markets and industrialization in the developing nations.[5] In this context, Puerto Rican development has frequently been cited as the archetypical example of an industrialization calamity. Puerto Rico has been passing through a stage of rapid industrialization based on the use of U.S. techniques; and while the outcome has included a dramatic increase in industrial output, it has also resulted in an absolute reduction in the number of employed industrial workers. This has been categorized as a case of laborsaving bias gone wild.[6] The problems are clear: how can one develop new technologies that match the manpower requirements of society, and how, if the most advanced techniques are used, can one expand the industrial sector to encompass a greater proportion of the society?[7] These are analogous to the work-force problems described for the U.S. economy, and obviously they are associated with a similar syndrome of allowing technology to determine social structure.

It is modish these days to advocate a new isolationism, arguing that the United States in its past interventions has caused more ill than good. The pattern is all too familiar: economic aid becomes military aid and a prop for military-landowner regimes; the green revolution immiserates the smallest farmers and reverses progress toward land reform; the exploitation of natural resources is encouraged and the aided country becomes a component in an international chain of production oriented to developed countries' needs.

Despite the bitter truth of this view and the neoimperialist complexion of past dealings with LDCs, it is impossible to ignore the depth of world poverty, and perhaps one can hope that eventually the U.S. will find itself a participant in constructive development efforts. This particular line would of course dovetail with the national objective of planned and directed research into control over the bias of domestic technical change and is, of course, research into the nature of technology itself.

Humane inquiry has advanced with pioneering work by a few leading technologists and industrial designers, but has not been supported in a significant way, i.e., as a space program with social impact aimed at bringing sophisticated but flexible techniques to a preindustrial economy.[8]

Urban Renovation

Chapter Ten has covered the fiscal side of the urban crisis and the required defensive tactics. It should also be recognized that urban development and redevelopment could become a critical avenue for growth. Again, the lines of solution appear natural and perhaps even too simple. The cities are now reservoirs of unemployed labor, and it makes a great deal of sense to begin transformational work-force programs within them. Greatly increased public sector employment is an obvious first step toward the rebuilding of an effective urban labor market, while the physical rebuilding of cities is an obvious vehicle for employment in the context of planned development and controlled technical change. These problems, of course, are not quite as simple in practical terms as they seem to be when we compare available resources with pressing needs. The existing tax laws, for example, provide incentives for suburban single-family construction and, within the cities, provide inducements (through depreciation schedules) for landlords to intentionally run down their properties.

This is not the place for a detailed discussion of the failures of past urban programs; there is an abundance of documents and opinion on the matter.[9] Among cited reasons for failure of urban-poverty-manpower-redevelopment programs are conflicts as to the level of subfederal political control over expenditures, the backlash, the drying up of expenditures themselves, the short duration of the programs, and the lack of a dynamic orientation to manpower development (the pattern of training for dead-end jobs). All of these factors seem apposite, and all connote the ineffectiveness of a day-to-day approach to a problem that must take generations to solve. A growth orientation focusing on the poverty populations within the cities has not really been tried; and the necessity of such an approach seems apparent, the past failures of OEO, HUD, and HEW notwithstanding.

There is an immense literature on urban needs and urban design; this book gives no specific endorsements. It is simply noted that housing construction, development of integrated work and residential living systems, and development of innovative multi-mode transportation systems are obvious program targets—and all of these can be the basis for system growth coordinated with manpower transformation and social requirements.*

GROWTH AND THE ENVIRONMENT

This book began with the argument that economic growth was a precondition for social change, but that if the environmental destruction wrought by industrial expansion could not be checked, there would be little point in pursuing the growth objective—there are, after all, no agreeable social arrangements on a lifeless planet. Up to this point we have been assuming that environmental safeguards could be installed; it is now time to examine the assumption that future growth can be compatible with environmental responsibility. It is difficult to be sanguine about clean growth at a time when the anti-environmental backlash has gathered force with a number of strong unions, oil companies, auto manufacturers, and the utilities in an entrenched political and bargaining position against ecological interests.

Environmental Programs as Growth Industries

To begin, let us consider the proposition that critical industries and activities tied to environmental responsibility may be a significant source of growth, and that growth industries may in fact be relatively clean in

---

* These are hardly trivial problems, since powerful groups have a vested interest in the established technology. For example, the automobile industry has not and probably will not endorse a transportation program that makes the private car into an unnecessary luxury; nor is it likely to invent the replacement product.

their environmental impact. A casual survey suggests that the more dynamic, high-technology industries are either relatively clean now or potentially so. If this proves to be true, a growth policy building heavily on the technologically progressive industries is likely to be relatively undemanding on the environment. For example, computers in use are antiseptic, and if reasonable care is taken over the recycling of printout paper, and if one can control some of the more toxic chemicals used in developing solid-state devices, the activities attaching to the computer would be relatively clean as well. This is only surmise, but many other high-technology fields seem to share the computer's cleanliness. This is surely true of the fast expanding "service" sector, which is to a significant degree associated with brainpower rather than industrial muscle; and of the "clean up" technologies such as the enzyme and bacterial agent systems just now emerging. There are also many techniques already in existence which cry for attention and broad development. Many should and would be picked under a mandate of clean development.

Broad Systems

Designs for economically and environmentally sane urban transportation systems exist on the drawing board, but neither industrial nor federal support has been generated. A "space program" approach to urban systems based on intelligent location, mass transportation for long hauls, exotic special purpose vehicles such as the surface-effect carriers in common use abroad, and personal (electric powered?) vehicles for short hauls and connections would have multiple favorable effects. On the environmental front, such an approach would reduce fuel energy demand, vehicular pollution, and the usurpation of living space by automobiles. On the growth track, such projects would employ critical technical work forces and generate general public-service employment within the urban labor market. In short, an environmentally clean urban transportation and locational system would also satisfy social conditions suggested for a dynamic manpower-growth policy.

Energy-Source Research

It is quite clear that the U.S. and other industrial nations have placed excessive reliance on conventional fossil fuel energy resources. Fusion, solar power, and geothermal gradients have theoretical potential as replacement sources, and it is likely that one or more of these will ultimately become basic means for producing power. Again, massive research expenditures on the space program model seem the appropriate line to take. Success in such a program would mean an instantaneous solution to several important pollution problems and simultaneously solve the "energy crisis" (whether real or concocted).[10] However, success would also disrupt the oil industry's systematic plan for long term exploitation of fossil fuel resources (the oil, coal, gasification, uranium sequence); so perhaps one should not be altogether sanguine on this matter.*

GENERAL ENVIRONMENTAL CONTROLS

The above conjectural lines of development are all amenable to a programmatic approach, all would have significant favorable environmental impact, and all would be compatible with social objectives. However, we have been considering programs that will induce broad growth, and one must be aware of the polluting potential in conventional industrial expansion. Recognizing that detailed prescriptions and recommendations for standards are outside the scope of this book, a few comments are still in order.

Antipollution Controls

The logical beginning is the question of guidance mechanisms. Economists have been among the first to recognize the externality and social-cost aspects of pollution (and the fact that standard national income accounting concepts vastly overstate true social product).† Nevertheless, the environmental movement has taken on a character uniquely its own, and the lines of remedial action fostered by the movement depart significantly from those that are advocated within economic classrooms and professional publications. The difference lies mainly in strategic approach to the problem. Economists have tended to favor a pricing or "market" approach to pollution (setting taxes on polluting activities or

---

* Many observers have been struck by the fact that the Nixon-Ford energy office had accepted the oil-company argument that their profits should be inflated so as to create a source of internal finance for "new energy development" (read, purchase of coal, gas, and uranium reserves). The concentration and "reconcentration" of wealth that is implied by the trillion-dollar scheme involves the largest (reverse) distribution program ever attempted in this country.

† Recall that all of the following are part of the GNP total: the activities of doctors and hospitals repairing the victims of pollution, the services of clean-up industries, the product of makers of pollution-control devices, the services of morticians, etc.

charging fees for "licenses to pollute"), whilst many environmentalists favor the setting of absolute restrictions and operating standards (allowable NO_2 levels, no sulphur-bearing fuel, maximum bacterial count, etc.).[11]

The two approaches can amount to the same thing in some instances. A tax set high enough can act as an absolute prohibition, and an environmental requirement that imposes costs can be examined in terms of those costs and the implied standard. Nevertheless, the two approaches differ significantly within the domain of political economy; however effective pricing signals may be as means to direct resources toward cleaner technology, they appear to lack the popular appeal, directness, and apparent equity of explicit prohibitions.

The "pricing" approach works best in an abstract setting of competing firms and relatively perfect markets and requires that the "taxing" agency accurately assess the social cost of the polluting activity.[12] Forcing costs back on the consumer seems to make some sense since, after all, the consumer is ordering the goods. But the consumer is not picking the mode of production and it is here that inequity creeps in. If firms are not competitive there is little to make them alter production techniques when they can shift a major portion of the burden.

In some instances, the standards approach has led to strikingly ineffective control, e.g., emission standards that result in gasoline-thirsty engine design, thus exacerbating refinery-based pollution. In other instances, the standards approach promotes bargaining from extreme positions; the industrial polluter protects his bargaining position by advocating a relatively dirty plant, whilst the environmentalist is forced to advocate an absolute prohibition of the activity and there is no path toward the middle ground (as in the Alaskan Pipeline controversies).

Yet we should recognize that the standards approach has had its successes and near successes. The cleaning out of particle, ash, and sulphur pollutants in Pittsburgh's and New York City's air was accomplished with comparatively little difficulty, even though the polluters acted out their hardship claims at every public occasion. In addition, automobile emission controls have resulted in substantial reductions of smog accumulation in certain areas. This experience has been a mixed success. One could perhaps argue that the short-term impacts of the standards approach were uneconomic (costly catalytic converters and gas-hungry flaccid engines); but there are promising prospects for the longer run. For example, foreign manufacturers (Honda and Mazda) have claimed the ability to design engines to meet the strictest U.S. pollution requirements.

Recall that nearly all engineering design involves an adaptation to multiple standards; for example, in the case of the automobile, guidelines handed down by the marketing department to govern desired performance, handling qualities, trunk space, and luxury options. My conjecture is that environmental restrictions in many fields are essentially no more inhibiting than such conventional restrictions (provided that ample lead time is given to the redesign stage). The polarized conflicts occur when a tight environmental standard is applied to a previously unconstrained technique (as in oil refinery disputes); so that environmental responsibility appears to have a high cost where clean-up devices are treated as add-on accessories to a previously polluting design. Again, this is largely conjecture, but it appears that with reasonable advance warning on tightening standards (and willingness to face adaptation of a foreign technology if the domestic industry fails to adjust), clean technology should be attainable with no more additional cost than is usually present in the development of a new model. There will always be a trade-off of attributes, but it takes time to learn about a new requirement and its technical implications and to redesign to accommodate a requirement that had previously been ignored.

CONCLUDING COMMENTS

I have argued that socially responsible growth is attainable, provided there is conscious concern with the dualistic-imbalance syndrome and explicit control to forestall it. Educational policy is crucial in any eventuality, but there is a fair choice among other activities as potential candidates to become the driving forces for growth. Renewed support for high technology industries is a structural necessity; but programs which focus on what are actually the critical problem areas of society also carry a positive growth potential.

Growth could develop out of reasonably well managed macrostabilization efforts; but the most effective economic regime would be one governed by an explicit development plan (presumably of the indicative type) that established growth consciousness and led to coordination of work-force development and technical research and design. This last matter seems most promising, but has somehow managed to escape professional and lay attention. Despite its novelty, the approach appears to be practical. The literature demonstrates that there is sufficient know-how and experience available to take a complex final product and develop from this a manpower and educational policy by use of crude forecasts of productivity change and projections of intermediate goods requirements derived from a standard input-output format. This methodology should be adequate to solve the inverted version of the problem: that of taking a projected social target and solving for the production patterns and educational policies that would support and advance the objective.

It should also be remembered that the redesign of production technology to accommodate social concerns is one focus of an international movement in industrial relations labeled variously: "job restructuring," "work reorganization," "industrial democracy," and "quality of working life." The flexibility of technology has been demonstrated in a number of widely publicized experiments—most notably, the use of autonomous work groups at Volvo and Saab installations, the elimination of machine pacing in the "mini lines" at IBM (Amsterdam), and the evaluation of the social content of jobs at Renault.[13] In much of industrial Europe, the principles behind the movement are endorsed by major firms, institutionalized in national politics, and routinely administered in pragmatic policy. However, despite early pioneering efforts in the United States, the matter of work design here tends to be a secondary bargaining issue for organized labor and is treated at the corporate level as a subject for sporadic experimentation. Accordingly, I have not presumed there to be an independent political impetus for technological reconstruction within this country. If macroeconomic and distributional concerns can trigger intervention into technical choices, the generally favorable experience with work restructuring will clearly mark the appropriate paths to follow at the implementation stage.

13

Conclusions:
A New Perspective on
the Modern Industrial Economy

MUCH of what is now written in economics on the subject of growth, capital, and distribution has as its underlying conception the nineteenth-century capitalist state. In the minds of the classical economists and their successors, this world was a simple one in which key elements were the rates at which machinery (capital) accumulated and technological progress improved each generation of the machine. In this world, the labor which worked the machines was easily described as an army of identical factory hands, and the owners of the machines as either accumulating capitalists or maximizers of wealth. The working and capitalist classes as economic groups corresponded closely enough to the social classes of the nineteenth-century industrial economy; so that for a time, at least, the economic picture was organically consistent with broad views of society formulated by both capitalist and Marxian scholars.

The perspectives in the nineteenth-century picture of capital accumulation were probably relevant well into the present century and a powerful armory of specific analytical techniques developed in conjunction with the broad picture. However, at the present time, the nineteenth-century perspective has become a cumbersome obstacle to an understanding of the nexus of economic and social problems within advanced economies and new orientations are needed. Economic characteristics which must be recognized in such reorientation include, at least: (1) the managerial coloring of the capitalist-entrepreneurial class; (2) the blurring of salary and profit interests; (3) growth of internal corporate finance; (4) increasing heterogeneity of labor inputs; (5) the emergence of "education" as a distinct factor of production; and (6) the organization of economic units around the production and implementation of advanced technology. With these characteristics in mind, a number of suggestions and recommendations on policy have been spotted at various points throughout the book, and it makes sense now to conclude with a compilation and amalgamation of these recommendations in a format that amounts to a program of socially oriented economic growth.

The General Policy Framework

The point has been made repeatedly that the structural setting assumed for policy evaluation is as important as the specific policy measures themselves. We will not review the dualistic-imbalance framework again; it should simply be noted that the model alerts the policy analyst to the following: (1) the necessity of considering transformational potentiality on issues involving poverty and the poor; (2) the need to recognize imbalance in cost trends, particularly with regard to services provided by the public sector; (3) the obligation to provide guidance to technological development, given the dependence of national growth on conditions within a few key sectors; (4) the possibility of altering technical conditions to fit a social objective; (5) the need to assess policies according to "management risk," given the inherent complexity of policies in this domain; and (6) an overwhelming need to recognize misperceptions of the system which cloud or distort the political setting. These are guiding precepts at the most general level and, admittedly, somewhat platitudinous. Let us move towards specific policy steps, arranged according to a few broad (and overlapping) problem areas.

Poverty Policy

The policies which have been presented here are designed to break the stagnant-sector syndrome and expedite labor-force transformation. Relief reform is a necessity and the text suggests rejection of the guaranteed-income, negative-tax format in favor of extensions of the existing system. The reasoning here is basically that maximum transformational possibilities per dollar of income support would be obtained from "controlled" as opposed to "free choice" systems of delivering benefits. In any case, full federal support for relief finances is a necessity; it is both cruel and insane to rely on the resources of the poorest districts for financing of major transfer programs. In terms of current program and candidate programs, strong opposition to the "workfare" approach is suggested; as currently formulated, the program provides subsidized relief for archaic technologies.

Among constructive approaches, the text supports the program concept of the original "War on Poverty" and "Great Society" as crystalized within the OEO. The program was aborted before there was any real chance to evaluate its performance (after all, a full generation is needed before one has any real throughput), and there were undoubtedly many "ripoffs" and examples of misdirected emphasis within it; but it was explicitly transformational and deserves, if not demands, resurrection. Surely, enough is now known of specific program weaknesses (e.g., training for dead-end or nonexistent jobs) so that the approach could be redesigned and reestablished in a politically palatable form, the issue of local or street control notwithstanding.

New inputs to discussion of poverty policy come from the dual-labor market theorists. Greatly increased public sector employment (including the need to redesign technologies to suit labor force requirements) is one constructive line of approach (which also contains within it explicit recognition of the starved public sector). Another step which could have enormous potential impact involves working through the minimum wage to force upgrading of technology in the present stagnant sector. Selective employment taxation and investment-tax credits, where the targets would be the small firms on the periphery of the economy could be another vehicle. All of these efforts, of course, should properly be part of a general manpower-information system (which already exists on paper), and all would seem feasible within the normal politics of the nation, as against the politics of the moment.

General Growth

Any constructive sectoral policies have to rely upon a background economy in reasonable health, both for material support through increased tax revenues and for the intangible support given to growth-generating activities by a heightened state of long-term anticipations. In this context health means growth, and here the problems are serious, since the current mismanagement of macroeconomic conditions has profoundly damaged the economy. The immediate remedial needs are for expansionary and growth-oriented investment, research, and education funding coupled with restricted consumer demand—all within a framework of fairly rigid price and wage restrictions. This can all be accomplished with the existing instruments for monetary and fiscal stabilization; however, for the longer run, growth must have a higher selective component, and this requires a move toward explicit indicative planning and work-force–priority planning. Channels for selective support of critical technology industries and activities, and for guidance of the developmental broadening of the system will be needed. To prepare the ground for these significant alterations of American practice, a period of familiarization is undoubtedly required.

Education

Education enters the framework of discourse in three ways: (1) as a means for transforming the employment potentialities of the lower social groupings; (2) as a means of extending the scale of the progressive sector through increasing the size of the technically adept work force; and (3) as an institution that of itself generates knowledge and technical change. The policy prescriptions are simple: increased support for all levels of education and awareness of the unbalanced-growth phenomenon which imperils education (and other social service categories) within the standard budgetary control systems. To finesse an outlook of recurrent budgetary crises, it would be desirable to link education to revenue sources that are themselves linked to growth. Of course, this argument applies to many other high-level stagnant activities and is, in effect, an argument for subsidizing "live performance" in its broadest construction.

The Urban Interest

All of the problem patterns just discussed are magnified within the urban setting, and it is likely that if lines of solutions are found in the areas of welfare, poverty, education, and controlled growth, the urban crisis as a pressing emergency will be significantly relieved. The cities, however, have taken a battering for a considerable period of time and there is a strong argument for selectively focused expenditure programs covering the renewal of the housing stock and renovation of public transportation. Such programs could be carried out in standard subsidy formats, provided that work-force–priority and critical-technology objectives were written into the contract specifications.

Critical Industries

Along with the industry groupings which can be classed with the urban interest are a number of other prospects for massive expenditures or programs. The environmental and energy-source fields, special technologies for LDCs, and biomedical technology are all strong candidates, having in common: a social raison d'être, a demand for technological advances that are likely to extend into general productivity increases, a requirement for high-level manpower, and (since the technological requirements are not fixed in advance) a potentiality for creating job opportunities of the transformational sort.

Institutional Change

Most of the suggestions just enumerated could be instituted within the existing political framework using established program formats (even those of NASA and DoD); but they involve a quite different orientation towards policy from that heard in recent years. The U.S. has not completed its economic development and has slack room to continue its growth and simultaneously correct its most pressing social problems. The issue is not guns *or* butter; the availability of undeveloped human resources allows for expansion without significant lost opportunities. In fact, attacks on the problem areas would pay off in immediate general growth provided that some recognition were given to work-force priorities. If this argument has any validity to it, one could probably operate primarily through persuasion, education, and intelligent leadership. However, alterations in institutions are proposed. The most significant would be explicit planning to coordinate work-force development with (presumed) rapidly changing technology and official guidance to firms as to technological needs, energy or work-force constraints, and the likely expansion path of the system as a whole. This type of guidance can be provided within a mixed private-public enterprise economy through indicative planning and coordinated forecasting. Development of an independent authority (equivalent in status to the Federal Reserve System) to direct this function could be a significant step towards managed prosperity and humane growth.

APPENDIX

An Economist's Model of

Modern Industrial Growth

I have claimed that the dualistic-imbalance model represents a new way of viewing socioeconomic phenomena. Yet many elements of the system are familiar features in a number of specialist literatures; so in a sense the overall scheme can be thought of as an eclectic compilation. The cost-pressure mechanism in unbalanced growth derives from Baumol's work; the treatment of corporate technostructure activity, from Galbraith and Marris; the treatment of poverty, from the dual-labor market theorists; the basic production and growth concepts, from the Cambridge school; the human-capital, individual-decision model, from Becker's school; while the scheme as a whole recalls themes in development economics. Each of these elements is controversial to a greater or lesser degree and each has gained both a constituency of support and a substantial fund of opposition and antagonism.

Unfortunately, however, the constituencies do not coincide; and we could take the pessimistic view that opposition accumulates and the union of economists who object to one or more elements in the scheme would make up to the entire profession. Neoclassical economists would object to theories based on market barriers and the neo-Keynesian coloring of the growth mechanism; while neo-Keynesians might object to the choice mechanism and tolerance of an (inferential) productivity basis for compensation. The right would object to the dual-labor market treatment of poverty; the radical left, to the departure from Marxian class categories.

Theoretical economists of all complexions would probably object to the endorsement of Galbraith.[1] These characterizations are not meant to be completely whimsical. None of the model elements has been thoroughly tested against the data by its proponent constituency; in fact, for some there may not be a feasible definitive test. Full empirical substantiation of each is obviously beyond the scope of this book; even a modest review of the literatures on evidence pertaining to particular model elements would more than double the length of this text without necessarily increasing its persuasiveness. The basic claim of this book, after all, is that the *synthesis* of these various elements provides a comprehensive, reasonable, and realistic picture of the system.

The claim goes further: since in the synthesis the elements cooperate fully and together form a realistic picture of the entire system, they are thereby individually supported and gain in individual plausibility, perhaps to the extent of offsetting gaps in the empirical record. In essence, I am arguing that each of the elements reflects a significant subdiscipline vision as to how an important component of the system operates in isolation. Each element is controversial with respect to the standard view of the system as a whole; but when integrated into the alternative view on system operation presented here, each gains in plausibility and extends its applicability.

For example, the dual labor market has usually been viewed as a static scheme without direct links to capital-theoretic processes. In the present model, the dual labor market becomes one of the critical distributional elements in a dynamic system. The existing literature on dualistic poverty is thus given a dynamic macroeconomic basis which it heretofore lacked.

Similarly, the Galbraith system, as originally projected in *The New Industrial State,* operates without any clear-cut distributional mechanism to link the technostructure factor to general economic welfare (or for that matter to the social trends documented in its predecessor, *The Affluent Society,* and its successor, *Economics and the Public Purpose*).[2] The claim is that the unbalanced-growth cost and wage mechanisms, along with the general distributional associations presented here, establish such linkages and, in generalizing the system, answer significant criticisms of the Galbraith format.[3]

In addition, the manner in which the modeled system can approximate to an equilibrium growth path is suggestive in another area of controversy over Galbraith's industrial state. Galbraith has claimed that the major industrial firms engage in significant forward planning, but suggests no mechanism (other than direct Department of Defense links with the aerospace industry) for coordination of plans among industries. This is an obvious weakness in his argument and critics have found the gap.[4] However, if the system can find its way to an equilibrium path of the sort suggested here, industrial firms can avoid gross conflicts and clashes by basing individual planning on a consensus growth rate.*

Continuing with the synthesis, we note that the present model applies growth reasoning (that which assigns the driving force to technological progress and firm investment behavior) to a broader social context and a more realistic class structure than is specified in the standard versions of the theory. The links with the human-capital model are interesting in this regard since the growth, educational-choice mechanism provides a plausible macro-dynamic explanation for returns to education as a factor of production within a general theory of distribution.

THE ELEMENTS OF THE MODEL

The essential motif of the dualistic imbalance model is the division of the economy into two distinct production regimes and two distinct work forces. These divisions lead to four subdivisions or model components:

(I)   A high-level (educated, technically skilled and experienced) work force with a progressive technique;
(II)   A high-level work force with a stagnant technique;
(III)   A low-level work force with stagnant technique; and
(IV)   A low-level work force with progressive techniques.

These subdivisions follow mechanically from the original division of productive activities and work forces. What matters is whether or not the taxonomy makes behavioral sense; whether the divisions and associated behaviors are empirically supported; whether the taxonomy is creative of additional structural insights; and whether or not further meaningful disaggregation flows from the scheme. We are, in effect, asking if it makes more sense to treat the economy in this fashion than to make a primary distinction between capital goods and consumer goods, and a primary distinction between profit recipients and wage earners. Further-

---

* As is argued in the final chapters, a formal indicative-planning system could provide the tighter coordination implicit in the Galbraithian tacit planning model. The present analysis does not contribute one way or the other to controversies over the Galbraithian "revised sequence" of firm influence over consumer tastes. The present model operates with or without this view; although perhaps it should be noted that modern marketing can be described as a reaction to unbalanced-growth cost pressures on personal salesmanship.

TABLE 2

Model Components and Characteristics

Component	1 Institutional-Industrial Setting	1a (Analogous Agricultural Setting)	2 Institutional Characteristics	3 Class and Social Associations	4 Technological Status
I. Progressive Technology, High-Level Work Force	Major firms; new high-technology firms	(Agribusiness; capital-intensive, progressive farms)	Significant educational and skill requirement; techno-structure; weak financial restrictions on firm activities	Executive, managerial sub-classes; links to classic ownership interests	Capital-intensity, progressive technology (productivity increases at net positive rate g)
II. Stagnant Technology, High-Level Work Force*	Educational institutions; performing arts; client-oriented governmental activities	(Academic research)	High educational requirements; subject to fiscal pressures	Academic, intellectual, civil-service bureaucracy	Stagnant technology; short-term "efficiency" improvements are possible
III. Stagnant Technology, Low-Level Work Force	Obsolescing industries; menial services; "hustles"; nonactivities	(Small subsistence farms; sharecrop, tenancy, field-hand operations)	Low sensitivity to mainstream economy; affected by focused selective policy	Displaced poor, agricultural poor; ghettos; racial poverty (reserve army and lumpen associations in Marxian class theory)	Unemployment or marginal employment in labor-intensive, non-progressive industry
IV. Progressive Technology Low-Level Work Force	Operative; laborer activities	(Marginal agricultural workers; migratory workers in agribusiness)	Increasing marginality, cyclical sensitivity; despite union sheltering, subject to "technical unemployment" and displacement, e.g., by shift to foreign manufacturing	Attenuation of traditional associations with the economic mainstream and traditions of upwards mobility, e.g., by European ethnic minorities; sensitivity to "dropping back" into deep poverty	Low skill requirement; ties to capital-intensive activities, but displaceable

Wage Prospects	Labor-Cost Prospects	Critical Market Characteristics	Growth-State Political Economy	Depressed-State Political Economy
Growth corresponding to productivity increase (exponential prospect $w_0 e^{gt}$)	Neutral; unit labor cost increase can be offset by productivity gain	Price behavior can be dynamically neutral and/or typically oligopolistic	Compensation self-determined subject to the scale constraint associated with the potential size of the technostructure-eligible work force; planning ties to national economy	Compensation and conditions sheltered by possibility of reverting to static, oligopolistic market strategies
Comparable to (I) in periods of growth via link to education requirements (wage prospect $mw_0 e^{gt}$; but highly sensitive to short-term market and budgetary pressure)	Increasing $ cost on unbalanced-growth logic; wage component passes into labor cost	Maintenance of level of activity requires combination of high-income elasticity and low-price elasticity; possible support from "adjacent" activities in progressive sector	Compensation determined by political budgetary system; treatment as infrastructural support for progressive sector	Political weakness in resisting crisis fiscal stringency
Stagnant sector wage w; interaction with welfare benefit level, minimum wage	Wage and labor cost frozen, else extinction of activity	Same as (II) if wage cost is passed through	Support level, compensation and conditions determined directly as a matter of national policy, e.g., explicit poverty policy, welfare policy, wage minima	Political constituency is weak; poverty objectives can be displaced from national political consciousness by stabilization and other problems
Varies with degree of sheltering, union strength; effective wage reduced because of cyclical sensitivity	Mixed; controllable by firm because of possible substitution of capital	Employment level subject to tenuring shelters; technological development, extent of multinational extension	Conditions subject to union strength *vs.* firm threat to displace work force; indirect influence of macroeconomic employment level	Persistence of unemployment can focus attention on preservation of job rights; Last In First Out (LIFO) hiring patterns can offset transitional gains made during growth periods

more, we are asking if building detail by working toward more elaborate labor, class, and occupational distinctions within the high-level population tells us more about the social structure than attempting to separate out different categories of profit recipients. This calls for review and recapitulation of the model components and associated behaviors. (For convenience the model structure and critical characteristics are given in capsule form in Table 2. Columns 1–4 cover the institutional setting.)

Component I: The Nexus of High-Level Work Force and Progressive Technology

To begin with, we should note that there is ample direct and inferential evidence of interindustry variation in growth rates and rates of productivity increase.[5] Growth rates differ and growth is intrinsically unbalanced. The key question of whether higher growth rates group on the technostructure or education factor, has received very little formal attention despite the broad currency of Galbraith's *New Industrial State* descriptions and the descriptions of the other major commentators on the modern corporation.[6]

A number of factors can produce the association between growth and education and the implicit separation of production into the two regimes of progressive and stagnant techniques which is modeled here. The evidentiary problem, as noted before, is that data are not organized in a way that readily allows us to identify the strength of these mechanisms; while the existing literature on contemporary production, as exemplified by the econometric production-function study, is predicated on the assumption of homogeneity of production forms across industries. Although these studies taken as a general body of literature do identify the growth-productivity-education association, with only a few exceptions they are uninformative about the causal links which one might say are embodied in the large-firm organization chart and the typical MBA curriculum. Again, one must examine the work of economic historians— both the specialists in technology and the quantitatively oriented "new economic historians"—to find significant inquiries into the causal interplay of education and the technical factor. In this regard, David's *Technical Choice, Innovation and Economic Growth* and the present book should be read as companion pieces, even though they are concerned with essentially different issues.[7] David's econometric analyses demonstrate the crucial role played by learning and adaptation processes in the leading edge industries, and provides a nearly perfect picture of the skill level-productivity nexus within an isolated activity.[8]

In contemporary analysis, this theme is carried forward in Finis Welch's study of the propagation of technical change in agriculture.[9] In Welch's model, the educated farmer has the ability to read, evaluate, assimilate, and apply the rich literature propagated by public institutions (agricultural schools, extension agents, and research bodies) and private agencies (equipment manufacturers, fertilizer distributors, etc.). The degree does not simply convey the latest technology, but rather opens up the door to a continuing stream of information that leads to efficient operation of existing techniques and timely adoption of newer techniques.

Welch's scheme and the learning adaptation process adduced by David apply to industries with relatively competitive market structures, as well as to industries dominated by large firms. Technical progress is not an exclusive attribute of size, nor am I arguing that any of the schemes just described embodies a thorough or completely reliable explanation of operations in the industrial sector. Nevertheless, it seems reasonable to use the working assumption that the education-productivity association is operative over enough of the system to trigger the trends which are the subject of this book. Where the large firm is also technically progressive, its economic weight alone is enough to make the process significant at a system level. But even where the firm is not progressive, but is simply one that trades on its market positions, it will have a like static distributional impact. Consider the institutional argument that the major firms tend to accumulate work forces of nonproduction workers and that the ticket of entry is educational status. Whether or not this additional input pays in *real* productivity increase, whether or not market position is the source of payoff to the firm; the payoff is sequestered within the large firm. Its ownership interest, its major management, and its associated, credentialed, educated staff are primary recipients and the primary agents determining overall distribution.[10]

Component II: High-Level Work Force/Stagnant Technique

This, the second category in the fourfold subdivision of system components, associates with education and a variety of social services that involve personal or "live" attention. Educational prerequisites at least as high as those in the progressive sector are implied for many activities.

Ordinary market forces would account for compensation in this component to roughly parallel that in the progressive sector (the teacher's wage cannot fall too far below that of the students). However, there are a number of qualifications to consider. Here, in summary form, we recapitulate materials introduced in Chapter Four:

Progressive-sector dominance: The compensation mechanisms rely on the progressive sector acting as the core of the economy so that progressive-sector economics dominate the wage structure and implicit and explicit bargaining. Compensation in the high-level, stagnant sector is thus a reflection of what goes on in the dominant sector.

Quasi-equilibrium growth: Our argument has been that compensation in this component parallels that in the progressive sector if employment demand for workers is maintained. That is, the starting salary and wage prospects for teachers must at least approximate those of their graduating students if the schools are to be staffed. However, if the basic growth in the system aborts, it is entirely possible for excess labor supplies to develop; and this component is particularly vulnerable. The current "glut in the academic marketplace" is a case in point. It seems clear that the real wage adjustments are being forced onto this sector.

Institutional factors: We should note, finally, that real wage structures and labor markets are rarely as clearly differentiated as they appear in abstract theoretical models. The markets in this component are particularly complicated by a variety of considerations including civil service status, job tenure, unionization, parity-pay, pensions, and others. For example, one has in the New York City system a complex of traditional and contractual links among pay schedules. There is no reason why "parity" established under one set of market conditions should be appropriate throughout a dynamic sequence; but nevertheless the principle exists as a fact of life. Some categories of low-skilled workers are apparently given a free ride on the progressive-sector wage structure (the sanitation department list is vastly oversubscribed, for example). In other instances, there may be a redefinition or upgrading of jobs and job requirements to fit the pay schedules. These "shelters," however, are idiosyncratic regardless of how dramatic their disclosure may be in a particular bargaining situation.[11]

Despite these important qualifications, the main point is clear: A sizable proportion of workers in education and social services must meet educational requirements and their work lacks technical progressiveness. Employees in the component will receive compensation that parallels that in the progressive sector during periods of growth; and at these times the unbalanced-growth cost argument is of great relevance. (During slack times, in what is essentially a "political" cycle, cost-cutting pressures may build.) Socioeconomic positions can not be disassociated from bargaining positions, budgetary positions, and special contractual status;

therefore, this group differs in a number of respects from the high-level work force in the progressive sectors. Nevertheless, there seems to be enough similarity in general status and overlap in labor-market positions for the groups to be classed together. Strong socioeconomic distinctions do emerge, however, as we look at the low-level work force.

Component III: Low Educational Level/Stagnant Technology

Characteristics of this grouping are considered in greater detail in Chapter Nine; but the essential argument is that the ghetto and agricultural poor, the low-skilled and subemployed, form a qualitatively distinct class within the general system. The research of dual labor market theorists provides abundant evidence on characteristic and distinct economic behaviors within this broad grouping. For example, in the urban ghettos, illegal activity—the hustle—provides the viable employment alternative for many; while in other subclasses, welfare or private transfers provide the earnings alternative. This research establishes that within the broad class of the poor there are many distinct subgroups and subclasses along with many distinct socioeconomic behaviors; but the key generalization over these groupings is that mainstream economic activities are rarely seen as viable or feasible options.

One key issue remains, however—the matter of associations between the lower component population and stagnant technology: It turns out that demonstrating the existence of the association is not a trivial exercise.* The population involved is to a large extent unemployed or subemployed—working sporadically or at a job that provides inadequate income for a minimal living standard. What is the "reference" employment for this population? To be sure, they may be unemployed with respect to certain low-skilled job categories, but it would not be incorrect to classify them as unemployed with respect to certain high-wage high-skill jobs as well. It is really only a convention that declares them as unemployed with reference to the lowest tier of jobs—those associated most closely with the marginal technologies.

---

* In pilot studies carried out by the author and colleagues of the Research Center for Economic Planning, the method followed has been that of taking stratified samples in ghetto and adjoining areas and comparing job associations there with those for the population at large. The hypothesized association with public-sector employment and "nongrowth" activities has been confirmed thus far.

Component IV : Low-Level Population/Progressive Technology

The preceding discussion and the need to complete the fourfold division begun earlier leads us to this category. There are many low-skilled jobs attached to major industries in the core of the economy. In addition, many of these jobs are protected by unionization and/or have pay scales linked to the progressive technology. The low-skilled operative on a production line, plant janitors, and a number of other categories come to mind. The argument here is that these situations are transitional and relatively unimportant within the economy and can be ignored in the general analysis. The "transitional" argument has three elements: first, that these categories are continuously on the verge of being extinguished by new technological developments. The more routine operations are usually the easiest to automate and the incentive to eliminate such jobs is high if they carry with them significant labor costs. The second argument is institutional in nature. Many firms have the ability to separate particular jobs from their basic pay structure. Such is the case, for example, if building maintenance for a progressive-sector firm is contracted to an outside firm so that the janitors are separated from the firm's "proper" employees. The third avoidance mechanism is that of "subcontracting" operations to low-level work forces abroad—a mechanism which has received much current attention with respect to the phenomenon of the multinational corporation.

There are many circumstances in which "good" progressive-sector jobs are held by low-level workers. After all, union protection and corporate responsibility to the residents of a company town are real institutional factors that may dominate other labor market considerations. However, these instances of sheltered jobs are the exception within our scheme; offering a possible path to adequate incomes for the poor and a line of potential social mobility for their children.

Recapitulation of Social Components

All in all, the view taken here is that the last component is a passive factor, essentially nondetermining in system dynamics. The critical elements are therefore: (1) the progressive sector and its associated high-level work force as the engine of technical progress and system dynamics; (2) the high-level work force in stagnant activities, such as education, as the governor of resources in the former sector and the conduit for social transformation; and (3) the low-level population in stagnant activities or the unemployed in conventional economic activities as the reservoir of social problems.* We have treated these components discursively, emphasizing their variegated structures, rather than insisting on homogeneity and like behaviors. The lack of homogeneity is a significant factor in the preparation of a base for methodology, since it points the way to a more detailed and realistic view of class structure within each of the population constellations (even though for analysis of system processes and dynamics it is helpful to stipulate component homogeneity and develop the model as if each of the subunits were made up of like individuals working like activities).

Inevitably the question must be confronted of whether the population division we are modelling corresponds to a delineation of social classes. There is no pat answer. It is generally believed that class structures have become amorphous compared to what they were in earlier times and in other places. (Surely there is no neat and acceptable description of classes in the contemporary United States to correspond to the Marxian description of nineteenth-century European socioeconomic structures or the conventional description of classes in much of contemporary Latin America). An effective socioeconomic class theory involves unique connections between social groups and economic activity or functions, held together with a view on class consciousness or recognized identity.† The present model is not complete in this sense: We have associated recognizable social groupings with distinct economic activities, but the groupings do not map directly onto expressed social identities or onto existing political structures. (Even the technostructure interest is not a separable element of the polity.) This leaves us short of a full class theory, but with a sketch framework on which viable class interests may form.

* These categories are catchall frameworks for variegated social structures. In the melting pot communities, for example, there is a tendency for public service employment to be the bridge to higher status of the first generation up from poverty. Thus we have the familiar succession of the Irish, Jews, and Blacks within the school systems of the major Eastern cities. The children of the first-generation teachers apparently filter into opportunities in the progressive sector core.

† Some scholars of the dual labor market emphasize the links between Southern subsistence farming, tenant farming, and the urban ghetto; with the latter serving as a holding pool of agricultural surplus populations. A number of radical theorists treat the groups as a "reserve army" or, at least, argue that the urban poor are so seen by the present-day counterparts of the Marxian capitalist. On this latter view, workers in the advanced sectors would regard the ghetto population as competition for jobs or a threat. The dual labor-market view, however, minimizes the threat construction on the grounds that there is significant economic distance between the two compartments of the economy.

COST, VALUE, AND INCOME TRENDS

The relationships among model components are shown in Table 2. Identified in abbreviated form are the institutional and industrial setting (columns 1, 1a), significant institutional characteristics (column 2), and class and social associations (column 3). The primary economic conditions in the model are summarized as technological status (column 4), wage prospects (column 5), and cost prospects (column 6). These conditions define the states of the system during a sustained growth phase of the economy and recapitulate the basic dualistic imbalance dynamic structure. The model is also recapitulated in mathematical form in Section Four, and some notations derived there appear in the table.

The key trend is progressive-sector compensation, which is assumed to increase at or around the net rate of productivity increase. Behind this assumption is a tale of bargaining strength and power: the Galbraithian story of the large firm in a tacit, cooperative, planning relationship with other firms possessing the market power to sequester the major part of gains from increasing productivity.

These gains are taken as conventional profits, managerial salaries, and wages to the technical and administrative work force. The firm is unlikely to be overly resistant to bargaining claims by its workers and, consequently, a substantial portion of the industrial labor force (component IV) will be geared into the pattern as well. The growth, profitability, and wage bargaining record for the major manufacturing firms from the late 1950s through the 1960s followed this line.* Once this pattern is established the unbalanced-growth cost-pressure trend for stagnant activities involving high-level work forces (component II) follows as a mechanical consequence. As noted in Chapter Four, there is direct evidence to substantiate both the basic cost trend and its fiscal implications; however, it is difficult to establish evidence for cost trends in stagnant private-sector activities (component III). It is not clear whether activities are being extinguished as higher wages are established or whether low-wage survivals are the rule. The key point is that employment and wage structures differ qualitatively for the high-level and low-level work forces. This seems to be

---

* It now appears that anticipations of major wage increases based on productivity increases had become institutionalized by the late 1960s. Such expectations when superimposed on static output may very well have aggravated the current inflation.

well established by the dual labor market studies and by direct investigations of the incentive structure implicit in overall income distributions.[12]

To a significant extent, the degree to which the dualism of the system can be sustained rests on dynamics affecting price structures. Here one has to rely on impressions and theoretical plausibility, since relative prices have not been formally studied with regard to underlying production conditions. The pricing mechanisms introduced thus far are conventional in the literature on unbalanced growth and imperfect markets. Column 7 of Table 2 summarizes assumptions as to market conditions consistent with dualistic imbalance. To the extent that progressive-sector firms are also the firms with the greatest market power, it may be impossible to disentangle pricing according to market strategy, cost-determined pricing, and pricing to support some other strategic objective. The most general assumption is essentially that pricing behavior and/or market-development strategy remains within the standard limits of the Galbraithian model or standard oligopoly theory, and that the firm, on its own, is not propelled to disturb the basic dualistic quasi-equilibrium. (The relevant characteristics were introduced in Chapter Eight and are summarized in columns 8 and 9 of Table 2.)

EQUILIBRIUM CONCEPTS IN THE MODEL

There are actually several concepts of equilibrium or "quasi-equilibrium" which apply to the system. The foundation concept is that of frozen class distribution as developed in the education models of Chapters Four, Five, and Six. The guiding mechanism is the human-capital model which, under the assumed conditions and sustained by cost and price trends, results in continuation of a preexisting class structure based on education and developed skills. The outcome of the process is a dynamic pattern in which two major socioeconomic groupings face quite different futures. The key indicator of the pattern is the ratio of progressive sector to stagnant sector wages. In the simplest form of the abstract model, the wage ratio can increase exponentially (if no other changes occur), thus intensifying economic and social pressures. But there exist other adaptations, counteractions, and trends which can modify the quasi-equilibrium frozen class division:

(a) *Remunerative wage increases in the stagnant sector.* If wages are not thoroughly bound by productivity considerations, stagnant sector wages can begin to rise, resulting in a rise in unemployment as the sector's cost position worsens. This pattern is one of the unpleasant variants of the continuing dualistic imbalance position with hardened class lines. Direct transfers or indirect transfers through industry subsidies would be needed to offset the employment effect.

(b) *Increases in the proportion educated.* This is an obvious step in a system in which the amount of educated manpower acts as a constraint. Lifting the limitation on educational places allows us to consider social, private, and firm human-capital investment programs that would expedite the transformation.

(c) *Technological adaptation.* The changing unit wage between the two groupings provides some incentive for research into alternative technologies that can better utilize less educated labor. This pattern suggests better utilization of the existing skill mix over growth with a fully developed labor force.

(d) *Hardening of the educational and class restrictions.* We are dealing with a system that can produce a dynastic class structure (children of the established higher class receive advantages that increase the likelihood that they would themselves be in that class upon maturity). The group is also likely to be politically dominant (again, the preconception is that the class will be large numerically within the dualistic system, rather than a small segment as in the archetype underdeveloped economy). For these reasons, it is possible to envisage the division becoming institutionalized and maintained for many years.

Effects (a) and (d) would be classified as perverse consequences of growth in an unmanaged system. Equilibria cultivated around concepts (b) and (c) are presumed for managed-growth sequences. The usefulness of these ways of looking at the system comes out in the final chapters, where it is shown that the dualistic imbalance scheme can provide an effective dynamic setting for a number of important themes in descriptive economics and social criticism that heretofore had not been integrated into a general system theory.

A MATHEMATICAL RESTATEMENT

As a strictly formal exercise, the trends generated by the model can be approximated with some nearly neoclassical calculations. I should stress that the model in this form is grossly oversimplified; even so, it says a good deal more about distribution than do the standard growth theoretic forms. I use the neoclassical notations with tongue-in-cheek since the model style is very far from neoclassical, and I am personally committed to a method of technical analysis that effectively denies the production function.[13] Yet it is interesting that all of the behaviors described here can be approximated by neoclassical production constructions aggregated into a two-sector model. I should also note that the formulations, complete with their blemishes, provide a useful framework within which to pose a critique of the human capital approach, set up calculations for work-force planning, and explicate the rather complex setting for urban finances. These elements are treated in the closing section of the Appendix.

The Basic Model

We can assume a single commodity (or standard composite commodity) with production carried out either with a "progressive" technique (designated by the prime sign in the notations that follow) or a stagnant technique. Exogenous technological change increases total factor productivity in the progressive sector at the rate of g percent per annum from some arbitrary beginning date. There is no such technological improvement in the stagnant activity. Using neoclassical notation for the production processes:

(1a) $$Q'_t = Q'\,(L'_t, K'_t)\,e^{gt} \quad \text{and}$$
(1b) $$Q_t = Q(L_t, K_t).$$

We isolate manpower characteristics most effectively if, for the moment, we make the grotesque assumptions that capital is completely malleable and can be used in either process, but that the L' labor force can only be drawn from the pool of educated manpower which will be designated as H_t: i.e., $L'_t \epsilon H_t$.

Education, however, is specified on narrower terms. The educational process is assumed to be satisfactorily approximated as a linear activity, as in equation (2):

(2) $$s_t = \theta f_t$$

Here s_t is the number of students and f_t, $f_t \epsilon H_t$ the number of educators. θ is thus the student/faculty ratio which produces graduates of some appropriate quality. For the time being we can take it that θ is fixed as a matter of tradition and conviction and that technological change does not alter the basic conditions of the classroom. To keep the analysis clean, we can ignore the need for physical capital to support the educational process and assume no population growth and an age distribution that is stable over time.

Since productivity in the progressive sector increases exponentially, the real wage of the L' labor force can increase exponentially as well. This wage prospect is written $w_0 e^{gt}$. In the one-commodity world, wages in the stagnant private activity cannot rise or the activity would become unprofitable; thus, the stagnant sector wage prospect is **w**. Education is also a technologically stagnant activity, but since it requires educated manpower as an input, it must pay the growing wage in order to continue to attract manpower. Hence, the wage rate in education will be $\phi w_0 e^{gt}$ (where ϕ reflects special nonpecuniary advantages of academic life or necessary market wage adjustments).

The "class" and distributional aspects of the model develop in this two-wage structure. The "higher" grouping H_t consists of those in L' and f employment. They start with the prospect of exponentially improving real economic welfare, while the lower grouping has as its basic wage the constant wage **w**. Members of H_t will also (by and large) be firm managers and the principal holders of direct and indirect equity claims against industry; so, whether an individual's income stems from profit, salary account, current earnings, or a pension would not matter particularly to the analysis. The wage bargain in the progressive sectors is thus notational rather than fundamental in its *general* welfare implications; although, of course, the economic positions of subgroupings in H_t will be affected. We will come back to this matter once some basic dynamics are established.

Saving and Accumulation

We begin with the convention that all saving flows from the H_t grouping and that the functions of saving are: (1) the financing of current education; (2) the financing of physical capital investment to suit the bias of technological change; and (3) the financing of capital deepening in either or both productive sectors. Rather than attempt separate motivations of saving and investment behaviors and then discuss their interaction in steady states of the system, we will consider a type of steady state first and discuss a range of realistic behaviors which are consistent with it. On this line, it is most convenient to develop the analysis in terms of the state in which the class structure remains stable over time: that is $H_t = \mathbf{H}$ a constant; and for this to occur, the proportions of the population in various occupations (L', L, s, f) also remain constant. The current expenditure on education is essentially equal to the faculty wage bill, $f\phi w_0 e^{gt}$ while total H_t income $= (f\phi + L')w_0 e^{gt}$. Therefore, the proportionate saving required to satisfy a stable class structure will be $f\phi/(f\phi + L')$. Whatever bias there is in the technological change that is impelling the system will alter the inducement to invest and (for constant underlying time preferences) the additional proportionate saving required to maintain a constant marginal product of capital over time will be B_t. For constant underlying bias, B_t will not vary with time; thus, we derive a constant saving propensity S (equation 3):

$$(3) \qquad\qquad S = f_\phi \,/\, (f_\phi + L') + B$$

S will be consistent with a class structure which is rigid over time. For the time being, we assume this saving propensity obtains and that this state is reached by adjustments (say in w_0/w) which will not affect accumulation.

Production

Note that in this scheme it does not matter particularly whether the technological change is disembodied or embodied in capital equipment (under conventional equivalence assumptions). The point is that the presence of educated workers is the *sine qua non* for the adoption of the technology, regardless of mode of transmission. Thus, equation (1a) could pertain to (a) an embodied technology which is chosen, installed, and operated by labor with highly developed skills; (b) disembodied technological changes associated with modern management; (c) the Galbraithian case discussed in the text; or (d) cases where the association between education and technological change is the result of social forces leading to hiring barriers rather than to any basic causal connection.

Otherwise, the production conditions within the model are of conventional types. The one-commodity assumption is a convenience. The results are qualitatively similar if there are many commodities, so long as the goods produced by the stagnant process labor force do not have strikingly high income elasticities and low price elasticities relative to the goods produced by the progressive force (or so long as the L force is not uniquely specialized in producing capital goods).

APPLICATIONS

We now turn to applications which are clarified by the formal specification. This section will consider the use of the model to establish a basis for a critique of the labor-augmentation perspective in human-capital theory and educational planning, a formal statement of the work-force–priority planning model, and an application of the model that integrates class and production phenomena with public finance in the specific setting of the urban crisis.

Education and the Human Capital Concept

The differences between the production specification in equations (1a), (1b) and that implicit in conventional human-capital formulations may require some additional clarification. The implicit production function in human-capital models is of the following general type:

$$(4) \qquad\qquad Q^*_t = Q^* (k, L^*_t)$$

where L^* is labor measured in terms of standard efficiency units. The number of efficiency units is, in turn, a function of the actual count of workers l_t and the amount of sunk human capital, k^*.

$$(5) \qquad\qquad L^*_t = \gamma(l_t, k^*_t)$$

The details of the function $\gamma(.)$ and the specification of various vintages of education need not concern us. The essence of the approach is that an untrained labor force l_0 can have the productive power of the force $L^*_0 (L^*_0 > l_0)$ with suitable investment in educational upgrading.

The distinction between models on the human-capital line and the present scheme becomes sharper when we introduce technological change. In our model, technical change is associated primarily with the production representation embracing educated manpower (1a). But a minimum of two sets of production conditions is needed to represent the entire system. In the implicit human-capital model, technical change involves a translation of (4) such as:

$$(6) \qquad\qquad Q^*_t = Q^*(K, L^*_t) e^{g^* t}$$

Only one family of production functions is specified, and in this formulation, technical change affects final output in the same fashion, regardless of whether the labor force consists of l_0 untrained individuals $(l_0 = L^*_0$ in efficiency units) or l'_0, a smaller but trained force, again with the efficiency value L^*_0. (The definition of "efficiency unit" is intrinsically circular in this formulation; but let us for the sake of argument say that we are satisfied with a calculation of the unit made at $t = 0$.) So far so good; but at this point, an intrinsic weakness of the labor augmentation basis of the human-capital scheme is exposed. Suppose it is discovered that one educated worker has the efficiency value of λ_t uneducated workers at $t = 0$; does the initial λ_t remain constant over time regardless of the shape of emerging technologies? This at best is a rather cumbersome condition. Alternatively, one should consider what is implied by the historical observation that the apparent rate of return to human capital remained constant during the period of greatest increase in the relative size of the pool of educated labor.

How does one explain a situation in which a greatly expanded labor force (in terms of implied efficiency units) continued to earn a nondecreasing marginal product? One possible explanation is that the expansion of physical capital was sufficiently out of step with the expansion of the efficiency of labor force so the marginal product condition was coincidentally met. A second possibility is that the efficiency measure changes, i.e., education itself is constantly improving, so that the efficiency coefficient of a later graduating class is sufficiently higher than that of an earlier class to counteract the higher numerical count of the labor force. The presumption of continually improving vintages may apply to a few technical fields, but it seems to contradict common sense impressions of what actually has been happening in the classroom generally. In summary, the following statements are offered:

(1)   The basic human-capital model is of enormous value as a decision scheme for the individual, as a descriptive framework for a broad population cross section, or as a framework for analysis of lifetime educational choices. However, the model leads to cumbersome and awkward constructions when applied to long growth sequences.

(2)   The difficulty lies primarily in the single production function specification which is implicit in the human-capital model. The present paper offers two (or more) production relationships: in one, education matters; in the other, it is irrelevant to productivity. This greater complexity in production relationships substitutes for implicit complexity in labor augmentation efficiency measurement. Occam's razor cuts as deeply into one specification as it does the other.

(3)   The model of this paper can embrace standard human-capital reasoning for individual decisions. A decision to take on schooling in order to move from the L to the H labor force can be couched in familiar human-capital investment terms. The return to education for the individual is the discounted value of the higher and increasing lifetime income which attaches to the H class. This return stream, however, can be determined outside of the individual-choice model by inspection of conditions of production at the macroeconomic level (given the basic dynamics of unbalanced growth).

(4)   A full reconciliation between the implicit labor augmentation basis of the human-capital production scheme and the bifurcated production scheme offered here is hardly needed. Suffice it to say that the present scheme offers a

partial explanation of some of the aggregate economic phenomena associated with education, and the standard human-capital formulation offers a useful line of attack on microeconomic phenomena. The links between education and technology are more complex than represented in either format, and it is likely that a blend of approaches may ultimately be the answer.

Educational Planning

Consider an economy within the basic structure described by the equations (1)–(3). A quasi-equilibrium state of the system in which the occupational proportions remain constant from generation to generation is illustrated by line segments along $a_o a_o$ in Diagram 1.

The segments f_o, l'_o, l_o and s_o represent, respectively, the proportion of educators, progressive sector workers, stagnant sector workers and students in the total working-age population. The 45-degree line shows the population proportion in the overall educated class. A second quasi-equilibrium steady-state with a high proportion in the educated classes is given by $a_1 a_1$. The line segment TE gives the proportion of students s_t required to maintain any steady-state educated population H_t; while line SS gives the population proportion in the accepted schooling years, a constraint. OF represents a constant faculty-student ratio applied to S_t to derive the required population proportion of faculty, f_t.

On the production assumptions given earlier (1a), (1b), and on the convention that education is not counted as a final product, production for the year t is given by the sum of stagnant sector and progressive sector production.

(7)
$$Y_t = Q'_t + Q_t$$

For initial conditions $Q'_o + Q_o$ a satisfactory working approximation is given by (8):

(8)
$$Y_t = Q'_o e^{gt} + Q_o.$$

But the general form will also be useful:

(9)
$$Y_t = Q'(l'_t, K_t) e^{gt} + Q(l_t, K_t).$$

For rectangular isoquants and Harrod-neutral technical change this becomes in per capita format:

(10)
$$Y_t = q'l'_t e^{gt} + q l_t.$$

Logarithmic production paths for steady state values of H_0 and H_1 are plotted as solid lines in Diagram 2. The transformation of a population from H_0 to H_1 is indicated by the trajectory curves in Diagram 1,

DIAGRAM 1

Class and Occupational Structure

Percent of
Population of
Working Age

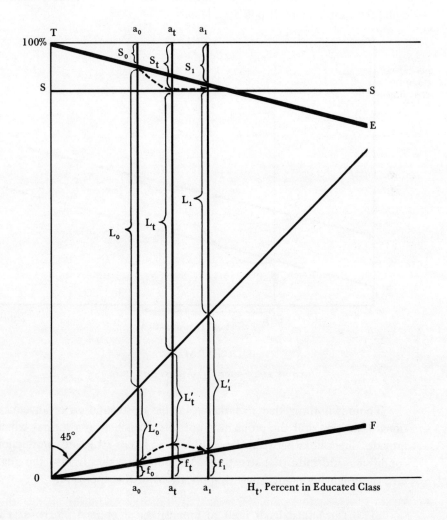

showing the increased requirements for faculty and increased student enrollment, and the income trajectory in Diagram 2. Obviously, the working
force in both sectors must fall and output must decline initially. The exact
calculation of output forgone can be obtained from more elaborate versions
of Equation (9), which take into account detailed information on the
mobility of capital and of potential faculty.

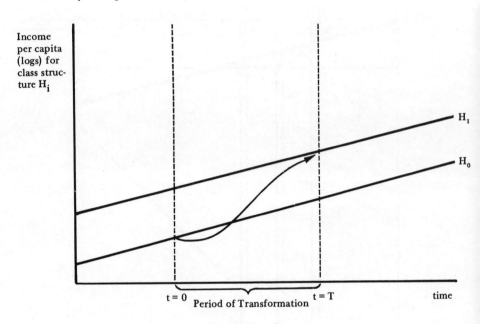

DIAGRAM 2

Income as a Function of Class Structure

There is nothing that remarkable in this representation of an educational transition; but the problem is not often couched in a format which
provides direct links between the education and class structure, production
conditions, and industrial structure. Without going deeply into the analysis, the following points suggest applications of the approach.

(1) The format lends itself to formulation of optimal programs. The
policies of educational transformation illustrated suggest turnpike paths, and
accordingly, least-time paths or output-maximizing paths for fixed horizons can
be calculated for specified target transformations. The distinction between
transitional phases and steady states is suggestive of recent experience: first
deficits, then surpluses in educational manpower and lack of anticipation in the
preparation of student bodies, etc. Theoretical discrepancies between observed

prices and shadow prices along turnpike trajectories are suggestive of difficulties in measuring rates of return to education and imputing appropriate faculty compensation.

(2) The model adopts in a straightforward way to detailed simulation and to considerable disaggregation. Areas of educational innovation, linked job and school programs, part time education, "continuing education," and education for older persons can be handled with relative ease, since a demographic profile is easily incorporated in the constraint structure of the model.

(3) The model transition which ends with a higher proportion of the population in the H class carries with it the expectation that those in the class will gain the progressive-sector income advantages. Actually, the expectations implied in the model are close to the expectations which were held by many students in recent years. Whether such expectations can be realized involves explicit industrial planning favoring progressive-sector activities.

Generalized Urban Models

To analyze urban trends we begin by assuming a fixed per capita requirement for government services. We also ignore wage differentials between progressive private industries and the government services. (The wage rate in both will be $w_0 e^{gt}$.) On this basis, we can predict S_t, the proportionate total cost on government service. A constant proportion of the population (M) will produce a constant output, but at the increasing unit cost $w_0 e^{gt}$. S_t, the cost of the program, is then $M w_0 e^{gt}$.

Equation (11) provides a crude projection of required tax rates by giving the ratio of cost (s_t, the numerator) to income (Y_t, the denominator).

$$(11) \qquad r_t = \frac{S_t}{Y_t} = \frac{M w_0 e^{gt}}{(R+M) w_0 e^{gt} + [1 - (R+M)] w}$$

Income in the city, Y_t, is the weighted sum of incomes at the increasing wage $(R+M) w_0 e^{gt}$ and incomes at the stagnant wage $[1 - (R+M)] w$.

By way of contrast, we imagine a modern suburb Prime, whose population is concentrated in the progressive sector. The " ' " designates conditions in Prime. The expression for r'_t, the tax rate in Prime, is identical to (11) except for the appropriate substitution of R' for R. The trick now is to calculate the ratio of tax rates for providing identical services in the two locales. This ratio, r'_t / r_t, is given by:

$$(12) \qquad \frac{r'_t}{r_t} = \frac{(R+M) w_0 e^{gt} + [1 - (R+M)] w}{(R'+M) w_0 e^{gt} + [1 - (R'+M)] w} .$$

The expression, in effect, is the ratio of incomes, Y'_t / Y_t, and the comparison is clearest in the limiting case where Prime is a one-class suburb;

i.e., where $(R' + M)$ is equal to unity. Substituting for $(R' + M)$ in (12), we obtain:

$$(13) \qquad \frac{r'_t}{r_t} = (R + M) + \frac{[1 - (R + M)]w}{w_0 e^{gt}}.$$

With time the second expression will diminish rapidly so the tax advantage increases towards the limiting proportion $(R + M)$.

$$(14) \qquad \lim_{t \to \infty} \left(\frac{r'_t}{r_t} \right) = R + M$$

This is the result described in Chapter Ten.[14]

Bibliographic Notes

CHAPTER 1

1. See Jonathan Shell, *The Time of Illusion* (New York: Alfred A. Knopf, 1976). Shell claims that Nixon's overt actions, the policies and programs of his administration, were guided by the same plan for assuming despotic control of the state that governed his covert actions and adventures. Economic policy was conceived of as a political modality, an instrument that could be used to foment divisions and isolate enemies.

2. See Robert L. Heilbroner, *An Inquiry into the Human Prospect* (New York: Norton, 1974). Heilbroner draws a terrifying picture of a near future in which the growth impulse has died: stagnation coupled with competition for insufficient product at both the international and national levels has repression of individual expectations and the establishment of totalitarian national states as its inevitable consequences.

3. It should be noted that "mismanagement" is an established analytical category within a taxonomy of crises associated with advanced capitalism. Jurgen Habermas in *Legitimation Crises* (Boston: Beacon, 1975) devotes considerable attention to the "steering problem" in state capitalism (pp. 61–68). In Habermas's scheme there can be a ". . . rationality deficit in public administration [which] means that the state apparatus cannot under given boundary conditions adequately steer the economic system" (p. 47).
It is chilling to note that in one very-official (but ostensibly private) circle blame for the "mismanagement" problem is assigned instead to the polity. See Michael J. Crozier, Samuel P. Huntington, and Joji Watanuki, *The Crisis of Democracy: Report on the Governability* [!] *of Democracies to the Trilateral Commission* (New York: New York University Press, 1975).

4. Geoffrey Barraclough, "The End of an Era," *New York Review of Books*, 27 June, 1974.

5. Michael Harrington, *The Accidental Century* (New York: Penguin, 1967).

6. Harrington, *Accidental Century*, p. 13.

7. Harrington argues that socialized production is the only defense against the technological imperative.

8. Michael Harrington, *The Other America* (New York: Penguin, 1962), pp. 15–19 and chapter 2.

9. Harrington's view on causation in a technically oriented economy oversimplifies an extremely complex historical process. The pattern of accidental adaptation is only one of many that emerge in a broad, fully developed history. See, for example, David

Landes, *The Unbound Prometheus* (Cambridge: Cambridge University Press, 1969), in particular, chapters 1 and 6, and pp. 546–49 in the general conclusion. The "accidental" reordering of society is also a theme in the work of Karl Polanyi, *The Great Transformation* (New York: Rinehart, 1944).

CHAPTER 2

1. This description of the "autonomous state" derives from a sophisticated and empirically satisfying Marxist literature surrounding the work of Nicholas Poulantsis. Michael Harrington, *The Twilight of Capitalism* (New York: Touchstone, 1976) provides a review and appreciation of some major themes following Poulantsis.

2. Edward Dennison, "United States Economic Growth," in Nathan Rosenberg, ed., *Economics of Technological Change* (Harmondsworth: Penguin Books, 1971), p. 375.

3. This thesis has been maintained by Seymour Melman for a number of years. For a recent statement, see his "Decision Making and Productivity as Economic Variables: The Present Depression as a Failure of Productivity," *Economic Issues* 10 (June 1976).

4. Kenneth Arrow, "The Economic Implications of Learning by Doing," *Review of Economic Studies* 29 (June 1962). The term, "learning," is used in a somewhat more restricted connection by Arrow. Arrow, however, fully develops the analytics of the interactions between newly introduced capital and the rate of learning.

5. On this point, see David Landes, *The Unbound Prometheus*, chapter 1.

6. This argument, which places primary emphasis on realized technical change and characterizes investment as a medium that may carry such change, represents the viewpoint of the growth economist and economic planner concerned with the ultimate sources of trends and economic change. This viewpoint is potentially misleading when it comes to describing the actual historical behaviors of a capitalist economy. Investment phenomena have behavioral primacy in a financially-directed capitalist system and technical change is an incidental matter that rarely touches the actual decision. Thus acts of investment may be the outcome of rational financial calculation within the firm, or the outgrowth of demented speculation. There is no guarantee as to whether financially-determined investment will be productive in the sense of carrying productivity change and expanding capacity. In addition, each act of enterprise investment leaves behind it a trail of financial claims (and memories) which set the conditions for the next round or rounds of investment. This legacy may at certain times be the determining fact of the economy. Chapter Eight carries this line of discussion forward. For the moment, note that Hyman P. Minsky, in *John Maynard Keynes* (New York: Columbia University Press, 1975), presents a clear and powerful picture of the interactions between financial structure and acts of investment.

7. Landes, *Prometheus*, p. 78. In addition Landes maintains that the process of design improvement was continuous and essentially involved the participation of innovative machinists, managers and owners with ties to the industry rather than to pure scientific investigation. *Prometheus*, pp. 105ff. And see below for further discussion.

8. The most obvious technology gaps were those between the Midlands and the South of England, and, of course, between England and the Continent. Landes, *Prometheus*, chapters 3, 4.

9. Paul A. David, "The Mechanization of Reaping in the Ante Bellum Midwest," in Henry Rosovsky, ed., *Industrialization in Two Systems* (New York: Wiley and Sons, 1966), cites the case of a grain-raking device which only raised the productivity of workers who were already operating mechanical reaping systems.

10. Landes, *Prometheus*, chapter 1.

11. The measurement of the relative importance of factors underlying productivity increase has been the subject of a sequence of empirical studies which follow from the pioneer work of Fabricant, Solow, and Denison. Virtually all of the studies on this

matter attribute to capital accumulation something less than 20 percent of the improvement in per-worker productivity. c.f.: Solomon Fabricant, "Economic Progress and Economic Change," National Bureau of Economic Research, Thirty-sixth Annual Report (New York, 1954); Robert Solow, "Technical Change and the Aggregate Production Function," *Review of Economics and Statistics* 39 (1957); Edward F. Denison, *The Sources of Economic Growth in the United States and the Alternatives Before Us* (London: Allen and Unwin, 1962).

12. John Kenneth Galbraith, *The New Industrial State* (Boston: Houghton Mifflin, 1969), various chapters (particularly chapters 5–8).

13. There is of course considerable controversy on the question of whether or not the Galbraithian technostructure does in fact have effective control over individual firms and a determining influence on overall productivity change and its bias. Detailed discussion is deferred to Chapter Eight.

CHAPTER 3

1. Joel Dirlam and Walter Adams, "Steel Imports and Vertical Monopoly Power," *American Economic Review* 54 (September 1964), provide the definitive study of big steel's procrastinations.

2. Fred Hirsch, *Social Limits to Growth* (Cambridge: Harvard University Press, 1976). Hirsch says what has to be said about the goods themselves, while Tibor Scitovsky, *The Joyless Economy* (New York: Oxford University Press, 1976), launches what I hope will be a successful campaign against the "more is better" doctrine which underlies so much of modern economic reasoning. I have not made an attack on sumptuary standards a necessary part of my basic argument; but it should be clear that my emphasis on education and knowledge-based activities is fully consistent with the Scitovsky position.

3. Lester G. Thurow, *Generating Inequality* (New York: Basic Books, 1975). See also Eva Mueller, *Technological Advance in an Expanding Economy: Its Impact on a Cross Section of the Labor Force* (Ann Arbor: Institute for Social Research, University of Michigan, 1969).

4. In the economic literature, such sustainable processes are described as growth equilibria. The magic condition which causes the desired expansion of the capital stock to just absorb new labor and the productivity increases from technical advance is termed Harrod neutrality following a convention in Roy Harrod, *Towards a Dynamic Economics* (New York: Macmillan, 1968).

5. Economists will note that the discussion in this chapter has been framed within the language of growth theory, but that my choice of the variables and phenomena to emphasize differs substantively from that in both the theoretical and policy-directed literatures. In many respects the descriptive treatment and focus derive from work of Schumpeter and the early students of the long cycle. See in particular Joseph Schumpeter, *The Theory of Economic Development* (1934; reprint ed. New York: Oxford University Press, 1961).

Many U.S. economists in their style of theoretical research have tended to play down the above arguments which feature control over technical change. Instead they have focused on a case in which technical change is presumed to be an exogenously given datum so that the natural rate is not the critical control variable. The focus of attention is usually capital intensity and, characteristically, growth is first viewed as a process of capital accumulation in response to a rate of saving which is institutionally or culturally given. There is, I think, something to the claim that the conventional U.S. view derives from overexposure to both neoclassical and neo-Marxian growth models which give greatest attention to the problem of reacting to the saving rate or finding the saving rate that implies the highest rate of per capita consumption over a steady growth path.

CHAPTER 4

1. This particular approach to dualism was first outlined by William Baumol, "Macroeconomics of Unbalanced Growth: The Anatomy of Urban Crisis," *American Economic Review* 57, no. 3 (June 1967). For his particular argument, it is also convenient to assume that technical progress is in Harrod-neutral form and has the effect of raising the apparent productivity of workers.

2. See P. A. David, "The Mechanization of Reaping."

3. This argument is borrowed from William Bowen and William Baumol, *Performing Arts, The Economic Dilemma* (New York: Twentieth-Century Fund, 1966).

4. Ibid.

5. See A. Wildavsky, *The Politics of the Budgetary Process* (Boston: Little Brown and Company, 1964); and O. Davis, M. Dempster, and A. Wildavsky, "A Theory of the Budgetary Process," *The American Political Science Review*, September 1966. Aaron Wildavsky, his students, and his coauthors show how the interplay among executive financial officers, program personnel, and legislators—all operating with rule of thumb "aids to calculation" and "balancing" principles—lead to budgetary outcomes in which the *status quo* (the previous budget) dominates the process. Dollar increments to this *status quo* tend to fall within a relatively narrow distribution of percentage increases.

6. David F. Bradford, Richard A. Malt, and Wallace E. Oates, "The Rising Cost of Local Public Services, Some Evidence and Reflections," *National Tax Journal* 22, no. 2 (June 1969).

7. Mao Tse-Tung, "Economic and Financial Problem," *Selected Works of Mao Tse-Tung* (Peking: Foreign Languages Press, 1965) vol. 3, pp. 111–112. Passage cited by John Gurley, "Formation of Mao's Economic Strategy," *Monthly Review*, July–August 1975, pp. 62–63.

CHAPTER 5

1. Garry A. Becker, *Human Capital* (New York: National Bureau of Economic Research, 1964); and Marc Blaug, "An Economic Interpretation of the Private Demand for Education," *Economica* 33 (May 1966). Section IV of the appendix shows in detail how the formulations here differ from those in the standard human capital tradition.

2. In later chapters the structural characteristics of the corporate research function are examined in more detail. See Richard R. Nelson, Merton M. J. Peck, Edward B. Kalachek, *Technology Economic Growth and Public Policy* (Washington, D.C.: The Brookings Institution, 1967).

3. See John Kenneth Galbraith, *The New Industrial State*, various chapters. The technostructure and the research and development function are discussed in greater detail in Chapter Eight herein.

4. These calculations derive from analysis in Peter S. Albin, "Poverty, Education and Unbalanced Economic Growth," *Quarterly Journal of Economics* 84 (February 1970). The function used is:

$$(1) \qquad V = -\int_0^M [\lambda W_o e^{gt} + W] e^{-kt} (dt) + \int_M^{65-(17+M)} [W_o e^{gt} - W] e^{-kt} (dt)$$

The left-hand integral represents the outlay for education. $\lambda W_o e^{gt}$ is the direct cost of education, tuition. As the formulation shows, tuition is tied to the wage level in the educational sector, and, by the proposition cited earlier, this cost factor grows exponentially. The constant, λ, is a proportionality factor tying tuition to the faculty wage. The second term in the square brackets, W, represents the indirect cost component, the opportunity wage for a worker in the depressed sector. The term outside the brackets is of course a discount factor, where the appropriate financing rate is k. The right-hand integral represents the benefit stream; the wage differential is within the brackets; the discount factor, outside. As the limits of integration show, the period of education is M years beginning at age seventeen, while the working lifetime is assumed to continue to age sixty-five.

CHAPTER 6

1. Present value calculated in year N, V_n, which we will term "contemporary value," will take into account the growth of both the direct cost component of outlays and the progressive sector wage. Equation (2) is a revised form of (1) (see Chapter 5) that specifies such revaluation.

$$(2) \qquad V_N = -\int_0^M [\lambda W_0 e^{gt(t+N)} + W] e^{-kt} (dt)$$
$$+\int_M^{65-(17+M)} [W_0 e^{gt(t+N)} - W] e^{-kt} (dt)$$

It can be shown that $d(V_n)/d(N)$ will be positive for a broad and plausible range of the parameters λ, k, M, g, and that it is reasonable to project that V_n will eventually become positive even for relatively high discount rates. Formal proofs of this contention are given in Albin, "Poverty, Education, and Unbalanced Growth."

2. See the *New York Times*, 26 October 1975, p. 1.

3. These figures were calculated from the formula given by equation (1) of the previous chapter.

4. The valuation formula appropriate to this case is given as:

$$(3) \qquad V' = -\int_0^{M'} \frac{M}{M'} \lambda W_0 e^{(g-k)t} (dt) + \int_{M'}^{65-(M'+17+\sigma)} [\phi_1 W_0 e^{gt} - W] e^{-kt} (dt) - \phi_2.$$

The changes from the formula given by (1) are as follows: the period of study is lengthened from M to M' years while the annual direct cost component is reduced proportionately. The indirect cost does not have to be met since the individual will be working to support himself while studying. As shown in the reduced upper limit of integration, the benefit stream will be truncated: first, by the longer period of study $(M'-M)$, and second, by a probable later starting point for the entire process $(17+\delta)$.

The benefit elements themselves will probably be reduced (by the factor ϕ_1, $(0 \leqslant \phi_1 \leqslant 1)$ to reflect the fact that the part-timer will have missed out on many lines of promotion and advancement by the time of his graduation. Finally, we should note the nonpecuniary element, ϕ_2, which reduces the value of the entire process. ϕ_2 reflects the disutilities of carrying out a double career and the likelihood that the full consumption benefits of education cannot be enjoyed under the circumstances.

CHAPTER 7

1. Most of the statistics given in this chapter appear in Seymour Harris, ed., *Economic Aspects of Education* (OECD.: Paris, 1964).

2. Robert J. Havighurst, *American Higher Education in the 1960s* (Columbus: Ohio State University Press, 1960).

3. For an example of a developed manpower-planning model, see Jan Tinbergen, "Educational Assessments," in UNESCO, *Economic and Social Aspects of Educational Planning* (Paris: UNESCO Publications, 1964), chapter 9 and accompanying appendices.

4. The endogenicity of the bias of technical change has been studied extensively by William Fellner, who concludes that the private sector already reacts to economic incentives during the design stage. Citations to the literature surrounding Fellner's work are deferred until the following chapter (reference 8).

5. For a constructive approach to job programs, see Robert Lampman, *Ends and Means of Reducing Income Poverty* (Chicago: Markham, 1971), p. 154 ff.

6. These and related questions are the subject of a growing literature on the management of research and development. Nelson et al., *Technology*, provides an excellent introduction to the field.

7. It is interesting to note that most of the research attention given to manpower development of this sort has been in a literature devoted to problems of the poor countries. The problem there becomes that of increasing advanced sector employment in the face of dominant laborsaving technologies imported from the leading industrial countries. See in particular: A. R. Prest, "The Role of Labour Taxes and Subsidies in Promoting Employment in Developing Countries," *International Labor Review* 103 (April 1971); Lloyd G. Reynolds, "Wages and Employment in a Labor-Surplus Economy," *American Economic Review* 55 (March 1965); S. F. Barry, "Economic Development with Surplus Labour," *Oxford Economic Papers* 21 (July 1970); O. Mehmet, "Benefit-Cost Analysis of Alternative Techniques of Production for Employment Creation," *International Labor Review* 104 (August 1971).

8. Harold L. Sheppard, Bennet Harrison, and William J. Spring, eds., *The Political Economy of Public Service Employment* (Lexington, Mass.: Heath, 1972), p. 399.

9. Economists will recognize that in this section I am describing a dynamic optimization problem of the turnpike type. The appendix gives the framework for formal analysis.

10. One should also note that the "alternative school movement" suggests that schooling has also been rejected by a fairly well educated and alert minority that is reacting to debased tendencies within standard education. For examples of the literature that has grown up around the avoidance of conventional public education, see: Paul Goodman, *Compulsory Miseducation* (New York: Horizon, 1964); John Holt, *How Children Fail* (New York: Pitman, 1964); Jonathan Kozol, *Death at an Early Age* (New York: Bantam, 1968); Herbert R. Kohl, *Teaching the Unteachable* (New York: New York Review Books, 1967).

11. I have described the need for educational planning as a matter for rational "policy" in the liberal, social democratic sense. See Habermas, *Legitimation Crisis.* Habermas sees the educational crisis as part of the larger "legitimation crisis" of advanced capitalism and unsusceptible to policy within that regime.

12. The golden rule was popularized by Edward S. Phelps through his fantasy, "The Golden Rule of Accumulation, a Fable for Growthmen," *American Economic Review* 51 (September 1961). In the case of capital accumulation, the rule describes a rate of saving that each generation should adhere to in order to obtain intertemporal equity among predecessor, current, and successor generations.

13. Habermas, *Legitimation Crisis*, p. 81.

CHAPTER 8

1. John K. Galbraith, *New Industrial State*. The statements in the text are, by and large, paraphrases of material in Galbraith; see in particular his chapters 5 and 15. Galbraith's view of the corporation derives from (or is compatible with) work by Marris, Baumol, Williamson, and others. See Robin Marris, *The Economic Theory of*

Managerial Capitalism (Glencoe: Free Press, 1964); William Baumol, *Business Behavior Value and Growth* (New York: Harcourt Brace, 1967), and Oliver E. Williamson, *The Economics of Discretionary Behavior* (Englewood Cliffs: Prentice-Hall, 1964).

Standard themes in the theory of the managerially oriented firm are surveyed and categorized admirably by M. Wildsmith, *Managerial Theories of the Firm* (New York: Dunellan, 1974). Control issues are reviewed by Peter S. Albin and Roger Alcaly in "Corporate Objectives and the Economy: Systematic Shifts between Growth and Profit Goals," *Journal of Economic Issues* 10 (June 1976).

2. Joseph Schumpeter, *Capitalism, Socialism and Democracy* (New York: Harper, 1950), p. 101 ff. The technically oriented firm possessing sizable material resources and operating in a controlled final market would seem to be a natural sponsor for innovative research. This was Schumpeter's original position and prediction. This viewpoint certainly emerges in Galbraith (possibly to excess) and in any number of studies which saw the innovative activities of oligopolists as a workable surrogate for market competition. Since Schumpeter's proposition was first disseminated in the 1920s, there has been a continuous stream of significant empirical studies of the relationship between innovation and firm size or mode of competition. The evidence is mixed. For example, there appears to be a threshold of firm size above which bigness no longer seems to spur innovative activity; see Jessie Markham, "Market Structure, Business Conduct and Innovation," *American Economic Review* 55 (May, 1965). In many new fields of applied science the fundamental innovations were conceived and developed by firms which started as vest pocket entities (Polaroid, Xerox, CDC, Syntex, and many others). In other areas (textile fibers, solid state devices), the large firm development model seems apposite. See Frederick Scherer, *Industrial Market Structure and Economic Performance* (Chicago: Rand McNally, 1970), chapter 15, "Market Structure and Technological Innovation." Scherer conducts an admirable survey of the varying themes in a chapter that sets a new standard for textbook exposition.

3. The interactions between macroeconomic conditions and shifting corporate objectives are explored in P. S. Albin and R. Alcaly, "Corporate Objectives."

4. To the list of economists already cited in this chapter we should add the social critics: Michael Harrington, *The Accidental Century*; Herbert Marcuse, *One Dimensional Man* (Boston: Beacon, 1964); and Jurgen Habermas, *Toward a Rational Society* (Boston: Beacon Press, 1970).

5. Marcuse, *One Dimensional*; Charles Reich, *The Greening of America* (New York: Random House, 1970). Habermas, *Toward a Rational Society*, provides a reasoned assessment of these potentialities.

6. Markham, "Market Structure," AER. Markham puts the size range for effective innovation at approximately $75 million to $200 million in annual sales (1965 prices); but the lower limit does screen out the glamor technology firms in their first growth phase and the classic venture-capital opportunity.

7. Schumpeter, *Capitalism*. This argument is a restatement of Schumpeter's main proposition (stated as a prognosis, not a prescription). The argument, in essentially the same form as given here, is central in Harrington, *Accidental Century*, chapters 1 and 9, and Galbraith, *New Industrial State*, chapters 9, 31, 35.

8. See William Fellner, "Two Propositions in the Theory of Induced Innovations," *Economic Journal* 71 (June 1961). Further developments in the context of neoclassical growth theory and profit maximization appear in the work of Charles Kennedy, "The Character of Improvements and of Technical Progress," *Economic Journal* 72 (December 1962) and "Induced Bias in Innovation and the Theory of Distribution," *Economic Journal* 74 (September 1964); and Paul Samuelson, "A Theory of Induced Innovation along Kennedy-Weisäcker Lines," *Review of Economics and Statistics* 47 (November 1965). This is a problem that is probably best handled theoretically or through case examination of specific technical artifacts. The statistical problems involved in identifying factor bias confound conventional regression analysis of production relationships. See Charles Kennedy and A. P. Thirwall, "Surveys in Applied Economics: Technical Progress," *Economic Journal* 82 (March 1972), p. 20 ff, for reports on this and other topics on empirical production research.

9. Galbraith, *New Industrial State*, chapter 15.

10. The list of references to research on the multinational firm is long and growing longer: John Kenneth Galbraith adopts his *New Industrial State* model to the multinational enterprise in *Economics of the Public Purpose* (Boston: Houghton Mifflin, 1973); Richard Barnet and Ronald Muller, provide an insightful general view of employment practices within multinationals that is relevant here in *Global Reach* (New York: Simon and Schuster, 1975).

11. See Hyman P. Minsky, *John Maynard Keynes* (New York: Columbia University Press, 1975).

12. Again, Minsky is a powerful advocate. See his "Investment in our Capitalist Economy" (unpublished manuscript). Minsky identifies the real and financial excesses of the boom as primary factors underlying structural inflation.

CHAPTER 9

1. Charles Sackrey, *The Political Economy of Urban Poverty* (New York: Norton, 1973), chapters 1 and 2. Sackrey gives some of the standard data on this phenomenon plus an overview of conditions affecting the economic condition of the urban poor. Extensive bibliographies on American poverty, particularly urban poverty, can be found in Sheppard, Harrison, and Spring, *Political Economy* and D. M. Gordon, *Theories of Poverty and Underemployment* (Lexington, Mass.: Heath, 1972).

2. A number of writers have produced evidence of a "discouraged worker" effect, in which workers who have repeatedly been denied employment drop out of the labor force, perhaps to reappear when job openings greatly expand at some later time. During the 1950s and 1960s, when new jobs were created, slightly more than half of the openings were filled by workers on the unemployment rolls and the remainder were filled by "new entrants" previously uncounted as seeking work. At the moment the number and proportion of uncounted workers seems greater still. In short, the *measured* unemployment rate vastly understates the *true* unemployment rate, which would take into account desired labor-force participation. Significant studies on this matter are: William G. Bowen and Thomas A. Finegan, *The Economics of Labor Force Participation* (Princeton: Princeton University Press, 1969); and Thomas Dernberg and Kenneth Strand, "Cyclical Variation in Civilian Labor Force Participation," *Review of Economics and Statistics* 46 (November 1964).

3. Sar Levitan and Robert Taggart, *Employment and Earnings Inadequacy: A New Social Indicator* (unpublished manuscript, Center for Manpower Policy Studies, George Washington University); Thomas Vietorisz, Robert Mier, and Jean-Ellen Giblin, "Indicators of Labor Market Functioning and Urban Social Distress," *The Social Economies of Cities: Urban Affairs Annual Review* 9 (1975).

4. Thomas Vietorisz, Robert Mier, Jean-Ellen Giblin, and Bennett Harrison, "Subemployment: Concepts, Measurements, and Trends," *Industrial Relations Research Association, Proceedings*, 1975.

5. Peter S. Albin, "Proposal: Interactions between Subemployment and Technical Progress" (unpublished manuscript, Research Center for Economic Planning, New York, 1974).

6. Levitan and Taggart, *Employment and Earnings*, chapter 4. Among the surprising findings of the Levitan-Taggart study are indications that subemployment is a general national problem with perhaps 10 percent of the work force so afflicted and that, if anything, income inadequacy is as serious in nonmetropolitan areas as it is in the major urban districts. In fact, except for the ghettoes, where subemployment reaches national maxima, unemployment rather than subemployment is the problem of the metropolitan areas.

7. Lowell Gallaway, "Foundations of the War on Poverty," *American Economic Review* 55 (March 1965). Henry Aaron, "The Foundations of the 'War on Poverty'

Re-examined," *American Economic Review* 57 (December 1967). Gallaway originally argued that "selective" anti-poverty measures could succeed in driving the poverty proportion down to some 6 percent of the population by 1980 (although 10 percent was not ruled out). To break that hard nut of the poor, the "backwash" from economic growth would have to be relied upon. Aaron's results suggest that the backwash has not materialized and in fact the sensitivity of the poverty proportion (properly measured) to aggregate growth is low.

On the specific question of racial poverty, Thurow clearly shows that "the emergence of a black middle class" as a phenomenon of growth is a chimera. Thurow, *Generating Inequality*, pp. 63–65 and chapter 7.

8. B. Harrison, *Education Training and the Urban Ghetto* (Baltimore: Johns Hopkins, 1972). T. Vietorisz and B. Harrison, *The Economic Development of Harlem* (New York: Praeger, 1970). See Gordon, *Theories of Poverty*, for additional bibliography.

A graphic description of the ghetto job situation in the 1976 partial recovery appears in Charlayne Hunter, "Black Teenagers' Jobless Rate Constant Despite U.S. Recovery," *New York Times*, 11 July 1976, p. 1.

9. The quotations appear in B. Harrison, "Public Employment and the Theory of the Dual Economy," in Sheppard, Harrison, and Spring, *Political Economy*. The quotations appear respectively on pages 52, 53, 57, and 60.

10. Lee Soltow, "The Share of Lower Income Groups in Income," *Review of Economics and Statistics* 47 (November 1965).

11. Peter Henle, "Exploring the Distribution of Earned Income," *Monthly Labor Review*, December 1972. Further confirmation of this pattern of income division is suggested by Henle's finding of increasing inequality in wage and salary income.

12. Harrington, *The Other America*, is the classic study of modern poverty.

13. A close reading of Keynes (see in particular H. P. Minsky, *John Maynard Keynes*) indicates that only a relatively small proportion of Keynes' insights were incorporated into the watered down versions which are labeled the "new economics" or "Keynesianism." The Keynes of the *General Theory*, for example, possessed an understanding and appreciation of the complexity of enterprise investment that is unequalled in any successor "translations."

14. Fritz Machlup, *International Payments, Debts, and Gold* (New York: Scribner, 1964), pp. 396–424. Machlup's republished papers from the 1920s along with his more recent work on similar topics point up the change in values that attach to the Keynesian revolution. It bears restating that the Nixon-Ford administration seemed attuned to attributes dated, say, 1928.

15. The early work of the National Bureau for Economic Research (NBER) is noteworthy here.

16. See Henle, "Exploring the Distribution."

17. Sheppard, Harrison, and Spring, *Political Economy*. See discussion and citations in Chapter Seven herein.

18. Thomas Vietorisz, "We Need a $3.50 Minimum Wage," *Challenge*, May-June 1973; Thomas Vietorisz, Robert Mier, and Bennett Harrison, "Full Employment at Living Wages," *Annals of the American Academy of Political and Social Science*, 1975.

CHAPTER 10

1. The uninhibited rhapsodies of this chapter reflect the author's sidewalk heritage. Jane Jacobs, *The Economy of Cities* (New York: Vintage, 1970), makes the case for the functioning of major cities and urban life with greater restraint.

2. Economists lack the basic analytical tools to deal with the sort of question which seems to suggest biological processes or abstract cybernetics (e.g., the question of what level of internal complexity must a computing machine reach before it has the capability

of building a machine which is an exact copy of itself). On these and related questions see: John von Neumann, *Theory of Self-Reproducing Automata* (Urbana: University of Illinois, 1966); Arthur W. Burks, *Essays on Cellular Automata* (Urbana: University of Illinois, 1970); and Peter S. Albin, *The Analysis of Complex Socio-economic Systems* (Lexington, Mass.: Heath, 1975).

3. Full calculations are given in Part V of the Appendix. These derive from Peter S. Albin "Unbalanced Growth and Intensification of the Urban Crisis," *Urban Studies* 8 (June 1971).

4. The budgetary mechanisms described here represent underlying trends. These trends were retarded in some localities by partial remedies such as the revenue sharing measures of the first Nixon administration; they were exacerbated on a regional basis by an expenditure pattern that reflected the "southern strategy."

An extraordinarily lucid comprehensive description of the New York City fiscal crisis and its underlying economic causes appears in Jason Epstein, "The Last Days of New York," in R. Alcaly and D. Mermelstein, eds., *The Fiscal Crisis of American Cities* (New York: Random House, 1977). The chapter originally appeared as an article in the *New York Review of Books*.

5. The theory of locational reactions to burden/benefit packages is crystalized in Charles E. Tiebout, "A Pure Theory of Local Expenditure," *Journal of Political Economy* 64 (October 1956). An elaborate model which develops locational factors in detail is described in Jerome Rothenberg, "Strategic Interaction and Resource Allocation in Metropolitan Intergovernmental Relations," *American Economic Review* 59 (May 1969). Industrial-location patterns are examined in John F. Due, "Studies of State-Local Tax Influence on Locations of Industry," *National Tax Journal* 14 (December 1961); while financial effects are analyzed in Wallace E. Oates, "The Effects of Property Tax and Local Public Spending on Property Values," *Journal of Political Economy* 77 (November 1969). For a general survey and bibliography, see Dick Netzer, "The Demand for Urban Public Services," in Harvey S. Perloff and Lowden Wingo, eds., *Issues in Urban Economics* (Baltimore: Johns Hopkins, 1968).

CHAPTER 11

1. The transition to C. II in the late 1950s and business's ostensible acceptance of the stabilization principle in the early 1960s are described and documented by Earl Cheit, *The Business Establishment* (New York: John Wiley & Sons, 1964).

James R. Crotty and Leonard A. Rapping, "The 1975 Report of the President's Council of Economic Advisers: A Radical Critique," *American Economic Review* 65 (December 1975), p. 793, suggest a Liberty-League ideology within the Ford Council of Economic Advisors.

2. A characteristic qualitative distinction between the two states is that in the cycle-prone economy, massive intervention is required to break the depression syndrome. However, once the syndrome is broken, it is possible that the full Keynesian policy apparatus actually becomes obsolete; investment behavior becoming far more stable and monetary policy proven ineffective in a cycle-prone system becoming a viable means of control. On this reasoning, the "neoclassical synthesis" or the "new monetary economics" are C. II phenomena applicable to one particular historical moment.

3. See Walter W. Heller, *New Dimensions of Political Economy* (Cambridge: Harvard University Press, 1966). I think this is a valid reading of Heller's memoir. There is nothing in the official documents and policy pronouncements of the early Kennedy years to suggest otherwise. Going beyond the words of the participant-observers, truly insightful views on the policy process appear in Charles E. Lindblom, *Politics and Markets* (New York: Basic Books, 1977) especially chaps. 14 and 23.

4. Arthur M. Okun, *The Political Economy of Prosperity* (Washington: Brookings Institution, 1970), chapter 1, suggests a policy set very much in keeping with the text.

5. See James C. Donovan, *The Politics of Poverty* (New York: Pegasus, 1967).

Donovan interprets the shift from the war on poverty to the war in Vietnam in terms of the limits of personal presidential power. It is clear from his account that Johnson was far from confirmed in C. III orientation although he had gone some of the distance.

6. See Keynes, *General Theory*; and Minsky, *John Maynard Keynes*.

7. There has been belated recognition of this occurrence within industry itself. See "The Breakdown of U.S. Innovation," *Business Week*, 16 Feb. 1976. The National Science Foundation and the General Accounting Office have made the technical leadership issue an area for serious study and have noted significant reversals in such indicators as the balance between domestic and foreign patents, numbers of "radical breakthroughs," and various measures of innovation cost. See "Whatever Happened to Independent Inventors," *Science News*, 24 July 1976.

8. Robert Lindsey, "Economy Mars Belief in the American Dream," *New York Times*, 26 October 1975, p. 1.

9. See, for example, the cover article, "Why Recovering Economies Don't Create Enough New Jobs," *Business Week*, 22 March 1976.

CHAPTER 12

1. The mechanics of indicative control systems and their use in macroeconomic regulation are discussed in Peter S. Albin, "Uncertainty, Information Exchange and the Theory of Indicative Planning," *Economic Journal* 81 (March 1971). This paper establishes the informational and control requirements for a decentralized economy with independent firms. Vera Lutz, *Central Planning in the Market Economy* (London: Longmans, 1969), presents arguments against the "practicality" of indicative techniques.

The organizational complexity required for control systems to be effective is a subject in my current research with Hans Gottinger (under a grant from the National Science Foundation).

2. See, for example, Taro Watanabe, "National Planning and Economic Development," *Economics of Planning*, no. 102 (1970); and Taro Watanabe and T. Uchida, "A Quantitative Appraisal of National Economic Policy," *Weltwirtschastliches Archiv* 106, no. 2 (1971).

3. P. S. Albin, "Uncertainty."

4. Again, see Tinbergen, *Educational Planning*.

5. See Nicholas Kaldor, *Strategic Factors in Economic Development* (Ithaca, N.Y.: Cornell University Press, 1967).

6. The examples abound. Gunnar Myrdal's *Asian Drama* (New York: Pantheon, 1968) has become the classic compendium.

7. Prest, "The Role of Labour Taxes," considered the use of selective employment taxation to offset laborsaving bias. The logic of such taxation is developed in Nicholas Kaldor, *The Causes of the Slow Rate of Economic Growth of the U.K.* (Cambridge: Cambridge University Press, 1966). Also note that an Office for Technology Assessment exists (on paper at least) as an information source to Congress on social impacts of technology.

8. Again, it should be emphasized that a massive United States program for development assistance would be viewed cautiously if not antagonistically by many LDCs. For views on nationalism in LDCs, see Gunnar Myrdal, *Beyond the Welfare State* (New York: Bantam, 1967), chap. 12.

High technology is only one avenue. See Victor Papanek, *Human Ecology and Social Change* (New York: Bantam, 1973). The radical design alternatives of Papanek, his students, and his colleagues provide elegant solutions to LDC technical problems, without demanding an advanced industrial base for their implementation.

9. See Donovan, *Politics of Poverty*, for an analysis of the deflection of the "Great Society." The failure of poverty programs and OEO innovations also has an extensive

bibliography. Daniel P. Moynihan, *Politics of a Guaranteed Income: The Nixon Administration and the Family Assistance Plan* (New York: Random House, 1973), is most frequently cited. See Edward C. Hayes, *Power Structure and Urban Policy* (New York: McGraw-Hill, 1972). Although inaccurate in some program details, Hayes' study of Oakland's recent history is informative on the politics of poverty at the local level.

10. For the "noncrisis" view, see Morris Adelman, *The World Petroleum Market* (Baltimore: Johns Hopkins, 1972).

11. Reliance on the price mechanism is a reflex that verges on idiosyncrasy. Planning theorists have demonstrated the equivalence of a number of alternative signalling and guidance techniques, and experience has not shown them to be ineffective. See Janos Kornai, *Anti-Equilibrium* (Amsterdam: North Holland, 1971), for a detailed and imaginative taxonomy of nonmarket information carriers.

12. The "pricing" approach comes out quite strongly in a book of readings edited by Robert Dorfman and Nancy Dorfman, *Economics of the Environment* (New York: Norton, 1972). This volume gives bibliographic references and a useful selection from the immense literature now developing on environmental consequences of growth. Walter Heller, "Coming to Terms with Growth and the Environment," *Forum on Energy, Economic Growth and the Environment* (Washington, D.C.: Resources for the Future, 1971), presents the ingredients of a clean growth plan using the pricing approach.

13. I apologize for the abbreviated treatment of this critical matter, but an adequate discussion of the political economy of work structuring would more than double the length of the book. A clear and insightful discussion of the complex political and social implications of specific restructuring operations appears in J. Friso Den Hertog, *Work System Design: Experiences with Alternative Production Organization* (Eindhoven, Holland: Phillips Eindhoven Ltd., 1976).

APPENDIX

1. See Charles H. Hession, *John Kenneth Galbraith and His Critics* (New York: Mentor, 1972), chaps. 7 and 8.

2. While on the subject we should mention again that the Galbraith scheme only really applies to a growth economy and that the firms involved have the option and ability to switch back to classic short-term shared-monopoly behavior when the situation warrants retrenchment.

3. See Hession, *Galbraith and His Critics*, for a review of the empirical evidence for and against particular mechanisms assumed by Galbraith.

4. Ibid., p. 168.

5. The census of industries and other tabulations according to standard industrial classifications (SIC Index) are not designed to locate the source of technical change, nor are they oriented toward the education-technostructure factor.

6. See citations in Chapter Eight herein.

7. Paul A. David, *Technical Choice, Innovation and Economic Growth* (Cambridge: Cambridge University Press, 1975). David's introductory essay on the methodology of production analysis could properly be appended to this Appendix.

8. *Ibid.*, introduction and chapters 1–3; see also the related unpublished work by Zevin described therein; and the general descriptions given in Landes, *Prometheus*.

9. Finis Welch, "Education in Production," *Journal of Political Economy*, (January/ February 1970). Welch's enterprising farm operator is an ideal subject for statistical analysis since he embodies both his firm as a business activity and his personal educational status as an input to production. The empirical problems are decisively greater when the inputs and performance have to be identified within a complex industrial structure or in a complex interfirm market environment.

10. Again, see the discussion in Chapter Four.

11. The concept of "sheltered" jobs has been advanced by Marcia Freeman in important unpublished work carried out at the Columbia Conservation of Human Resources Project. Workers seek shelter from job market risks as well as earnings, and progressive-sector civil service and technostructure jobs are seen as providing these benefits. The number of sheltered opportunities for the uncredentialed is seen as seriously declining.

12. See the discussion of Soltow's research in Chapter Nine.

13. Albin, *Analysis of Complex Socioeconomic Systems*.

14. Further extensions of the analysis appear in Albin, *Unbalanced Growth*.

INDEX